# Analysing Social Media Data and Web Networks

# Analysing Social Media Data and Web Networks

Edited by

Marta Cantijoch
*University of Manchester, UK*

Rachel Gibson
*University of Manchester, UK*

Stephen Ward
*University of Salford, UK*

palgrave
macmillan

First published 2014 by
PALGRAVE MACMILLAN

Palgrave Macmillan in the UK is an imprint of Macmillan Publishers Limited, registered in England, company number 785998, of Houndmills, Basingstoke, Hampshire RG21 6XS.

Palgrave Macmillan in the US is a division of St Martin's Press LLC, 175 Fifth Avenue, New York, NY 10010.

Palgrave Macmillan is the global academic imprint of the above companies and has companies and representatives throughout the world.

Palgrave® and Macmillan® are registered trademarks in the United States, the United Kingdom, Europe and other countries.

ISBN 978–1–137–27676–6

This book is printed on paper suitable for recycling and made from fully managed and sustained forest sources. Logging, pulping and manufacturing processes are expected to conform to the environmental regulations of the country of origin.

A catalogue record for this book is available from the British Library.

A catalog record for this book is available from the Library of Congress.

# Contents

## Part III Mixed Methods and Approaches for the Analysis of Web Campaign

# Figures and Tables

## Figures

## Tables

# Contributors

**Robert Ackland** is an Associate Professor in the Australian Demographic and Social Research Institute, Australian National University (ANU), Canberra. He has degrees in Economics from the University of Melbourne, Yale University (where he was a Fulbright Scholar) and ANU, where he gained his PhD in 2001. Since 2002 he has been working in the fields of network science, computational social science and web science, with a particular focus on quantitative analysis of online social and organisational networks. He leads the Virtual Observatory for the Study of Online Networks project (http://voson.anu.edu.au) and teaches on the social science of the Internet, statistics and online research methods. He has been chief investigator on a number of Australian Research Council grants, and in 2007 he was a UK National Centre for e-Social Science Visiting Fellow and James Martin Visiting Fellow at the Oxford Internet Institute. He is the author of *Web Social Science* (2013).

**Nick Anstead** is Assistant Professor in Media and Communication at the Department of Media and Communications, London School of Economics and Political Science, UK. His work focuses on the relationship between political institutions and ideas, and new technologies. Nick's work has been published in a number of journals, including the *Journal of Information Technology Politics and Information, International Journal of Press/Politics* and *Information, Communication and Society*. In 2009, he co-edited (with Will Straw) the Fabian Society book *The Change We Need* which examined lessons for British politics from Barack Obama's 2008 election victory, and featured a foreword by the then UK Prime Minister Gordon Brown. He has appeared on BBC television news, BBC Radio 4 and BBC Radio 5 Live, as well as numerous regional and international media outlets. He blogs at nickanstead.com/blog and tweets as @nickanstead.

**Marta Cantijoch** is Lecturer in Politics at the University of Manchester, UK. She is also a member of the Manchester Q-Step Centre. She has published several articles on the effects of digital media on citizen politics.

**Gema García-Albacete** is a Postdoctoral Fellow at the Department of Political Science and International Relations, Universidad Autónoma de Madrid, Spain. Until 2012, she worked at the University of Mannheim where she also completed her PhD. Her research relates to citizens' political behaviour and attitudes. She is particularly interested in the processes by which political participation and political orientations develop. Her work on young people's political participation in western Europe *Continuity or Generational Change?* was awarded the 'Lorenz von Stein' and the 'Juan Linz' prizes, published by Palgrave Macmillan. She has also published her research in international journals such as *Acta Politica* and *American Behavioral Scientist*.

**Rachel Gibson** is Professor of Political Science at the Department of Politics, University of Manchester, UK. She has held visiting positions at universities in Australia, Germany and Spain. She has published several books and articles on the use of digital media in political communication, particularly by parties, and for election campaigning and participation.

**Todd Graham** is Assistant Professor in Political Communication at the Groningen Centre for Media and Journalism Studies, University of Groningen, the Netherlands. His research interests include: (1) the use of new media in representative democracies; (2) the intersections between popular culture and formal politics; (3) online election campaigns; (4) social media and participatory journalism; (5) forms of online deliberation and political talk; (6) online third spaces and forms of civic engagement; (7) public sphere and deliberative democratic theory. He has published widely in these areas in a number of journals, including the *European Journal of Communication, Journal of Computer-Mediated Communication, Journalism Practice* and *Journal of Information Technology and Politics*.

**Daniel Hardt** is Associate Professor of Computational Linguistics at the Department of IT Management, Copenhagen Business School, Denmark. His research deals with language from a theoretical and practical point of view. His main theoretical interests involve the formal mechanisms underlying the construction of meaning in language. This theoretical work provides the underpinning for topics of practical interest to business and society: in particular, automatic translation, sentiment analysis and social media analytics.

**Abid Hussain** is a PhD fellow at the Department of IT Management, Copenhagen Business School, Denmark. His research interests are in computational social science. His PhD project focuses on the design, development and evaluation of an abstract data model, methods and tools for social data analytics of Facebook walls and Twitter streams.

**Zeshan Ali Jaffari** is a PhD fellow at the Department of IT Management, Copenhagen Business School, Denmark. His research interests are in social media management. His PhD project focuses on the methods and tools for social media management in order to address current operational issues and managerial challenges in the perception, adoption and use of social media in organisational settings.

**Andreas Jungherr** is a research fellow at the Chair of Political Sociology at the Otto-Friedrich-Universität, Bamberg, Germany. He is the co-author of *Das Internet in Wahlkämpfen: Konzepte, Wirkungen und Kampagnenfunktionen*. His articles have been published in *Journal of Communication, Internet Research, Social Science Computer Review* and *Policy & Internet.*

**Pascal Jürgens** is a research fellow at the Department of Mass Communication, Johannes Gutenberg-Universität, Mainz, Germany. His research interests include political communication, social networks and fragmentation phenomena on the Internet. A second focal point lies in the development of methods suited for the study of digital behavioural data.

**David Karpf** is an Assistant Professor in the School of Media and Public Affairs, George Washington University, USA. He conducts research on the Internet and political associations, with a particular interest in the new generation of 'netroots' advocacy groups. His work has been published in *Journal of Information Technology and Politics, Policy & Internet* and *Information, Communication, and Society*. He is also the author of *The MoveOn Effect: The Unexpected Transformation of American Political Advocacy* (2012). He is now working on a second book that focuses on analytics in political activism. He tweets as @davekarpf and blogs at shoutingloudly.com, and his research can be found at davidkarpf.com.

**Benjamin J. Lee** is a Research Associate in the Department of Politics and International Relations, University of Leicester, UK. He completed his PhD in the Institute for Social Change at the University of Manchester in 2013. Using a mixed-methods approach, his thesis measured and attempted to explain the use of web campaign tools in constituency campaigns during the 2010 UK general election. Since moving to Leicester, Benjamin has been working on a Europe-wide project mapping and analysing online communication by populist political groups, and he retains a strong interest in online political campaigning. Benjamin's work has been published in *Politics* and *New Media & Society*.

**Ben O'Loughlin** is Professor of International Relations and Co-Director of the New Political Communication Unit at Royal Holloway, University of London, UK. He is Specialist Advisor to the UK House of Lords Select Committee on Soft Power and the UK's Influence. He is co-editor of the Sage journal *Media, War & Conflict.* His most recent book is *Strategic Narratives: Communication Power and the New World Order*. He has carried out projects on media and security for the UK's Economic and Social Research Council and the Centre for the Protection of National Infrastructure. He recently completed a project with the BBC examining global responses on Twitter to the 2012 London Olympics. He has contributed to the *New York Times, Guardian, OpenDemocracy, Sky News* and *Newsweek*. He tweets as @ben_oloughlin.

**Jamsheed Shorish** is Chief Technology Officer at Uberlink Corporation and founder and CEO of Shorish Research. He is a computational economist, with a PhD from Carnegie Mellon University, USA. Prior to his entrepreneurial activities, he was Science Officer for the Information and Communication Technologies Domain at COST (the European Cooperation in Science and Technology) in Brussels and a professor at the Institute for Advanced Studies, Vienna, and the University of Aarhus, Denmark. Jamsheed has a background in complex systems analysis and dynamic optimisation, with published work appearing in journals such as the *Journal of Economic Theory, Journal of Economic Dynamics and Control, Economic Theory* and *Computational Economics*. He is currently an associated faculty member at the Institute for Advanced Studies, where he teaches on a regular basis. In 2007, he was a UK National Centre for e-Social Science (NceSS) Visiting Fellow at the University of Manchester, UK.

**Rosalynd Southern** is a final-year PhD student in the Centre for Census and Survey Research, University of Manchester, UK. She has been with the university since September 2008 when she began a Masters in research methods. Her PhD research is centred around online campaigning at the constituency level at the 2010 UK general election, with a focus on the adoption and use of personal websites, social media and email by candidates. Her main research interests include electoral campaigning, civic engagement, constituency-level campaigns and the use of new forms of media for political communication, assessed using quantitative methods.

**Laura Sudulich** is a research fellow at the Centre d'étude de la vie politique (Cevipol), Université Libre de Bruxelles, Belgium. She holds a PhD from Trinity College Dublin, and she previously worked as a postdoctoral research fellow at the University of Amsterdam and the European University Institute. Her research interests include new technologies and electoral campaigns, electoral behaviour, public opinion and voting advice applications (VAA). Her research has been published in *British Journal of Political Science, Electoral Studies, Parliamentary Affairs, Journal of Information Technology and Politics* and *Journal of Elections, Public Opinion and Parties*.

**Mike Thelwall** is Professor of Information Science and leader of the Statistical Cybermetrics Research Group at the University of Wolverhampton, UK, and a research associate at the Oxford Internet Institute. Mike has developed tools for gathering and analysing web data, including hyperlink analysis, sentiment analysis and content analysis for Twitter, YouTube, blogs and the general web. His publications include over 220 refereed journal articles, 7 book chapters and 2 books, including *Introduction to Webometrics*. He is an associate editor of the *Journal of the Association for Information Science and Technology* and sits on three other editorial boards.

**Yannis Theocharis** is a researcher at the Mannheim Centre for European Social Research (MZES), University of Mannheim, Germany. He was a Humboldt postdoctoral fellow at the University of Mannheim in 2011–2013. His research interests are political participation, protest politics, new media and social capital. He has published in the area of Internet and politics in journals such as *New Media & Society, Journal of Information Technology and Politics* and *Information, Communication & Society*.

**Ravi Vatrapu** is Professor of Human Computer Interaction and Director of the Computational Social Science Laboratory (CSSL) at the Department of IT Management, Copenhagen Business School, Denmark. He is also Professor of Applied Computing at the Norwegian

School of Information Technology (NITH), Norway. His basic research programme is to conduct theory-based empirical studies of socio-technical affordances and develop an empirically informed theory of technological intersubjectivity. His applied research areas are social media management and technology-enhanced learning. His current research projects are on social data analytics, teaching analytics and comparative informatics.

**Matthew Wall** is Lecturer in Politics at Swansea University, UK. Prior to arriving at Swansea, he worked as a Postdoctoral Research Fellow at the Université Libre de Bruxelles as part of the 'Electoral System Change in Europe since 1945' (ESCE) research project. He is a Marie Curie Research Fellow, having completed a year's postdoctoral research as part of the Training Network in Electoral Democracy (ELECDEM) initial training network at the Free University, Amsterdam. He completed his PhD thesis on African electoral and party systems at Trinity College Dublin. His research interests include VAA websites; online politics; electoral campaigns; electoral system effects and reform; comparative politics and Irish politics. Matthew has published several research articles on these topics in a number of journals, including *Electoral Studies, Party Politics, Parliamentary Affairs, Irish Political Studies, Journal of Information Technology and Politics* and *Journal of Elections, Public Opinion and Parties*.

**Stephen Ward** is Director of the Politics and Contemporary History Group and Reader in Politics at the School of Arts and Media, University of Salford, UK. He was previously a Research Fellow at the Oxford Internet Institute. He has published widely in areas such as political participation, campaigns and elections online along with parties' use of digital technologies.

**Scott Wright** is Senior Lecturer in Political Communication at the University of Melbourne, Australia. In 2012, he was Mid-Career Fellow of the British Academy, when this research was conducted. He has two principal research interests. The first focuses on government-led e-participation exercises such as online consultations and e-petitions. The second focuses on the 'new' agenda for online deliberation: everyday political in non-political, third spaces. His articles have appeared in *Journal of Computer-Mediated Communication, New Media and Society, British Journal of Politics and International Relations* and *Journal of European Public Policy*.

# Introduction: The Importance of Method in the Study of the 'Political Internet'

*Laura Sudulich, Matthew Wall, Rachel Gibson, Marta Cantijoch and Stephen Ward*

In this introduction, we outline our understanding of the 'political Internet' and present the methodologically focused approach that we take to the topic in this volume. We then discuss the growing social and political relevance of the Internet and examine the characteristics of the contemporary 'Web 2.0' Internet, before outlining the general methodological challenges and opportunities that it presents for researchers. We argue that three key characteristics of online political information in the Web 2.0 era shape and constrain any study of the political Internet. These characteristics are (1) extremely large volume, (2) heterogeneity and (3) plasticity. We contend that this combination creates what we term a 'dynamic data deluge' for social scientists, which makes distinguishing and recording meaningful information generated by the political Internet a methodologically challenging endeavour. We then discuss how the chapters collected here attempt to make sense of the dynamic data deluge that the political Internet presents. In the course of doing so, we build a picture of what distinguishes social media from earlier types of digital communication and discuss how social media content can be assimilated and processed by social science. We touch on epistemological concerns arising from this discussion before outlining the structure of the book and providing details of the individual contributions.

## A focus on methods for studying the 'political Internet'

The purpose of this volume is to describe and evaluate the methodologies that are available to social scientists who study political phenomena using data generated in the contemporary online environment. We use the term 'political' to refer to the realm of governance in its broadest sense, encompassing citizens, institutions and intermediary actors, as well as pertaining to their interactions and interdependencies. We thus use the term 'political Internet' to designate a system of globally interconnected computer and mobile devices that both provides a novel space for political interactions and interdependencies to occur and makes possible new forms of communication between political actors. Our principal concern in this introduction and in the chapters that follow is empirically capturing and dissecting the politically relevant information that the Internet generates, as well as providing some guidance to researchers on how best to approach this task for themselves, using a new suite of freely available methodologies.

Because the Internet is a multi-functional medium capable of facilitating communication, mobilisation, organisation and networking on a multitude of scales, from the local to the global, it has inspired a range of reactions, interpretations and predictions in both academic and popular literatures (for an example of two radically divergent viewpoints from the popular literature, see Shirky 2010; Morozov 2011). Our goal here, however, is not to explore the Internet's capabilities and properties from a substantive and interpretive perspective. Instead, the chapters included in this book focus primarily on showcasing methods for measurement and analysis of the political Internet, in particular the new processes of adoption and adaptation that are occurring due to the rise of social media. As such, we sit quite firmly in the behaviourist tradition of social research, focusing on observable and measurable political activities that are occurring in the social media environment. According to this tradition, 'scientific' social research should make the procedures employed freely available to the public for scrutiny and reproduction; indeed, the methods employed during the research process are a core element of the research content (King et al. 1994, 8–10). It is this methodological openness that allows for the accumulation of public knowledge in areas of social or political interest. We therefore emphasise in this volume the need to develop methods that are both transparent and reproducible in order to systematically increase our understanding of the political Internet.

This emphasis on 'praxis' or the 'how to' of studying the political Internet constitutes something of a departure from existing work on the topic. Early studies in particular (but also more recent scholarship) eschewed an empirical focus entirely and concentrated instead on addressing broader questions about what the emerging technology meant for underlying power relations that define modern political society. Some enthusiastic visionaries such as Negroponte (1995), Mosco and Foster (2001) speculated that the profoundly levelling consequences of the growth of computer-mediated communication (CMC) would radically transform political configurations and institutions around the world. As the field has evolved, however, scholars have taken to addressing these wider questions in a more empirically focused manner, by applying standard social science methods, as well as an emerging array of methods specifically tailored for the online environment to the study of various 'slices' or components of political life online. However, this progression has occurred with relatively little methodological introspection, a lacuna that is all the more keenly felt given the unique challenges and opportunities that data generated by the 'Web 2.0' or social media Internet offers to researchers. Our focus on the methodological challenges posed by the political Internet thus sets this collection apart from previous contributions in the field. Nonetheless, it is important to provide context and motivation for this study of the political Internet at the outset, which we seek to do in the next section.

## The growing social and political relevance of the Internet

A simple indicator of the growing social relevance of the Internet is the increasing volume of individuals around the world who use it. Internetworldstats.com, a website that amalgamates Internet use statistics from around the world, estimates a global total of over 2.4 billion Internet users as of June 2012; with particularly strong penetration levels in North America (78.6 per cent), Australia/Oceania (67.6 per cent) and Europe (63.2 per cent). These figures reflect a rapid growth in numbers of Internet users since the beginning of the twenty-first century, with the same website reporting an increase of just over 566 per cent from their estimate of 360 million users in December 2000. This trend is due both to a widening of access across all sectors of society as the technology becomes cheaper and easier to use (DiMaggio et al. 2004) and to the cohort effect whereby highly 'wired' younger generation gradually replaces those generations that relied on the more traditional media of radio, television and newspapers (Howe and Strauss 2000). The shift in generations is not simply one in the quantity of use of digital media, however, it is also one of quality. As we will discuss in the next section, the advent and spread of so-called 'Web 2.0' platforms, combined with new mobile Internet technologies in particular, have created a more immersive media experience.

The ongoing growth in numbers using Internet technologies and the increased intensity of many users' engagement with these technologies mean that the Internet offers ever more advantages to politicians and those seeking to occupy governing office. In political terms, while the Howard Dean campaign's innovative use of online technology in the 2004 Democratic primary pointed towards the potential of online campaigning (Hindman 2005), the US 2008 presidential campaign is widely recognised as having signalled the 'arrival' of the Internet into the mainstream of politics, with Barack Obama having shown how online technologies could generate substantial revenues and drive a successful campaign. Recent evidences from the UK general election of 2010 (see Southern and Lee in this volume; Lilleker and Jackson 2010; Southern and Ward 2011) and Australia in 2011 (Gibson and McAllister 2011) demonstrate that the use of e-campaigning techniques has become almost universal in established democracies, at least among candidates from major parties.[1]

Political organisations are also increasingly reliant on 'back end' web-based systems that are used to store data about voters, supporters and donors. Nielsen's ethnographic research on American congressional campaigns led him to conclude that the day-to-day organisation of such campaigns is 'deeply dependent on back-end logistics and increasingly tied in with new information and communication technologies' (2012, 27). Certainly, we have seen considerable divergence in the enthusiasm with which political parties and governments have adopted web technology; however, in some newly emerging social and political movements, the Internet is integral to organisational infrastructure and collective decision-making mechanisms. The German Pirate Party, for instance, is using a range of online softwares such as 'Pirate Pad' (a collaborative text editor) and 'Liquid Feedback' (a tool for proposing and ratifying policy proposals) to collaborate on policy platforms (Meyer 2012), while Beppe Grillo's Italian *Movimento 5 Stelle* argues for a form of direct democracy 'recognising to all users of the internet the role of government and direction that is normally attributed to a few' (Grillo 2011, 1). Technocentric parties are achieving some success at the polls: the German Pirate Party recently surpassed the 5 per cent threshold imposed by the German electoral system to win seats in several German state assemblies while the *Movimento 5 Stelle* won over 25 per cent of the popular vote in the 2013 Italian elections, the largest share won by any single party. There is little in principle to stop larger, more established parties adopting similar methodologies – though few have chosen to do so to date. Whether such tools can overcome Michels' (1915) 'Iron Law of Oligarchy' remains to be seen.

Overall, there is little doubt that the Internet is 'here to stay' within the political realm and wider society, and, indeed, is likely to become even more pervasive in the short to medium term. The extent to which the medium has now penetrated the daily lives and organisations of the key actors in political life means that it warrants sustained academic attention as an object of study. While there was arguably a lag between the reality of the Internet as an important political phenomenon and its uptake as a legitimate topic for academic study in the mid to late 1990s, there is little doubt that in the last few years, as Chadwick and Howard note, 'the politics of the Internet has entered the social science mainstream' (2009, 1). The 2000s have seen an ever-growing number of publications in monographs and mainstream journals exploring the Internet–politics nexus, as well as the emergence of several specialist journals, including *Information, Communication and Society*; *Information Polity*; *International Journal of Electronic Governance*; *Journal of Information Technology & Politics*; *Policy and Internet*; *New Media and Society*; and *Social Science Computer Review*.

However, as noted here and as the chapters that follow make clear, the embedding of the web into our daily lives creates a fundamental tension for those seeking to explore the online dynamics and processes. The Internet is an environment where 'everything flows' at an unprecedented pace, with content and connections constantly being created, amended and deleted. There is thus an emerging disjuncture between the Internet's permanence as an element of social (and political) life and the large-scale, diverse and highly ephemeral nature of its content. As we discuss in the next section, over the course of its incarnation as a mass medium, the Internet has evolved dramatically in terms of the interactive opportunities that it offers to users as well as the volume and structure of data that it generates for social scientists.

## The Internet, Web 2.0 and social media as objects of study

The Internet is now an established technology that has evolved rapidly in terms of its availability and diversity of uses. The Internet is most easily understood from a technological perspective as a global network of millions of computers (mobile or fixed platforms) connected through a set of protocols and a broad array of electronic, wireless and optical networking technologies. First established in the 1960s as a 'failsafe' communication device to serve the U.S. Department of Defense, the Internet now serves as a basic infrastructure that supports an increasingly extensive range of information resources and services. The World

Wide Web constitutes one of the most popular and widely used services running on the Internet. Invented by researcher Tim Berners-Lee in the late 1980s at the Swiss particle physics laboratory, the European Organisation for Nuclear Research (CERN), the Web is a collection of interconnected documents and other resources that are written in specialist computer code (primarily, hypertext mark-up language or html) and stored across multiple hosts worldwide. Through the software of a web browser and the hypertext links embedded in the documents they are easily accessed and retrieved through the 'point and click' of a mouse.

The visually exciting and user-friendly nature of the Web meant that the Internet rapidly became a mass medium from the mid-1990s onwards, accessed by millions for a wide range of recreational, commercial and educational purposes. Although the Web was originally conceived as a technology that would allow all users to view and edit pages, a decision was made in the early stages of the development of Web browser technology to remove the 'edit' function (Anderson 2007). This meant that most web users viewed or interacted with content (primarily, pages of text and graphics) produced by the 'webmasters' – those individuals within an organisation or institution who had mastered html. However, by the middle of the first decade of the twenty-first century, webmasters were to lose their elite status as new software and services were developed that allowed ordinary users to generate, edit, tag and post content in what Kaplan and Haenlein describe as 'an evolution back to the Internet's roots' (2010, 60). This shift to a more bottom-up, user-generated and interactive version of the Web was captured in abstract terms as a move from a Web 1.0 era to Web 2.0 (O'Reilly 2005).

Kaplan and Haenlein (2010) identify Adobe Flash animation and multimedia software, Really Simple Syndication (RSS) web feed formats and a set of technologies and practices known as Autosynchronous Java Script + XML (AJAX) as the technical underpinnings of Web 2.0. Anderson (2007) notes that the Web 2.0 environment is characterised by the presence of several applications and services that facilitate user generation, sharing, editing and tagging of content, as well as the creation of networks of connected users – such services and applications include blogs and blog-creating software, wikis, multimedia-sharing sites, tagging and social bookmarking sites, podcasting and social media sites. These technologies both emerge from and contribute to a series of 'big ideas' that underpin the Web 2.0 Internet – most notably a focus on facilitating the production and sharing of user-generated content, but also a deep awareness of network effects and the 'power of the crowd', as well as a focus on using large-scale data as a technical and economic resource (O'Reilly 2005; Anderson 2007).

In this volume, the concept of 'social media' is of particular importance, and we therefore clarify what the term means here. While social media sites are often conflated with social networking sites such as MySpace, LinkedIn, Facebook and Twitter, we understand social networking sites to be a sub-category of a broad conceptualisation of 'social media'. Boyd and Ellison identify the articulation of a list with whom users wish to share a connection as a defining criterion of a social network site, arguing that 'what makes social network sites unique is not that they allow individuals to meet strangers, but rather that they enable users to articulate and make visible their social networks' (2007, 211). We adopt Kaplan and Haenlein's (2010, 61) more encompassing definition of social media as 'a group of Internet applications that build on the ideological and technical foundations Web 2.0, and that allow the creation and exchange of User Generated Content', meaning that blogs, wikis and content community sites (such as YouTube) are classified alongside social networking sites such as Facebook and Twitter as 'social media'.

A key take away from the preceding discussion for our purposes is that the Internet, the web and social media, while clearly interrelated and interdependent, are not one and the same thing. They form a chronological and technological line of progression whereby the Internet forms the underlying infrastructure and 'root' network that supports the outward 'skein' of the Web, upon which are laid various applications, some of the most popular and widely used of which are social media platforms. From a sociopolitical perspective, they can be seen as an increasingly democratised means of undertaking digital communication, with social media now forming the most widely used entry point into the online world for most people.

From an historical perspective, this development can also be located in a wider narrative developed by Bimber (2003), which argues that periods of relative stability in terms of the political control of information and political contestation ('information regimes') are punctuated by dramatic technological changes influencing the costs of acquiring and transmitting political information ('information revolutions'). Bimber argues that each information revolution that has taken place to date in America has led to dramatic changes in patterns of political contestation. Interestingly, the period between such revolutions appears to be contracting in the Internet age. With rapid advent of Web 2.0

from the mid-2000s onwards, and talk (among some) of a Web 3.0 era emerging (see, for example, Hendler 2009), we may be in a period of semi-continuous information revolution, which has implications for methodologically rigorous study of online politics, especially in the domain of reliability.

While this process is fascinating from a theoretical and normative perspective as noted earlier, our concern here is with how, in practical terms, we can make sense of the growing chaos of bits and bytes that it has released into the world of data analysis. The rise of social media in particular presents a new frontier for social science research methodology to confront. In the subsequent discussion in this chapter, and throughout the contributions collected for this volume, we argue that, in its current form, the Internet presents new opportunities for the study of politics and society, providing digitised and instantaneous data on processes and phenomena that were previously extremely difficult to study empirically. However, this medium also poses novel challenges for researchers seeking to abide by the standards of transparency, generalisability and replicability that underlie the 'scientific' claims of empirically orientated social and political research. As we discuss in the next section, a combination of volume, heterogeneity and plasticity makes the contemporary political Internet a unique research target for social scientists, necessitating considerable methodological care.

## Methodological challenges and the 'Political Internet': volume, heterogeneity and plasticity

Above, we have referred to three innate characteristics of the Internet that we consider to have significant methodological implications for any empirical study of the political Internet. These are the overwhelming supply of information that it presents, the heterogeneity of that information and the plasticity or changeability of that content. These overarching features of Internet-based political data are particularly prevalent in the era of social media and present major new challenges and opportunities for data collection, processing and analysis. We elaborate on these core characteristics below and outline how the chapters collected in this volume illustrate some of the key problems and possibilities that they raise with respect to the study of political actors, institutions and events.

### Volume

First, the sheer quantity of Internet-generated data creates a unique set of methodological questions for social science research. Social media promote the flow of an unprecedented amount of information, leading to the emergence of the term 'big data' in discourses surrounding what can be gleaned about individuals and societies from their digital imprints. Big data is collected into large datasets where online transactions become the unit of analysis. This particular type of data often involves capturing real-time messaging, such as tweets, chat-streams, blog posts and their comments, and Facebook walls' content and timelines.

In the pre-digital era, political scientists were primarily responsible for the generation of data that preserved as much as possible of the quality of social and political phenomena via a systematic process of measuring and recording. Such a constraint was useful in that it allowed analysts to exercise a degree of control over the size and quality of the information that they created. However, this process also introduced a certain degree of 'artifice' and gave a manufactured quality to data that social scientists were able to generate. The Internet, and computer technology more generally, has introduced a previously unimaginable level of automated or 'natural' data production, which occurs as a by-product of the interactions that take place online. The Internet generates an enormous corpus of politically relevant information, and the digital quality of this information means that it can be captured to faithfully reflect its original content. The capacity of online processes to generate enormous tranches of data introduces some novel issues that students of the political Internet must address.

Hargittai (2000) argued that the emergence of the Internet as a popular communication medium created a paradox whereby information abundance leads to a situation of attention scarcity among users. We build on this insight by focusing on the abundance of potentially interesting information for political scientists created by the Internet versus the relative scarcity of systematic methods to capture such data. While there is an enormous amount of data available, much of what is collected is 'noise', that is, meaningless data having little to do with the political phenomena that we are interested in. Karpf (2012) points out that large portions of the data that can be harvested online are 'fake' having been generated by 'bots' created to systematically distort online data. Worryingly for political analysts, Karpf goes on to argue that 'there is an inverse relationship between the reliability of an online metric of influence and its financial or political value' (ibid. 650), meaning that the most relevant metrics for political scientists are precisely those that are most likely to be distorted by professional computer scientists seeking to game the system for financial gain. Even leaving these considerations to one side, the vast majority of data generated online are non-political – postings about the weather, sports events and celebrity gossip being some examples. It is therefore essential that social scientists studying the political Internet should devise strategies for parsing – allowing them to collect data relevant to their topic of interest, as well as to distinguish such data from non-relevant 'noise' in their analyses.

Chapters by García-Albacete and Theocharis and Jungherr and Jürgens studying Twitter content in this volume show how this can be done through detection of discernible elements embedded in the users' imprint, such as 'hashtags' – keywords explicitly marked with the symbol # used by twitterers to categorise the content of their own messages. By identifying these hashtags, researchers take advantage of the features of the medium for data collection purposes, and they do so from an extraneous, non-interventionist position: Twitter users employ and develop hashtags for the sake of communication efficiency, unaware of the researcher's presence.[2] Beyond the case of Twitter, the Thelwall and Vatrapu et al. chapters approach the task through a pilot or case study approach, taking a small 'slice' of the social media world – comments on a particular YouTube video or on the Facebook wall of a small number of politicians – and then subjecting this text to analysis with purpose built new software tools that parse and extract essential aspects such as tone, focus and demographics of those commenting.

It is also important to note that, despite its ever-widening reach and the growing volumes of data that it is capable of producing, the Internet is not entirely ubiquitous either within or across national societies. Even within industrially and economically well-developed countries, there remain substantial portions of the public without Internet access, and among those with access, there are sections of the population that never or very rarely use the Internet. More recent studies have therefore suggested that the nature of this 'digital divide' problem is evolving, from one of unequal access in the 1990s to one of 'differentiated use' (DiMaggio et al. 2004) in the 2000s, with Hargittai and Walejko finding that 'neither creation nor sharing (of online content) is randomly distributed' (2008, 239). Although the implications for social science research of this divide are widely appreciated as a key normative and substantive question for research (Norris 2001), from the methodologically centred perspective of this book, the key concern arising from the 'digital divide' phenomenon is that it gives rise to systematic biases in information gathered online that limit the extent to which social scientists can extrapolate to trends and views in wider society. Indeed, almost all of the chapters in this volume make clear the limitations of their analysis in relying solely on online-generated data, when one is seeking to make generalisations about wider populations of interest. The methodological question of interest is whether the large volume of data generated online can be leveraged in order to produce either transformed datasets or subsamples that can be used to make inferences about out-of-sample populations.

## Diversity

The second feature of the political Internet that we focus on here is the extremely heterogeneous character of social media data. Data can be transmitted in graphic, textual and audio formats. In order to capture such a diverse mass of content, new tools have to be designed to fit the complexity of the object of study. While this aspect of online political data presents daunting challenges and trade-offs, it also holds the promise of generating data that were previously unavailable to political and social science. From websites to complex and extremely dense Twitter networks, the digital medium provides for a fresh insight into established subjects of study. The home pages of candidates, for example, as the chapters by Lee and Southern in this volume demonstrate, provide a new publicly accessible and self-defined 'one stop shop' and window of insight into campaigns and parties' core business and goals (Druckman et al. 2009, 345). Social media offer new global and aggregate sources of data on popular behaviour and trends. Search tools, links, comments and 'like buttons' on social network profiles all present new means of measuring popularity and public interest in people, organisations and events.

Tracing patterns of interaction and connection through hyperlinks and Twitter or YouTube networks, as undertaken in the chapter in this volume by Thelwall, can open up the 'weak ties' that bind individuals to a cause or movement. Given the myriad of new types of data that are being generated online, it is not possible for one book to contain and describe them all. We can, however, impose a degree of order and aggregation on what exists and based on the analyses undertaken here we divide Internet-based data into two types – network data and textual data.

*Network data*

While use of network data in social science was present prior to the arrival of the Internet (Borgatti et al. 2009), the development of the Web and social media has seen an escalation of interest in this type of analysis. Initially, this interest was fired by the new connectivity made possible through the presence of hyperlinks on sites and weblogs, whereby organisations and individuals could interlink on a global scale. Further enthusiasm for the collection of network data has been stimulated by the rise of social media sites dedicated specifically to social networking, such as MySpace, Facebook and LinkedIn, as well as a host of slightly more instrumental social media platforms such as YouTube, Flickr and Twitter that focus on sharing of particular media content such as video, photos and news media updates. Thus, in addition to approaches designed to map and measure the broader properties and structure of the networks built online, the focus is now also upon methods that can extract and make sense of those interactions that occur within the new social spaces being created on the Web.

The chapters assembled here focus on both. The chapters by Ackland and Shorish and Karpf adopt the structural perspective in mapping the architecture and characteristics of the political blogosphere. Ackland and Shorish address the new opportunities opened up by the Internet in the study of homophily, a widely discussed concept in the pre-Internet sociological research agenda describing how the structure of connections among individuals and actors typically displays patterns of preferences on the basis of similarity in personal attributes or political affiliation. Using social network analysis techniques, they map processes of political homophily in the blogosphere and discuss how web data collection and analysis is advancing the classic studies of network structures and properties. Karpf's chapter introduces us to the Blogosphere Authority Index, a ranking system for the elite political blogosphere through the systematic measurement of changing traffic, hyperlink and community activity patterns among major blogs. The chapter discusses four main themes related to the structure and properties of this particular network: overall system stability, left–right comparative rankings, changes in blog architecture and overall blog professionalisation. Vatrapu et al. takes an alternative approach, offering a closer look at the interactions occurring within those networks. Thelwall mixes the two in that he not only examines the structure of the networks that exist around YouTube videos in regard to their size and density but also provides some in-depth understanding of dynamics within those groups through a pilot study of comments on a speech by Barack Obama.

*Textual data*

The process of extracting substantively meaningful information from textual data represents one of the major challenges for social scientists studying the political Internet. Content analysis of texts in political science dates back over 50 years and is seen as one of the most powerful techniques to derive meaningful generalisation from textual data (Hopkins and King 2010). In the pre-digital era, while texts could be multiple and extensive, they were more finite in nature. Only a predictable amount of newsprint, for example, was produced on any one day. As such a multiplicity of methodological choices were open to researchers, starting with simple small N manual approaches that developed into sophisticated large-scale computer-based techniques. In the digital era, the abundance of data available renders the former approach somewhat obsolete as a primary mode of extracting meaning (see Jurgherr and Jürgens in this volume).

This loss of the 'personal touch' is one that needs some consideration. The differences between human coding and computerised coding in terms of reliability versus validity have been summarised well by Benoit and Laver (2006) in relation to the study of election manifestos. Whereas computerised techniques can claim perfect reliability, human coding provides a higher level of validity, as human coders with an awareness of the context can make inferences about content that are (currently) impossible for machines to reach. All in all, 'it is clear that we need to take advantage of continuing advances in computational techniques for analysing social media, while ensuring that we make the most effective use of methods that rely on human expertise' (Procter et al. 2013, 209).

Automated coding requires a certain structure and volume of textual data and can be somewhat ambiguous in its output – often requiring subjective substantive interpretation to be usable as a source of meaningful political analysis. While of course this doesn't mean that human coding is precluded for digital data as a number of the chapters included here show, it does mean that a bias towards more automation is inevitably introduced to minimise loss of information. One potentially promising avenue of research that seeks to address this trade-off is the crowd sourcing of data coding, with large numbers of non-expert coders being used either alongside or instead of automated coding for large volumes of political text (Benoit et al. 2012). However, with large-scale textual data generated online, human coding is increasingly used as a post-hoc check or confirmatory exercise on the results derived from computer-based methods.

The chapters included in this volume reflect this tension. The social media analysis of Vatrapu et al. uses the new software of SODATO (Social Data Analytics Tool) to apply a fully automated coding scheme to Facebook wall posts to measure their tone, subject and length. Conversely, automated systems are used by Jungherr and Jürgens and García-Albacete and Theocharis in their studies to only retrieve information from Twitter. The authors then turn to manual coding protocols to discern and classify the content of the messages.

### Plasticity

The third key feature of the political Internet that we draw attention to is its dynamic nature, or what we term *plasticity*. The web, unlike previous electronic and print-based forms of media, is an ever-changing space. Much of the data that it generates are ephemeral and can be subject to almost instantaneous change. Schnieder and Foot (2004, 115) have pointed out that the transience of the Internet as a medium involves two dimensions: content and construction. The content generated online may only appear there briefly and often cannot be traced back (retrieved) over a long period of time. This means that once something is not accounted for at the beginning of the data collection process, it is most likely that it will be irretrievable afterwards. Such a major *caveat* has potentially dramatic consequences for research outcomes, and poorly designed data collection can easily bias results or produce invalid estimations. In terms of construction, Schnieder and Foot point out that 'web content, once presented, needs to be reconstructed and represented in order for others to experience it' (ibid.). However, the structures of websites and social networking platforms are not constant – some activities and types of interaction are altered and discontinued, while others are introduced. This means that the reconstruction of collected online content is not always straightforward for data collected over an extended time period, and changes in file formats and software can make it difficult to reconstruct and represent stored digital data in its original format (*Economist* 2012).

The authors assembled here have tackled this challenge with varying degrees of success. Vatrapu et al., for example, study the Facebook walls of politicians daily across a two-year period. Karpf reports the results for the Blogosphere Authority Index over a two-year period as well, although his indicators were measured monthly – blogs' dynamism moving at a relatively slower pace than that of social networking sites.

While there are concerns about the permanence of data produced by social media, it also needs to be acknowledged that social media sources facilitate the recording and measurement of phenomena that were previously impervious to capture. For instance, public conversations around a particular event or issue that occur on Twitter or the daily output of campaigns are now accessible and recordable, allowing us to measure aspects of human interaction that were hitherto out of reach. And as Ackland and Shorish discuss in their chapter, the longitudinal character of the datasets collected online, albeit challenging, constitutes a new advantage for the study of dynamic social processes of preference and tie formation.

These new dimensions of volume, diversity and plasticity that characterise Internet data raise important issues for research design and the steps of the research process – data selection, capture and analysis. As we have outlined, the methodologically oriented pieces in this volume have developed an array of replicable approaches designed to maximise the opportunities presented by these characteristics of online data, as well as to mitigate the difficulties that such data present. In the final section of this chapter, we outline some important epistemological considerations that flow from this discussion of the characteristics of the political internet.

## Epistemological considerations

We argue that moving forward with the task of extracting meaningful information from web-based data requires a radical re-thinking of the optimal manner of approaching the research design process. Specifically, we need to revisit the choice between inductive and deductive approaches. The changeability of the Internet means that web scholars must be observers of emerging patterns and regularities, as well as builders of generalised theory and testable hypotheses. The dichotomy separating induction and deduction as methods of understanding empirical phenomena dates back to Aristotle. From its origins as a philosophical classification, the induction/deduction divide has been transmogrified into a core cleavage in philosophy of science. Francis Bacon pioneered the view that induction based on observation and experimentation is the true 'scientific' method (Moses and Knutsen 2012, 47). According to Bacon, scientific knowledge begins with observation – particularly observation of consistent patterns linking cause to effect – with intuitions based on these observations being verifiable by public and transparent empirical demonstrations employing the experimental method. Popper's 'positivist' conception of the scientific method, on the other hand, is characterised by an alternative process. According to Popperian logic, scientific hypotheses should be based on deductive inference – scientists develop generalised theoretical accounts of empirical/social phenomena based on logic and on the findings of previous research, rather than through direct observation. These hypotheses must be specified in a manner that can be falsified by specific, measureable observations (ibid.). Deductive methods are driven by prior ideas, which are used to generate falsifiable hypotheses, which are then tested against empirical observations. Inductive methods employ data to generate ideas, which are then used to generate hypotheses, which are then tested against subsequent observations. In other words, the deductive approach is theory driven, whereas the inductive approach is 'data' or 'observation' driven.

It should be acknowledged that modern political science is dominated by the Popperian 'positivist' approach. In line with this tradition, most studies of the political Internet have adopted a deductive approach, based on the classification and interpretation of web content on the basis of theoretical speculations. While this logic deeply characterises social science research, its application to web-originated data is somewhat more problematic than to other type of data. This is principally due to what we describe above as the 'plasticity' of online data. As we outlined above, the Internet and associated technologies have rapidly changed during its relatively short life as a mass medium and, the audience using these technologies has expanded rapidly. While a hypothesis may be valid at one point in the development of the Internet as a medium, there is no guarantee that it will remain so for a significant amount of time. Furthermore, certain hypotheses may only emerge in the light of fresh technological or audience developments while others may cease to make sense. Karpf (2012, 642) argues that this rapid and continuous changes in both the audiences using online technologies and the types of participation and interaction that those technologies offer – combined with a relatively glacial grant application, research and publication cycle – means that many research findings about the political Internet are 'rendered obsolete by the time that they are published'. These considerations would point towards an indicative and highly conditional approach to the study of the political Internet.

However, such an approach comes with associated costs. For instance, the lack of universally accepted theoretical classifications of online politically relevant material has produced a multiplicity of rather inconsistent empirical methods of data classification and analysis. While Gibson and Ward (2000) sought to produce a systematic theoretical and empirical roadmap for further studies of similar nature, the field has deviated from such a template in a rather chaotic fashion, which makes cross-country and longitudinal comparison extremely difficult. We ought to regard such a lack of consistency as a shortcoming of inductive and ad hoc theoretical and methodological development in the study of the political Internet.

## Organisation of the book

In Part I, the first four chapters look at the capture and analysis of structural features of social media use by social and political actors in the shape of hyperlinked policy networks, blog-based networks and YouTube commenter's networks. Ackland and Shorish examine the structure and social implications of online networks forged through hyperlinks and demonstrates how a particular statistical social network analysis technique (exponential random graph modelling) can be used to map and analyse patterns of homophily in the US political blogosphere. Karpf follows up with an overview of empirical efforts to define and capture the blogosphere and the influence of individual political bloggers. He applies his index of blog influence across a two-year period in the United States to highlight the changes and challenges facing researchers in the field. Thelwall presents a purpose-built software tool, Webometric Analyst, that can extract and analyse comments on YouTube videos and map the network relationships between commenters and comments. These diagrams offer important insights into the extent to which social media generate new patterns of connections between previously unconnected individuals or build communities of opinion and dissemination. The tool is significant in that it allows for an in-depth and systematic analysis of the circulation of and response to individual and collections of videos on one of the most widely used social media platforms.

In Part II, the analysis turns to the substantive interactions occurring within these online networks. Vatrapu et al. use a newly developed web resource, Social Data Analytics Tool (SODATO), to capture and sentiment analyse Facebook group participants and discussion in a recent Danish general election. They compare the consensual nature of online political discussion across the two countries in the lead-up to recent national elections through analysis of the comments expressed on the Facebook walls of the main candidates and the extent of cross-wall postings. The findings reveal an interesting picture of divergence, suggesting that social technologies do not necessarily suppress but actually may reflect cultural differences in political participation. García-Albacete and

Theocharis, and Jungherr and Jürgens turn the attention to the content of Twitter discussion. Key questions posed are the extent to which the Twitterverse can provide a means of tracking and tracing the evolution of offline protest: can Twitter messages be used as a barometer for public opinion on key political events such as protest movements? García-Albacete and Theocharis develop several indicators used to compare mobilisation processes in three related but different movements: the 15M or *Indignados* movement in Spain, the Greek *Aganaktismenoi* protests and the 'Occupy Wall Street' movement in the United States. They show and discuss how data can be collected and analysed to study the aims, repertoires of action and tactics of different protest movements as well as evaluations and attitudes of Twitter users towards them. Jungherr and Jürgens illustrate the potential of social media for event detection. They examine Twitter messages posted during one of the heaviest episodes of clashes between demonstrators and the police in Germany's recent history – the contentious protest against the project 'Stuttgart 21'. They apply four distinct approaches for event detection on data collected from Twitter during the protest to develop a timeline of the events occurring offline. By comparing the results produced by these different methods, they show how it is possible to identify various discrete steps of the protest, its build-up and its aftermath using web data. Finally, Wright and Graham probe more deeply the question of the nature of debate occurring online, and particularly in informal third spaces, with a multi-method approach that combines scraping posts from sites to identify 'super participants' and level of equality of debate within a given forum. This automated element is triangulated with qualitative coding and interviews to better understand the motivations and outlook of individuals who dominate online discussion.

In Part III, in two chapters, Southern and Lee examine a specific area of innovation in the use of social media – election campaign communication efforts by parties and candidates. Both authors aim to develop and apply innovative coding schemes to produce quantitative data to compare and characterise parties' web campaign content. Southern's chapter focuses on parties' use of external Web 2.0 platforms in the 2010 UK general election and proposes a new classification schema for measuring their interactivity online. She makes a case for extension of the analysis into a mixed-methods approach that triangulates the quantitative site data with qualitative data from a candidate email study and elite interviews. The chapter by Lee identifies some key methodological considerations associated with identifying and researching local level social media campaigns. Through a study of candidates' web use in the NorthWest region of the United Kingdom during the 2010 general election he concentrates on the challenges faced by researchers in first locating all facets of an official web campaign. He then establishes a new set of conceptual and empirical criterion for judging the authenticity of candidates' engagement with the new digital media.

The book concludes with a chapter by Anstead and O'Loughlin that provides a historical perspective on current methodological debates. By examining the narratives surrounding the development of public opinion polling, particularly in its formative years, they draw parallels for the understanding of new semantic opinion polling (the mining and analysis of large amounts of social media data to make statements about public opinion). Anstead and O'Loughlin argue that new semantic polling offers significant challenges to the orthodoxy of public opinion polling by: blurring the distinction between qualitative and quantitative data; challenging the methodological individualism of traditional public opinion surveys; and even questioning our basic understanding and definition of what constitutes public opinion.

## Notes

1. Further anecdotal evidence to support the growing importance attributed to the medium by politicians can be seen in the recent dispute between the two main candidates for the London mayoral election – Boris Johnston and Ken Livingstone. A heated argument emerged in the campaign over the former's appropriation of the @MayorofLondon Twitter account, which was re-named @BorisJohnson for his re-election campaign. The resultant furore led Johnson to establish a separate @BackBoris account to promote campaign activities (though he nonetheless used the @BorisJohnson feed to promote this new account) (Mulholland 2012). While appearing on the surface to be perhaps a trivial spat, the Livingstone camp clearly felt that the account's 250,000 plus followers represented a significant political resource.
2. This may, in turn, raise relevant ethical issues.

## References

Anderson, P. (2007) 'What Is Web 2.0? Ideas, Technologies and Implication for Education', JISC Technology and Standards Watch Report, February.

Benoit, K., Conway, D., Laver, M. and Mikhaylov, S. (2012) 'Crowd-sourced Data Coding for the Social Sciences: Massive Non-expert Human Coding of Political Texts', paper presented at the 3rd annual 'New Directions in Analyzing Text as Data' Conference, Harvard University, Cambridge, MA, 5–6 October.

Benoit, K. and Laver, M. (2006) *Party Policy in Modern Democracies* (London: Routledge).

Bimber, B. (2003) *Information and American Democracy: Technology in the Evolution of Political Power* (Cambridge: Cambridge University Press).

Borgatti, S., Ajay, M., Daniel, B. and Labianca, G. (2009) 'Network Analysis in the Social Sciences', *Science*, 323 (5916), 892–895.

Boyd, D. and Ellison, N. (2007) 'Social Network Sites: Definition, History and Scholarship', *Journal of Computer Mediated Communication*, 13 (1), 210–230.

Chadwick, A. and Howard, P.N. (2009) 'Introduction: New Directions in Internet Politics Research', in A. Chadwick and P.N. Howard (eds.), *Routledge Handbook of Internet Politics* (Oxford: Routledge), pp. 1–11.

DiMaggio, P., Hargittai, E., Celeste, C. and Shafer, S. (2004) 'Digital Inequality: From Unequal Access to Differentiated use', in K. Neckerman (ed.), *Social Inequality* (New York: Russell Sage Foundation), pp. 355–400.

Druckman, J., Kifer, M. and Parkin, M. (2009) 'Campaign Communications in US Congressional Elections', *American Political Science Review*, 103 (3), 343–366.

*The Economist*. (2012) 'Digital Archiving: History Flushed', 28 April 2012.

Gibson, R.K. and McAllister, I. (2011) 'Do Online Election Campaigns Win Votes? The 2007 Australian "YouTube" Election', *Political Communication*, 28 (2), 227–244.

Gibson, R.K. and Ward, S.J. (2000) 'A Proposed Methodology for Studying the Function and Effectiveness of Party and Candidate Websites', *Social Science Computer Review*, 18 (3), 301–319.

Grillo, B. (2011) 'The 5 Star MoVement (sic.) Between Utopia and Reality.' Beppe Grillo's Blog (English version), posted 23 June 2011, available at: http://www.beppegrillo.it/en/2011/06/the_5_star_movement_between_ut.html, date accessed 11 March 2013.

Hargittai, E. (2000) 'Open Portals or Closed Gates? Channelling Content on the World Wide Web', *Politics*, 27 (4), 233–253.

Hargittai, E. and Walejko, P. (2008) 'The Participation Divide: Content Creation and Sharing in the Digital Age', *Information, Communication & Society*, 11 (2), 239–256.

Hendler, J. (2009) 'Web 3.0 Emerging', *Computer (IEE Computer Society)*, 42 (1), 111–113.

Hindman, M. (2005) 'The Real Lessons of Howard Dean: Reflections on the First Digital Campaign', *Perspectives on Politics*, 3 (1), 121–128.

Hopkins, D. and King, G. (2010) 'Extracting Systematic Social Science Meaning from Text', *American Journal of Political Science*, 54 (1), 229–247.

Howe, N. and Strauss, W. (2000) *Millenials Rising: The Next Great Generation* (New York: Vintage).

Kaplan, A. and Haenlein, M. (2010) 'Users of the World, Unite! The Challenges and Opportunities of Social Media', *Business Horizons*, 53, 59–68.

Karpf, D. (2012) 'Social Science Research Methods in Internet Time', *Information, Communication & Society*, 15 (5), 639–661.

King, G., Keohane, R.O. and Verba, S. (1994) *Designing Social Inquiry: Scientific Inference in Qualitative Research* (Princeton, NJ: Princeton University Press).

Lilliker, D.G. and Jackson, N.A. (2010) 'Towards a More Participatory Style of Election Campaigning: The Impact of Web 2.0 on the UK 2010 General Election', *Policy & Internet*, 2 (3), 69–98.

Meyer, D. (2012) 'How the German Pirate Party's "Liquid Democracy" Works' published on www.tecpresident.com's 'WeGov' section, available at: http://techpresident.com/news/wegov/22154/how-german-pirate-partys-liquid-democracy-works date accessed 12 March 2013.

Michels, R. (1915) *Political Parties: A Sociological Study of the Oligarchical Tendencies of Modern Democracy,* translated into English by Eden P. and Cedar P. (New York: The Free Press).
Morozov, E. (2011) *The Net Delusion: The Dark Side of Internet Freedom* (London: Allen Lane).
Mosco, V. and Foster, D. (2001) 'Cyberspace and the End of Politics', *Journal of Communication Inquiry*, 25 (3), 218–236.
Moses, J. and Knutsen, T. (2012) *Ways of Knowing: Competing Methodologies in Social and Political Research,* second edition (Houndmills: Palgrave MacMillan).
Mulholland, H. (2012) 'Boris Johnson Backs Down Over London Mayoral Twitter Account', *The Guardian,* 20 March.
Negroponte, N. (1995) *Being Digital* (New York: Vintage Publishing).
Nielsen, R.K. (2012) *Ground Wars: Personalized Communication in Political Campaigns* (New Jersey: Princeton University Press).
Norris, P. (2001) *Digital Divide: Civic Engagement, Information Poverty and the Internet Worldwide* (New York: Cambridge University Press).
O'Reilly, T. (2005) 'What is Web 2.0: Design Patterns and Business Models for the Next Generation of Software.' O'Reilly website, 30 September 2005 O'Reilly Media Inc. available at: http://www.oreillynet.com/pub/a/oreilly/tim/news/2005/09/30/what-is-web-20.html , date accessed 13 April 2013.
Procter, R., Vis, F. and Voss, A. (2013) 'Reading the Riots on Twitter: Methodological Innovation for the Analysis of Big Data', *International Journal of Sociological Research Methodology,* 16 (3), 197–214.
Schnieder, S.M. and Foot K.A. (2004) 'The Web as an Object of Study', *New Media and Society,* 6, 114–122.
Shirky, C. (2010) *Cognitive Surplus: Creativity and Generosity in a Connected Age* (New York: Penguin).
Southern, R. and Ward, S.J. (2011) 'Below the Radar: Online Campaigning at the Local Level at the 2010 Election', in D. Wring, R. Mortimore and S. Atkinson (eds.), *Political Communication in Britain* (Houndmills: Palgrave Macmillan), pp. 218–241.

# Part I
# Structure and Influence

# 1

# Political Homophily on the Web

*Robert Ackland and Jamsheed Shorish*

Homophily is a central concept within sociological research and describes the preference of actors in social networks to form ties on the basis of shared attributes, such as gender and race, as well as subjective characteristics such as political affiliations and desires for certain consumer goods. The study of homophily can provide important insights into the diffusion of information and behaviours within a society and has been particularly useful in understanding online community formation given the self-selected nature of the information consumed.

In this chapter, we introduce the concept of homophily and show that in order to accurately measure homophily, one needs to control for factors such as group size and the existence endogenous network ties. We then provide a discussion of how Web data can be used to advance research into political homophily, which is the phenomenon whereby people seek out others who share their political affiliation. We contend that the Web provides several unique opportunities for political homophily research, but there are associated challenges that must be taken into account.

Any research involving Web data for understanding social and political behaviour should first establish that the observed online behaviour is a valid or meaningful representation of its offline counterpart – this has been referred to as the requirement that there be a 'mapping' between the online and offline world (Williams 2010), or that the online data have 'construct validity' (Burt 2011). Our chapter discusses the construct validity of Web data for political homophily and offers three tests of such validity.

One of the tests is that the Web data display *differential* homophily, where communities exhibit idiosyncratic tie preferences within their community, rather than a uniform tendency of flocking for the population at large. In this context, we revisit the well-known 'Divided They Blog' 2004 weblog network data of Adamic and Glance (2005) and show how a particular statistical social network analysis technique (exponential random graph modelling or ERGM) can be used to quantitatively characterise political (uniform and/or differential) homophily in the blogosphere. We use the VOSON (Virtual Observatory for the Study of Online Networks) hyperlink network research tool to construct a network of the US political blogosphere in 2011 and assess how political homophily has changed since 2004. Complementing the traditional insights gained from qualitative network visualisation techniques, we show that differential homophily has become more characteristic of the political landscape exhibited by weblogs from 2004 to 2011.

## Assortative mixing and homophily

Assortative mixing in social networks refers to a positive correlation in the personal attributes (age, race, ethnicity, education, religion, socio-economic status, physical appearance, etc.) of people who are socially connected to one another. There is strong evidence that people assortatively mix when it comes to forming friendships, marriages and sexual partnerships – this is, the 'birds of a feather flock together' phenomenon (see, for example, McPherson et al. 2001 for a review).

With regard to marriage, research reviewed in the aforementioned McPherson et al. (2001) shows that Americans exhibit a preference for 'same-race alters' far in excess of preference for similarity based on other characteristics such as age and education. There is also evidence that people assortatively mix on the basis of political preferences, and recent work by Alford et al. (2011) shows that the correlation between spouses' political attitudes is larger than for other personality and/or physical traits.

A tendency towards politically homogeneous social interactions affects the degree of exposure to different political perspectives, and this can have an impact on, for example, the operation and effectiveness of municipal councils and civic associations ('crosstalk'; see, for example, Weare et al. 2009). In addition, the concept of assortative mixing assists in the classification of political networks and the factions they represent, as discussed in, for example, Kydros et al. (2012). And in the wake of the mass shooting tragedy in Newtown, Connecticut, in December 2012, network visualisations have permeated mass-media outlets to such an extent that the gun control debate in the United States is also best understood – and presented – from an assortative mixing perspective (cf. Stray 2013).

Assortative mixing is thus an important and fundamental aspect of social networks and consequently has received much research attention. However, assortative mixing is simply an empirical measure that describes the structure or composition of a social network (that is, which types of nodes have a higher probability of being connected) – it says nothing about the exact processes that have led to the formation of a particular social network. While it is reasonably easy to measure the level or extent of assortative mixing in a social network, it is much more difficult to discover *why* people are mixing on the basis of shared characteristics. We outline three main reasons why a given social network might exhibit assortative mixing.[1]

First, there might be *homophily* – a term first coined by Lazarsfeld and Merton (1954) which refers to people forming a social tie because they prefer to be connected to someone who is similar to themselves. Homophily can, in principle, operate with respect to any attribute – physical characteristics such as race and gender, 'cultural preferences' over books and music, and political attitudes. However, when the person has choice over the attribute then it is harder to distinguish whether 'birds of the feather are flocking together' (attributes are influencing friendship formation) or whether someone is becoming more like their friends (friendships are influencing attitudes and preferences).

Second, there are *opportunity structures* that influence social tie formation. In particular, *group size* is important: the smaller a particular group (for example, racial category) the more likely (all other things considered) that its group members will form social ties outside of the group (Blau 1977). If group size is not controlled for, then there can be erroneous conclusions about the 'homophilous' behaviour of different groups. Independent of group size, the *propinquity mechanism* can also influence whether two people form a social tie – these shared 'foci effects' might relate to spatial proximity (for example, living in the same neighbourhood) or shared institutional environments (for example, working in the same organisation) – see, for example, Feld (1981) and Mouw and Entwisle (2006).

Finally, there are *endogenous network effects*, which are mechanisms that are not directly related to the attributes of individuals, but exert influence on social tie formation. First, there is the process of *sociality*: two people might become friends simply because they are both social people and like to form lots of social ties. Second, social networks tend to exhibit two properties: (1) *reciprocity* – if A extends the hand of friendship to B, there is good chance that B will reciprocate the friendship; and (2) *transitivity* – the tendency for friends-of-friends to become friends (this is referred to as *triadic closure*). It has been argued by the proponents of balance theory (see, for example, Davis 1963) that the social norms reciprocity and transitivity reduce the social and psychological strain that arises from unreciprocated ties and being in a situation where one's friends are not themselves friends.

Reciprocity and transitivity can also impact on the measurement of homophily: if a particular group does have a genuine preference for forming in-group ties, then this preference will be amplified by the processes of reciprocity and transitivity. Furthermore, if there are differences between the extent of reciprocity and transitivity across different social groups (for example, one race has a cultural tendency to reciprocate friendships or introduce friends to each other), then this may obscure the cross-group comparison of homophily.

The problem for researchers studying homophily is that both opportunity structures and endogenous network effects can 'mask' the true level of homophily in a social network. Currarini et al. (2009) demonstrate one approach for constructing measures of homophily where differences in group size are controlled for. Below, we demonstrate a statistical technique that provides estimates of homophily in a social network, where both group size and balance mechanisms are controlled for.

## The Web and political homophily

It was mentioned in the previous section that there is evidence people are more likely to be socially connected to other people who share a political affiliation. This section considers how research using Web data is providing new insights into political homophily. First, we discuss how Web data from social network sites (such as Facebook), blogs and microblogs (such as Twitter) provide several key opportunities – and sometimes challenges – for studying political homophily. Next, we examine evidence for whether political homophily exists on the Web and if so, whether it has characteristics that are similar to political homophily in the offline world. Finally, we consider whether Web data may provide insights into how political attitudes are formed, and we also ask the question: might the Web itself contribute to political homophily?

### Opportunities for studying political homophily

Web data provide several opportunities and challenges for social networks research. This section provides a summary, with particular focus on research into political homophily. First, Web data are created in a naturalistic environment, and so there may be less problem of recall error and respondent burden with regard to the collection of social tie data. However, there is the additional problem that all relevant social network ties may not be observable to the researcher. If the research aims to, for example, understand the role of social networks in political preference formation using Facebook data, it may be that significant offline social ties are not represented in the data (for example, friends and family who are not on Facebook).

The naturalistic nature of Web data also poses both challenges and opportunities for collecting data on the key attribute of interest: political affiliation. Focusing once again on the example of Facebook, data on the political preferences of an individual will only be available to the researcher if the Facebook user has decided to fill out the appropriate profile fields, and there may be something different about such individuals that make them less representative of the population under study (they may be more politically motivated or active than the average person in the population). Also there is a potential issue of the accuracy of the political preference data: with certain populations of study (for example, university students), there may be social pressure to display a particular political affiliation in the Facebook profile that doesn't reflect the person's true political preferences.

With this caveat in mind, a second major advantage of Web data is that it is often possible to collect complete network data (where links between all actors in the network are recorded). This allows the computation of both *node*-level metrics (such as degree, betweenness and closeness centrality) and *network*-level metrics (such as density and centralisation) that may be important to understand the phenomenon being researched. Whole network data are necessary for being able to model 'supra-dyadic' phenomena, that is, where it is not just the direct ties between a person ('ego') and his or her social contacts ('alters') that are important in understanding that person's behaviour or outcomes, but also the connections between alters themselves (and, indeed, connections between people more two or more degrees of separation from ego).

However, while Facebook might provide an opportunity to collect complete network data for a particular population, for example US college students, it needs to be recognised that this population cannot be representative of the general population. Hence, conclusions that are drawn about the extent of political homophily among college students may not be able to be generalised to a wider population.

It also needs to be recognised that for some Web data sources, it may not be feasible to identify a bounded population from which to collect complete network data. For example, in research on the blogosphere, investigators often need to use 'snowball' sampling in order to build their network data because there is no sampling frame from which to randomly sample observations. Non-probability sampling techniques such as snowball sampling typically cannot be used to make inferences about population statistics – it may not be valid to make strong conclusions about the extent of political homophily in the political blogosphere, for example, when snowball sampling has been used. Further, the fact that snowball sampling may be required to construct the complete network may also make it difficult to assess the population share of, for example, conservative and liberal US political bloggers, and this can have implications for the measurement of political homophily (see the following paragraphs).

A third and final major advantage of Web data for studying political homophily is the fact that many Web datasets are longitudinal: research subjects' political and other attributes are recorded over time, as are their social network data. This opens up the possibility for studying how political preferences and social networks co-evolve over time, allowing potential insights into the social processes underlying political preference formation.

However, there are associated challenges involved with the use of time stamped Web data in the context of research into political homophily. First, it has been noted that while Web environments such as Facebook provide useful data for social tie *formation*, they are less useful as sources of data on tie *dissolution*: people do not tend to 'unfriend' in Facebook, because the costs of maintaining a Facebook friendship are minimal. Noel and Nyhan (2011) have shown that homophily in Facebook friendship retention can confound causal estimates of social influence. The implication is that one needs to be cautious when using longitudinal Web data (for example, from Facebook) for researching how social ties impact on political preferences, since homophily in friendship retention (people with shared political preferences are less likely to unfriend one another) can exert upward bias on estimates of the extent to which political preferences are transmitted through social networks.

Another potential problem with time stamped social network data (both online and offline) is that people can drop out of the sample over time, and if the rate of attrition is related to the political behaviour of interest then differential rates of attrition can impact on research findings. While differential rates of attrition may not be a concern when one is studying mainstream political behaviour, it may be more of a problem if the focus of study is on radical or extreme behaviour. That is, a Facebook user who has recently started engaging in radical political behaviour might be more inclined to change his or her profile to private and thus become invisible to researchers, or stop using Facebook entirely, and this will impact research into social influence and political behaviour.

**Is there political homophily on the Web?**

For online data to provide useful insights into offline social and political phenomena, it needs to be demonstrated that the behaviour of interest online has similar characteristics as its offline counterpart. In the context of virtual worlds, Williams (2010) refers to the need for a 'mapping' between the virtual and real world, and Burt (2011) argues that virtual world data need to have 'construct validity' in order for them to be useful in social networks research:

> Do social networks in virtual worlds have the same effects observed in the real world? The advantages of network data in virtual worlds are worthless without calibrating the analogy between real and inworld. If social networks in virtual worlds operate by unique processes unrelated to networks in the real world, then the scale and precision of data available on social networks in virtual worlds has no value for understanding relations in the real world. On the other hand, if social networks in virtual worlds operate just like networks in the real world, then we can use the richer data on virtual worlds to better understand... network processes in the real world.
>
> (Burt 2011, 5)

While Williams (2010) and Burt (2011) were referring to virtual worlds such as Second Life and massively multiplayer online role-playing games (MMORPGs), the issue of construct validity is relevant for any type of Web data that are used for social and political research. In the context of using Web data to study political homophily, it is therefore pertinent to ask: is there political homophily on the Web, and does it have the same characteristics as political homophily offline?

Adamic and Glance (2005) demonstrated that it was possible to identify assortative mixing within political weblog networks, delineating between blogs identified as politically conservative and those identified as politically liberal. The authors constructed two datasets. The first was a single day's snapshot of around 1500 political blogs collected by searching through several blog catalogue websites, and manually coded by political affiliation (750 liberal and 726 conservative

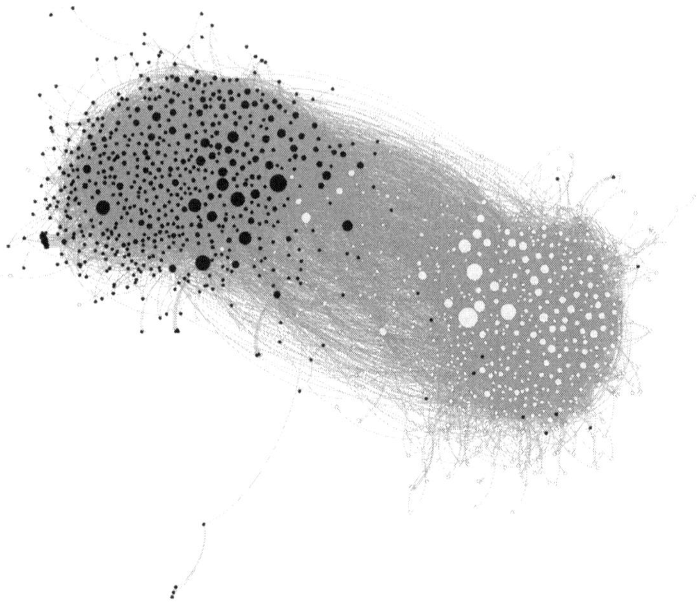

*Figure 1.1* US political blogosphere 2004
*Note*: Black = 'conservative', white = 'liberal'; node size indicates degree.
*Source*: Data are from Adamic and Glance (2005). Visualisation by the authors.

bloggers). On 8 February 2005, the authors then extracted all hyperlinks from the front page of each blog – there was no distinction between hyperlinks made in blogrolls (blogroll links) and those made in posts (post citations). Figure 1.1 presents a visualisation of the 1204 non-isolate weblogs, where the 'Divided They Blog' phenomenon identified by Adamic and Glance (2005) is clearly displayed.[2]

Qualitative analysis (visualisation) of the one-day snapshot clearly showed that there was assortative mixing on the basis of political preferences in the US political blogosphere. This was not an unexpected finding, but it is certainly a necessary one if blog data are to have construct validity for political homophily research.

A second way of testing the construct validity of blog data for political homophily research is to establish whether there is *differential* homophily, that is, are the mixing patterns of the two political subpopulations different in ways that make sense? Alford et al. (2005) provide evidence for the existence of two broad political 'phenotypes' (observable characteristics of individuals that are determined by both genes and environmental influences): 'absolutist' or conservative who tend to be more suspicious of out-groups, and 'contextualist' or progressive who exhibit relatively tolerant attitudes towards out-groups. Drawing from this, one would expect conservatives to display greater political homophily than liberals in their linking behaviour in the blogosphere, and this is therefore another way of testing the construct validity of blog data for political homophily research.

The work by Adamic and Glance (2005) also provides some insights into the extent of differential political homophily in the US blogosphere. The authors constructed a second dataset from a subset of 40 prominent weblogs ('A-listers') and, in contrast to the larger dataset of bloggers mentioned above, this second dataset consisted of blog posts over a two-month period leading up to the 2004 US presidential election. While the larger dataset used both blogroll links and post citations as ties between bloggers, the second A-lister dataset only used post citations. Adamic and Glance (2005) argued that since blogroll links tended to get 'stale', post citations were a more accurate indicator of linking behaviour, and this can be seen as a methodological response to a problem that is analogous to the 'unfriending problem' that Facebook researchers encounter (discussed above).

Adamic and Glance (2005) found evidence that conservative weblogs tended to cite other conservative weblogs more frequently than liberal weblogs cited other liberal weblogs.[3] In other words, the sub-network of liberal weblogs had more connections to conservative weblogs than vice versa:

> Through... visualizations, we see that right-leaning blogs have a denser structure of strong connections than the left, although liberal blogs do have a few exceptionally strong reciprocated connections.
> (Adamic and Glance 2005, 40)

It should again be noted that Adamic and Glance (2005) did not provide a formal test of differential homophily, but rather used evidence from visualisations in support of this thesis. One of the challenges of formally testing for political homophily using blog data is that one would need to control for differences in group size (it was noted above that different population shares can obscure true levels of homophily) and with blog data, especially when collected using snowball sampling, it is very hard to know whether the population shares are accurate.

A final test of the construct validity of Web data for political homophily research, which is related to the above two, is establishing whether the observed actors are representative of the underlying population of interest. It was mentioned above that snowball sampling may not be representative of the overall population of political bloggers. But what if the objective is to use Web data to say something about the political behaviour of, for example, the voting-age population and not just the subset of the voting-age population who are also political bloggers?

It needs to be recognised that political bloggers and people engaging in politically oriented conversations on Twitter are most certainly *not* representative of the voting-age population. For example, Mitchell and Hitlin (2013) compared US nationally representative survey data with data collected from Twitter in order to gauge the public response to eight major political news events and found that the response on Twitter was much more extreme (both on the political right and left), compared with that in the national polls. Any conclusions about the extent or dynamics of political homophily based on blog or Twitter data need to be qualified, given the sampled observations are not generally representative of the offline population.

The above discussion on the construct validity of Web data for political homophily research has focused on blog data. However, political homophily research has also used other types of online data. For example, Gaines and Mondak (2009) found evidence of ideological clustering in a subset of members of the 'UIllinois' Facebook network, which consists of registered users affiliated with the University of Illinois at Urbana-Champaign.

Huber and Malhotra (2012, 1) used data from a US online dating site to assess the extent of political homophily and found that 'people find those with similar political beliefs more desirable and are more likely to "match" with them compared to people with discordant opinions'. The authors argued that online dating sites provide a unique source of data for political homophily research because they allow the research to observe political preferences (expressed in profiles on the dating site) *before* sorting occurs. This overcomes a limitation of, for example, data on married couples where shared political affiliation may have resulted from homophily (common political preference was a factor in their union), shared environment (the couple were exposed to similar exogenous factors, for example, mass advertising or changes in the economy) or attitude conversion (one member of the couple influenced the other to change political preferences).

## Social influence and political affiliation

Unlike some individual attributes (such as age and race), political preferences are not immutable: a person can change his or her political affiliation, and a potential source of change is influence from people in his or her social network. But identifying social influence using observational data is not straightforward: without detailed time stamped data on both behaviour and social networks, it is difficult to know whether two people share an attribute such as political affiliation because of social influence (one person influenced the other person to change political preferences), social selection or homophily (the two people became socially connected because of their shared political preferences) or because both people were exposed to the same exogenous or environmental conditions that influenced them to jointly change political affiliation.

There is an active agenda of research into social influence using both offline and online social network data. With regard to online data, for example, there has been research on the spread of health behaviour in an online health community (Centola 2010) and product adoption in an instant messaging network (Aral et al. 2009). While we are not aware of a study that has attempted to understand social influence and political affiliations using Web data, the offline study by Lazer et al. (2008) may provide insights into how such research could be conducted using timestamped Web data. Lazer et al. (2008) collected data on research subjects' political views before and after their exposure to one another, and they argued that this allowed them to show how social interactions influence political views.

Finally, there has also been interest in whether the extent of political homophily may be in fact *influenced* by the Web. In the early days of the Web, two radically different predictions regarding the impact of the Web on politics were advanced. Some (for example, Castells 1996) argued that the Web would lead to a new era of *participatory democracy* (broad participation in the direction and operation of the political system). In contrast, authors such as Putnam (2000) and Sunstein (2001) argued that the Web would lead to increased isolation and the loss of a common political discourse, leading to *cyberbalkanisation* – a fragmenting of the online population into narrowly focused groups of individuals who share similar opinions and are only exposed to information that confirms their previously held opinions. In this context, Hargittai et al. (2008) used a dataset on A-list political bloggers to test whether the amount of cross-ideological linking among blogs is declining over time (this is proposed as a direct test of the 'fragmentation' hypothesis), and found no support for this hypothesis over a ten-month period.

## ERGM analysis of homophily in the political blogosphere

While Adamic and Glance (2005) had a large impact on the search for and analysis of homophily on the Web, there is to our knowledge no follow-up research to indicate (1) whether or not differential homophily is a continuing phenomenon within the political weblog community and (2) whether or not network formation models such as ERGM can provide a good fit for such models, that is, whether or not *quantitative* evidence for differential homophily can be obtained.

To address both issues, we revisit the political weblog phenomenon originally treated by Adamic and Glance (2005). We collect new weblog data in 2011 using a similar data collection technique and then estimate several ERGMs to ascertain whether differential homophily is statistically significant. In addition, we apply the same ERGM approach to the original weblog dataset from Adamic and Glance (2005). We find that differential homophily is demonstrated in the updated dataset, and that the ERGM analysis indicates support for its statistical significance.

### Data and methodology

Weblog data for politically conservative and politically liberal weblogs were collected on 27 October 2011, from two websites which catalogue weblogs, 'BlogCatalog' (www.blogcatalog.com) and 'eTalkingHead' (www.etalkinghead.com). These two sites provide catalogs of 'conservative' and 'liberal' websites and provided a total of 973 unique websites, similar to the ca. 1464 such websites collected by Adamic and Glance (2005).

With the explosion of weblogs over the past decade, there is no guarantee that these sites would necessarily hyperlink to each other – to help circumvent this, Adamic and Glance (2005) 'snowballed' their original sample by an additional 30 weblogs which were cited at least 17 times by the initial collection. As the total number of weblogs collected was then 1494, these additional 30 weblogs comprise about 2 per cent of the total. By contrast our approach does not utilise blogroll data to examine numbers of citations for snowballing the initial collection of 973 weblogs, and we take these sites as given. The premise here is that there may be a degree of self-selection by weblogs to have their data collected and stored by BlogCatalog and eTalkingHead, and that this self-selection is an ex ante form of snowballing at the level of the blog

*Figure 1.2* Political blogosphere 2011
*Note*: Black = 'conservative', white = 'liberal'; node size indicates degree.

catalog. Future research can, however, take the 973 sites as 'seed' sites for a larger analysis of hyperlink citations.

The 973 weblogs so collected were then analysed by the VOSON software for hyperlink network analysis[4] to generate a full network between them. When isolated weblogs are omitted, the resulting Web network is depicted in Figure 1.2, with the circles depicting weblogs and the ties depicting citations (hyperlinks) to or from other weblogs. The size of the circles reflects how many of these citations there are for each weblog, or the weblog's 'degree'. Without the snowballing methodology of Adamic and Glance (2005), the number of weblogs which cite at least one other weblog (or which are cited by at least one other weblog) is 315, or about one-third the number of sites initially collected. The figure clearly depicts a separation between weblogs which labelled themselves as 'conservative' and those which labelled themselves as 'liberal', and reproduces the qualitative feature of Adamic and Glance (2005, Figure 1, 37).

Although the graphical depiction is promising, it is unclear whether or not the separation between conservative and liberal weblogs is a symmetric or asymmetric feature, that is, the graph cannot immediately provide information about differential homophily. To answer this question requires fitting a model of network formation, and we select ERGM fitting for what follows.

### Measuring homophily: Controlling for endogenous network effects

ERGM can be used to control for balance mechanisms in social networks. While a detailed introduction to ERGM is beyond the scope of this chapter, it is useful to understand what ERGM is designed to do.[5]

ERGM is a statistical technique that allows for the explicit modelling of the dependence among the units of observation, that is, network ties or dyads. By means of illustration, say we have three people: Ann, Sue and David. Assume that Ann and Sue are friends and Ann and David are friends. Earlier statistical approaches to modelling social networks required the implausible assumption that the probability of Sue and David forming a friendship is the same as it would be if Ann was not friends with either of them. This is implausible because it overlooks a basic mechanism in social behaviour, *triadic closure*, which is the tendency of friends of one individual to become friends themselves.

There are two types of features in social networks. Above we introduced *endogenous network effects* – these are network ties that have nothing to do with actor attributes, but are more to do with social norms. The second major feature in social networks is *actor-relation effects* – these are network ties that are created because of the characteristics or attributes of actors. There are three further sub-types of actor-relation effects:

- *Sender effects* show the impact of presence or absence of a particular actor attribute on the propensity to create, or 'send', ties (a significant and positive sender effect indicates that actors with the attribute send more ties than expected by chance).
- *Receiver effects* are analogous to sender effects, but refer to the propensity of receiving ties.
- *Homophily effects* occur when actors with an attribute are more likely than chance to send ties to other actors who also share the attribute.

To illustrate the above ideas, assume we are conducting an analysis of friendship formation in a school, and we have collected information on 'friendship nominations' (for example, person $i$ nominates person $j$ as a friend), gender and age. Assume that three of the actors are $i$ (female, 12 years old), $j$ (female, 12 years old) and $k$ (female, 14 years old), and the friendship nominations between these actors are $i$ nominates $j$, $j$ nominates $k$ and $i$ nominates $k$.

These three network ties together form a *transitive triad*, which is a very common structure in social networks. Why did this transitive triad form? In particular, what social process is behind the tie from $i$ to $k$?

There are two potential reasons. First, the tie from *i* to *k* could be an actor-relation effect (*k* is older than *i* and children are often keen to show that they hang out with the 'big kids'; *k* also shares *i*'s gender and there is strong evidence of gender homophily especially amongst children). However, the tie from *i* to *k* could also be an endogenous network effect: the fact that *i* nominates *j* and *j* nominates *k* means there is a higher likelihood that *i* will also nominate *k* ('a friend of my friend is also my friend'). The main point is that it is difficult to discern actor-relation effects from endogenous network effects if the social network is only observed at a single point in time. We do not know if *i* became friends with *k* first, or after *j* became friends with *k* (for example, *i* might have met *k* via *j*).

An exponential random graph model is essentially a pattern recognition device which breaks a given network down into all of its constituent network 'motifs' or 'configurations', and then tests whether particular configurations occur more (or less) frequently than would be expected by chance alone. In a manner similar to standard regression techniques, the model estimation produces parameter estimates and associated standard errors and confidence estimates. If a particular network motif occurs at greater or less than chance levels, we can then infer that the associated social relation has had a significant role in the development of the social network. Not controlling for endogenous or self-organising network properties may lead to a spurious conclusion that the attributes of actors are driving social tie formation when, in fact, it is endogenous self-organisation. In the context of homophily research, ERGM allows one to 'control' for endogenous network effects such as reciprocity and transitivity and thus accurately measure the homophily actor-relation effect.

### ERGM analysis

We fit five different ERGMs, in order to test the hypothesis that the political blog dataset exhibits differential homophily.[6] The baseline model (Model 1) excludes homophily from consideration and simply assumes that the likelihood of the given network realisation is a function of the edges ('ties') in the system, along with the number of reciprocated (or 'mutual') ties. Next, we fit a model of homophily without distinguishing between weblog type (Model 2) – this is the most naïve model for homophily, as it treats both conservative and liberal weblogs symmetrically and only asks if assortative mixing is observed. Model 3 refines this by allowing for differential homophily, that is, it fits a model whereby different rates of attachment are distinguished by weblog type.

Although Model 3 may appear to be sufficient to treat the question of the existence of differential homophily in the data, there is the possibility that a model without such behaviour nevertheless appears to exhibit homophilic behaviour. This is because of the scale or group-size effect mentioned above – if one community of weblog types is much larger than the other, then any modelling environment (such as ERGM) where links are formed at random will tend to link weblogs to weblogs of the larger community type. This leads to the result that the smaller community appears to have a different rate of attachment. In other words, it exhibits homophily different from the larger community, when in fact this is an artefact of random network formation.

To alleviate this requires an additional statistic to capture and control for the relative size effects of the two communities – this statistic counts the total number of times a weblog belonging to a particular community is connected, as a directed inbound link, to any other weblog. Thus, larger communities will receive more connections, and this statistic can then be used to adjust the relative degree of differential homophily. Model 4 contains both the differential homophily statistic and the community link count (inbound) statistic.

Finally, we would like to ask how 'dense' these communities of weblogs are within the network, by appealing to 'clustering' or 'triangle formation'. Unfortunately, the Maximum Likelihood Estimation (MLE) techniques used to estimate ERGMs can lead to a degenerate outcome, if the model is misspecified by assuming homogeneous behaviour across the network for clustering and triangle formation. Hence, we use the *geometrically weighted edgewise shared partner distribution* (GWESP) statistic to allow for heterogeneous triangle formation; this statistic counts the number of shared partners by edges between two weblogs and so creates a distribution rather than a single network-wide attribute. This has been shown to alleviate the degeneracy problem in MLE over a wide range of ERGM estimation problems. We fit a model both with (Model 5a) and without (Model 5b) reciprocated links, as a priori we might expect that GWESP captures link formation better than reciprocation if cluster formation (rather than bilateral relationship formation) is more dominant in the network.

The models were fit using the ERGM routine from the 'statnet' (2003) package for R (2011).[7] The results for all five models are presented in Table 1.1. From this, we may infer that Model 5 (a and b), incorporating differential homophily corrected for scale and heterogeneous clustering provides the best fit to the data, as both the Akaike Information Criterion (AIC) and the log-likelihood are significant improvements over

*Table 1.1* ERGMs for 2011 political weblog dataset

| Coefficient | Model 1 | Model 2 | Model 3 | Model 4 | Model 5a | Model 5b |
|---|---|---|---|---|---|---|
| Links | −4.89453** | −6.4380** | −6.4353** | −6.9334** | −7.0349** | −7.0007** |
| Reciprocated links | 2.08626** | 1.6376** | 1.5448** | 1.5768** | −0.1146 | – |
| Political spectrum, symmetric | – | 2.0942** | – | – | – | – |
| Political spectrum, conservative | – | – | 1.8277** | 2.3395** | 2.1723** | 2.0755** |
| Political spectrum, liberal | – | – | 2.5745** | 2.1817** | 1.5105** | 1.4624** |
| Indegree count, liberal | – | – | – | 0.8824* | 0.85373* | 0.8132* |
| GWESP ($\tau = 0.2$) | – | – | – | – | 1.7131** | 1.7851** |
| AIC | 9077.5 | 8573.8 | 8491.6 | 8482.3 | 7546.3 | 7527.9 |
| Log likelihood | −4536.8 | −4283.9 | −4241.8 | −4236.1 | −3767.1 | −3759.0 |

*Note*: ** $< 0.1\%$ significance; * $< 1\%$ significance.

Models 1–4. We also see that in Model 5 (a and b) the log-odds for link formation are influenced to a greater degree by conservative weblog homophily than by liberal weblog homophily, reinforcing the notion that (on the margin) conservative weblogs reference other conservative weblogs more often than liberal weblogs reference other liberal weblogs.

We note that in Model 5a, where GWESP and reciprocating links are both offered as explanatory statistics, reciprocation ceases to be statistically significant. Moreover, Model 5b (where reciprocation is removed from the model) has the lowest AIC and highest log-likelihood of all models, which provides evidence in favour of selecting this model as the best ERGM fit to the data.

By comparison, results of the same analysis for Adamic and Glance's (2005) dataset from 2004 are presented in Table 1.2. We note again that Model 5 provides the best fit, again according to the AIC and log-likelihood – in this case, including reciprocating links was a strong log-odds predictor of link formation, and so only one version of Model 5 was fit. For the 2004 data, although there is evidence for differential homophily, it is weaker than for the 2011 data: for instance, it is roughly 8 times more likely that a conservative weblog will link to another conservative weblog in 2011, while in 2004 it is only about 1.75 times as likely. The values for liberal weblogs are about 4.3 times

*Table 1.2* ERGMs for 2004 political weblog dataset

| Coefficient | Model 1 | Model 2 | Model 3 | Model 4 | Model 5 |
|---|---|---|---|---|---|
| Links | −4.6022** | −5.1064** | −5.1096** | −5.0771** | −5.7380** |
| Reciprocated links | 3.4742** | 3.3725** | 3.3557** | 3.3574** | 2.4980*** |
| Political spectrum, symmetric | – | 0.8062** | – | – | – |
| Political spectrum, conservative | – | – | 0.9382** | 0.9017** | 0.5517** |
| Political spectrum, liberal | – | – | 0.7608** | 0.7952** | 0.7168** |
| Indegree count, Liberal | – | – | – | −0.0588+ | −0.0517** |
| GWESP ($\tau = 0.2$) | – | – | – | – | 1.2440** |
| AIC | 191646 | 188372 | 188215 | 188233 | 166127 |
| Log likelihood | −95820.9 | −94182.9 | −94103.6 | −94111.7 | −83057.3 |

*Note*: ** < 0.1% significance; * < 1% significance; + < 10% significance.

as likely (2011) and 2 times as likely (2004), respectively. The effect of including the GWESP statistic was roughly the same for both the 2004 and 2011 models, as was the impact of links (of any kind).

## Conclusion

This chapter has focused on how homophily, as a major contributor to assortative mixing on the basis of political affiliation, may be conceptually defined and empirically identified in Web data. It is worth noting that we have used as our point of departure the existence (or lack thereof) of the *characteristic* of homophily, rather than first specifying the micro-level choices of individuals comprising a Web network that would lead to homophily. By so doing, we have replaced the actual decision-making process of individuals, which is exceptionally complex for networks of the size and variety discussed here, by a behavioural assumption – that 'like prefers like'.[8] But this assumption nevertheless carries with it a rich set of implications for network types and topologies, which can replicate many sets of interactions observed in real networks.

This chapter first provided a background on homophily and its measurement, showing how homophily (people having a preference to be connected to other similar people) differs from assortative mixing (an empirical statement of whether like are connected to like) and, is in fact, one of several reasons why a given social network may display assortative mixing. We then focused on how Web data can provide new insights into political homophily and discussed the opportunities (and challenges) of Web data in this context. The concept of 'construct validity' of Web data was introduced, and we provided three tests of whether Web data have construct validity for political homophily research. We also briefly discussed how Web data are being used for research into social influence and pointed to future opportunities for such research in the context of political affiliations.

As part of this review, we also examine the role that digital media may play in increasing the fragmentation of views within a population, by allowing those of similar opinions to more readily 'flock together', a process which has become known as 'cyberbalkanisation'. The resulting emergence of narrow online communities of like-minded interests is a growing concern for policy-makers due to the perceived potential of weakening levels of social cohesion, inclusion and tolerance.

Our review of homophily and its measurement identified the need for statistical social network analysis for conducting rigorous test of homophily. We demonstrated how the ERGM technique can be used for quantifying homophily in the context of political weblogs, and applied ERGM to both the weblog data collected by Adamic and Glance (2005) and a more current dataset that was constructed for this chapter. Provided that the fidelity of the data is high enough to provide meaningful statistical inference, we contend that the Web will increasingly be a source of data for political homophily research, and we have shown that Web collection and analysis tools such as those provided by VOSON are of great importance in obtaining this quality of data.

## Notes

1. See Wimmer and Lewis (2010) for a detailed review.
2. Visualisations in this chapter were created using *Gephi* (Bastian et al. 2009), an open-source network visualisation platform.
3. Ackland and Shorish (2009) propose an economic model of link formation that can explain the existence of differential political homophily in the blogosphere, where the link formation behaviour of bloggers is influenced by the underlying distribution of political preferences.
4. For more information on the VOSON software and associated methods, see, for example, Ackland (2011), Ackland and O'Neil (2011) and Ackland and Gibson (2013).
5. See Robins et al. (2007) for a detailed introduction.

6. See Lusher and Ackland (2011) for an introduction to using ERGMs to study hyperlink networks.
7. R v. 2.13.2 64-bit on OSX 10.7.2. MLE and Markov Chain Monte Carlo (MCMC) with sample size of one million per iteration, maximum 15 iterations for each model.
8. Compared with Ackland and Shorish (2009), where such micro-level foundations are explored.

## References


Ackland, R. (2011) 'WWW Hyperlink Networks', in D. Hansen, B. Shneiderman and M. Smith (eds.), *Analyzing Social Media Networks with NodeXL: Insights from a Connected World* (Burlington, MA: Morgan-Kaufmann), pp. 181–200.

Ackland, R. and Gibson, R.K. (2013) 'Hyperlinks and Networked Communication: A Comparative Study of Political Parties Online', *International Journal of Social Research Methodology*, 16 (3), special issue on Computational Social Science: Research Strategies, Design & Methods, 231–244.

Ackland, R. and O'Neil, M. (2011) 'Online Collective Identity: The Case of the Environmental Movement', *Social Networks*, 33, 177–190.

Ackland, R. and Shorish, J. (2009) 'Network Formation in the Political Blogosphere: An Application of Agent Based Simulation and e-Research Tools', *Computational Economics*, 34 (4), 383–398.

Adamic, L. and Glance, N. (2005) 'The Political Blogosphere and the 2004 US Election: Divided They Blog', in KDD '05: The Eleventh ACM SIGKDD International Conference on Knowledge Discovery and Data Mining. Chicago, IL, 21–24 August, pp. 36–43.

Alford, R., Funk, C. and Hibbing, J. (2005) 'Are Political Orientations Genetically Transmitted?', *American Political Science Review*, 99, 153–167.

Alford, J.R., Hatemi, P.K., Hibbing, J.R., Martin, N.G. and Eaves, L.J. (2011) 'The Politics of Mate Choice', *The Journal of Politics*, 73, 362–379.

Aral, S., Muchnik, L. and Sundararajan, A. (2009) 'Distinguishing Influence-based Contagion from Homophily-driven Diffusion in Dynamic Networks', *Proceedings of the National Academy of Sciences*, 106 (51), 21544–21549.

Bastian, M., Heymann, S. and Jacomy, M. (2009) 'Gephi: An Open Source Software for Exploring and Manipulating Networks', in International AAAI Conference on Weblogs and Social Media.

Blau, P. (1977) *Inequality and Heterogeneity: A Primitive Theory of Social Structure* (New York: Free Press).

Burt, R. (2011) *Structural Holes in Virtual Worlds* (Chicago: Booth School of Business, University of Chicago, Working Paper).

Castells, M. (1996) *The Rise of the Network Society. The Information Age: Economy, Society and Culture*, Volume I. (London: Blackwell).

Centola, D. (2010) 'The Spread of Behavior in an Online Social Network Experiment', *Science*, 329, 1194–1197.

Currarini, S., Jackson, M.O. and Pin, P. (2009) 'An Economic Model of Friendship: Homophily, Minorities and Segregation', *American Economic Review*, 77 (4), 1003–1045.

Davis, J.A. (1963) 'Structural Balance, Mechanical Solidarity, and Interpersonal Relations', *American Journal of Sociology*, 68, 444–462.

Feld, S.L. (1981) 'The Focused Organization of Social Ties', *American Journal of Sociology*, 86 (5), 1015–1035.

Gaines, B. and Mondak, J. (2009) 'Typing Together? Clustering of Ideological Types in Online Social Networks', *Journal of Information Technology & Politics*, 6 (3–4), 216–231.

Hargittai, E., Gallo, J. and Kane, M. (2008) 'Cross-ideological Discussions Among Conservative and Liberal Bloggers', *Public Choice*, 134, 67–86.

Huber, G. and Malhotra, N. (2012) 'Political Sorting in Social Relationships', Working Paper, available at: http://huber.research.yale.edu/materials/38_paper.pdf, date accessed 14 April 2013.

Kydros, D., Magoulios, G. and Trevlakis, N. (2012) 'A Network Analysis of the Greek Parliament and some Socio-Economic Issues', *MIBES Transactions*, 6, 27–38.

Lazarsfeld, P.F. and Merton, R.K. (1954) 'Friendship as a Social Process: A Substantive and Methodological Analysis', in M. Berger (ed.), *Freedom and Control in Modern Society* (New York: Van Nostrand), pp. 18–66.

Lazer, D., Rubineau, B., Katz, N., Chetkovich, C. and Neblo, M. (2008) *Networks and Political Attitudes: Structure, Influence, and Co-evolution* (Cambridge, MA: Harvard University, John F. Kennedy School of Government, Working Paper rwp 08–044).

Lusher, D. and Ackland, R. (2011) 'A Relational Hyperlink Analysis of an Online Social Movement', *Journal of Social Structure*, 11, available at: http://www.cmu.edu/joss/content/articles/volume11/Lusher/.

McPherson, M., Smith-Lovin, M. and Cook, J.M. (2001) 'Birds of a Feather: Homophily in Social Networks', *Annual Review of Sociology*, 27, 415–444.

Mitchell, A. and Hitlin, P. (2013) 'Twitter Reaction to Events Often at Odds with Overall Public Opinion', Pew Research Center Report, available at: http://www.pewresearch.org/2013/03/04/twitter-reaction-to-events-often-at-odds-with-overall-public-opinion/, date accessed 14 April 2013.

Mouw, T. and Entwisle, B. (2006) 'Residential Segregation and Interracial Friendship in Schools', *American Journal of Sociology*, 112 (2), 394–441.

Noel, H. and Nyhan, B. (2011) 'The "Unfriending" Problem: The Consequences of Homophily in Friendship Retention for Causal Estimates of Social Influence', *Social Networks*, 33 (3), 211–218.

Putnam, R.D. (2000) *Bowling Alone* (New York: Simon & Schuster).

R Development Core Team (2011) *R: A Language and Environment for Statistical Computing* (Vienna: Foundation for Statistical Computing).

Robins, G., Pattison, P., Kalish, Y. and Lusher, D. (2007) 'An Introduction to Exponential Random Graph (p*) Models for Social Networks', *Social Networks*, 29 (2), 173–191.

Stray, J. (2013) 'The Whole Dysfunctional National Conversation About Guns – on Twitter...in One Interactive Graph', *The Atlantic*, 26 February 2013, available at: http://theatlantic.com, date accessed 5 April 2013.

Sunstein, C. (2001) *Republic.com* (Princeton: Princeton University Press).

Weare, C., Musso, J. and Jun, K-N. (2009) 'Cross-Talk: The Role of Homophily and Elite Bias in Civic Associations', *Social Forces*, 88 (1), 147–173.

Williams, D. (2010) 'The Mapping Principle, and a Research Framework for Virtual Worlds', *Communication Theory*, 20 (4), 451–470.
Wimmer, A. and Lewis, K. (2010) 'Beyond and Below Racial Homophily: ERG Models of a Friendship Network Documented on Facebook', *American Journal of Sociology*, 116, 583–642.

# 2

# Blogosphere Authority Index 2.0: Change and Continuity in the American Political Blogosphere, 2007–2010

*David Karpf*

Political blogs have emerged as a vibrant component of the information ecology of American politics. Previous scholars have described bloggers as 'agenda seekers' or as the digital equivalent to Op-ed columnists (Hindman 2008; Davis 2009). Researchers have investigated the motivations of bloggers and their attentive readers, the impact of blogs on elections, the demographics of reader bases and the mass participatory and agenda-setting impacts of the medium (McKenna and Pole 2004; Wallsten 2007, 2008; Pole 2009; Gil de Zuniga et al. 2009; Gil de Zuniga et al. 2010; Lawrence et al. 2010). A few scholars have also explored structural differences between the left and right blogospheres (Karpf 2008b; Benkler and Shaw 2010). Once a passing curiosity with a funny name, blogs today have become a well-established piece of the political landscape. They have been replaced by Twitter as the funny-sounding social media object of fascination. Blogs have been incorporated into existing media and political institutions, even being termed 'passé' in some circles.

Today, there effectively is no such thing as a single, overarching 'blogosphere'. As the medium has diffused, it has also changed. Early political blogs were a monoculture. All sites shared a host of overlapping structural elements. They were authored by individual bloggers, usually operating under pseudonym, who used online self-publishing to challenge a variety of existing media institutions. Today, the top ten blogs that are included in Technorati.com's popular web-tracker are media institutions. The *Huffington Post* (#1) hires reporters from the *New York*

*Times* and was recently acquired by aol.com for $315 million. Gawker (#4) is a gossip empire and has been the subject of a feature-length story in the *Atlantic*.[1] These modified news organisations have more in common with mainstream news venues than they do with www.shoutingloudly.com (an unremarkable and entirely standard academic blog). Meanwhile, community blogs like DailyKos.com operate as quasi-advocacy groups (Karpf 2008b, 2012a). They endorse and fundraise for candidates, select issue priorities and even hold an annual in-person convention. DailyKos.com is a blog, but the activity on that site has little in common with the old Pyra Labs software (blogspot) that once defined the medium.

In November 2007, I launched the Blogosphere Authority Index (BAI)[2] as a tool for studying elite political blogs. The BAI tracks blog 'clusters', identified through the network ties created in blogrolls. It does not attempt to track the entire 'blogosphere', because it was already clear in 2007 that the boundaries between a blog and any other website had become hopelessly blurry. Instead, I intended to craft a ranking mechanism for tracking and comparing the top political blogs on the left and right. The system was automated in August 2008, was updated monthly through March 2012, when it was put on hiatus for redesign. It is a simple system, and intentionally so. The BAI has played a role in several publications, both by myself (Karpf 2008a, 2008b, 2009, 2012a) and others (Benkler and Shaw 2010; Barzilai-Nahon et al. 2011, Barzilai-Nahon and Helmsley 2011). It also has served as a resource for student projects at several universities and is used as a reference point by the research community at large.

Much has happened in US politics since the initial launch of the BAI. Twitter existed at that time, but had a trivial user base. Barack Obama was still a long shot challenger to presumed nominee Hillary Clinton. Tea Parties were reserved for little children and eighteenth-century-history buffs. Today, with over two years of data, it is high time to ask two major questions: how has the blogosphere changed, and how can the tracking system be refined, improved and adapted?

This chapter serves to answer those two questions. The bulk of the chapter is devoted to the analysis of two years of BAI data. It evaluates not only the overall stability of the top political blogs and looks at structural changes within the left and right blogging communities, but also the comparative strength of each community over time. Several interesting findings emerge from the data (Karpf 2009). First, the rankings have remained surprisingly stable over time. The top blogs of the left and right in 2008 are, for the most part, the top blogs of 2010 and 2011. What's more, the fifth largest blog of 2008 is still (approximately) the fifth largest blog of 2011. Following Hindman's prediction of a stable, power law dominated system (Hindman et al. 2003; Hindman 2008), the elite blogosphere exhibits a small number of large-scale hub sites, relatively few new entrants and relatively little change in rank order. Second, the gap between progressive and conservative blogs has remained substantial, despite the emergence of the Tea Party movement and supposed outpouring of grassroots online conservatism. Claims that conservatives have gained parity or better with progressives online (Ruffini 2009, 2010) are not supported by the BAI dataset. Conservative blogs have become more popular, but they have failed to catch up with their progressive equivalents, which have grown as well. Third, elite political blogs have exhibited a trend towards increasing sophistication and professionalisation, migrating to new quadrants of the 'Understanding Blogspace' typology (Karpf 2008b). A few brief case examples will flesh out the most noteworthy institutional advancements among these political blogs. A final segment of the chapter will provide a self-critique of the BAI methodology and offer speculation on new techniques and features to be included in a second version of the system, 'BAI 2.0'.

## The BAI methodology

The BAI is a ranking mechanism for 'neighbourhoods' or 'clumps' of interlinked blogs. It is important to note at the outset a few things that the BAI therefore does *not* accomplish. First, the BAI necessarily ignores the millions of blogs that are either non-elite, non-political or not considered *by their peers* to be part of the progressive or conservative political community. This can yield some noteworthy exceptions. Ron Paul bloggers, for instance, were shunned by the elite conservative blogs during the 2008 primary season.[3] As a result, though they clearly were political in nature, and several attracted substantial traffic, the BAI identifies them as an empirically distinct neighbourhood. Conservative and Progressive refer not to objective ideological indicators, or even revealed partisan preferences, but rather to elite networks of actors who read and interact with each other. Borrowing from Adamic and Glance (2005), political preference in the blogosphere can be observed by the company you keep. According to this perspective, if a conservative blog author is rarely listed in blogrolls of their peers, then they are treated as an outlier or a member of some other, unexamined blog neighbourhood.

This design choice offers two substantial benefits. First, it removes the need for researcher-imposed ideological classification – a time-consuming process which can introduce biases into the population definition process. Second, it allows the bloggers themselves to determine what is and is not a blog. The Drudge Report, for instance, is a highly trafficked and highly influential 'protoblog' (Perlmutter 2008; Wallsten 2011; Karpf 2012). It has some blog-like qualities, but lacks others. Some researchers include it in their blog listings, others don't. Likewise, the Huffington Post is considered a blog by some and a media organisation by others. The line between those two categories is fuzzy. Indeed, many bloggers do not list the Huffington Post and similar 'bridge blogs' in their blogrolls, likely because they consider it not to be a 'blog', per se. It definitely was a blog at one point. Now it is basically AOL. Sometime in between, it drifted. Rather than selecting a researcher-imposed definition, the BAI allows members of the cluster self-determine their peers. This also makes the BAI methodology eminently portable. It can be usefully applied to *any* neighbourhood with an identifiable central hub site. For the purposes of my research, I only apply it to the two politically prominent neighbourhoods dominated by DailyKos and HotAir. DailyKos, founded in 2003, is the top community blog on the American left. HotAir, founded in 2006, is the top blog on the American right.

After identifying this networked clump of associated blogs, the BAI gathers three other types of authority information. Hyperlinks, site traffic and comment activity each represent a different form of blog strength, each with their own strengths and pitfalls. Rather than seeking to independently determine how many site visits a hyperlink is equivalent to, we convert each measure (including the sociometric network centrality measure) to an ordinal ranking. This is designed to be a 'plug and play' system, such that we take the best publicly available system for ranking these three forms of proxy data, then convert to rankings. At present, for instance, Technorati provides the best measure of hyperlink patterns. If, years from now, another system rises to prominence and provides better data on hyperlinks, we can seamlessly swap data sources without overturning the tracking system. So long as the raw data can be converted to ordinal rankings, it can be used by the BAI. This feature potentially makes the BAI more durable than competing tracking systems as new features of the Internet rapidly develop.

Blog data collection is a fundamentally noisy endeavour. There is monetary gain to be found in launching spam blogs or 'splogs' to artificially boost a site's Technorati score, or in using bots to artificially boost site traffic. Either of these can help generate additional revenue for site owners. With talented coders fighting an ongoing war to game the system and keep it accurate, any single measure of blog influence is vulnerable to manipulation (Karpf 2012b). The final BAI measure is calculated by the formula [FinalRank = Rank1+Rank2+Rank3+Rank4−LowestRank],where each of the contributing ranks consists of an ordinal ranking along the metrics of Network Centrality Score, Hyperlink Authority Score, Site Traffic Score and Community Activity Score. This allows blogs that do not allow comments, blogs which are not tracked by Technorati or blogs whose site traffic is not publicly available to be included in the rankings. It also allows bridge blogs like HuffingtonPost and Townhall, which systematically receive low NCS scores, to overcome their artificially low scores in this area. Dropping the LowestRank from the formula creates some degree of artificial stability (as does converting raw data into ordinal rankings, then merging rankings), but it is preferable to excluding important blogs that happen to lack reliable site traffic data.[4] Observed up close, all publicly available Web data takes on a 'swiss cheese' character. My intention with the BAI has been to keep these limitations transparent, while also providing a valuable data service.

For the purposes of this study, it is important to note that blogs which lack *two* of these inputs are excluded from the BAI. Thus 'The Corner', a popular conservative site hosted by National Review Online, is not included because its site traffic cannot be determined and it does not allow comments.[5] Also, since blogrolls are rarely and slowly updated, new sites such as FiveThirtyEight.com can, in practical terms, become an oft-cited member of a blog community before the system can record it as such. The Site Traffic and Community Activity measures can exhibit heavy week-to-week fluctuation, while the Network Centrality and Hyperlink Authority measures change more slowly. Finally, in order to capture popular blogs that do not rank highly in the original Network Centrality rankings, the system gathers data on twice as many blogs as it reports. I have set the BAI to report top 25 rankings for each blog network, so it gathers data on the 50 most-central blogs in each network. The number 25 is an arbitrary cut point, but reflects what I believe to be a reasonable size for capturing all of the major sites in a neighbourhood. The names and Web addresses of all blogs included in these top 25 rankings are listed in the appendix of this chapter.

The BAI data collection has been automated since August 2008. It recorded weekly rankings during the course of the 2008 election season and has recorded monthly rankings ever since. The complete dataset therefore currently includes 40 rankings, including 13 entries of weekly data spanning from 22 September to 14 December (data is calculated and posted on Sunday for the preceding week) and 27 entries from January 2009 to February 2011.[6] Each of these postings includes a progressive top 25, a conservative top 25 and a combined top 50 that allows for comparison of network centrality, hyperlinks, traffic and comments between the two blog communities. All ranked data is publicly available at: www.blogosphereauthorityindex.com, and all raw data is free to researchers upon request.

## Stability and change: 2008–2011

### Stability

A 2009 report examined systemic stability, using a transition matrix to examine the likelihood that site rank X at time T would remain at rank X at time T + 1. It found the top of the rankings to be overwhelmingly stable, while the lower rankings exhibited a bit more variance. This is in keeping with the power law distribution exhibited in the raw data – the gap in site traffic between Huffington Post and DailyKos is in the millions, while the gap in site traffic between Shakespeare's Sister (rank 20 in the latest rankings) and Crooked Timber (rank 21 in the latest rankings) is in the hundreds or the dozens. Tables 2.1 and 2.2 provide the average rank, top rank, bottom rank and standard deviation for each progressive and conservative site that appeared in at least half of the BAI rankings in 2009 and 2010.

In keeping with the findings from 2009, the standard deviation increases as we move down the top 25 lists, with standard deviations of less than one among the top five progressive sites and less than two among several of the top conservative sites. BigGovernment represents a notable departure among the top conservative sites, as it was only launched in September 2009, and has since risen through the rankings. Little Green Footballs, on the other hand, is a former conservative top-five site that publicly broke ranks with the conservative blogging community in November 2009.[7] Its rankings subsequently decreased.

Among the progressive sites that have the largest standard deviation, three are due to underlying data flaws and site migration. FiveThirtyEight.com was founded during the 2008 election season and developed a strong subsequent following. In the summer of 2010, Nate Silver joined the staff of the *New York Times*, migrating his blog to their platform. In so doing, his site traffic was no longer technically measurable, causing his ranking to artificially crater. Likewise, Ezra Klein moved to the *Washington Post*, rendering his traffic ranking untrackable, and Matt Yglesias moved under the banner of ThinkProgress. The other

*Table 2.1* Progressive rankings, 2009–2010

| Site | Average rank | Minimum rank | Maximum rank | Standard deviation |
|---|---|---|---|---|
| Huffington Post | 1 | 1 | 1 | 0 |
| DailyKos | 1.5 | 1 | 1 | 0.5 |
| TalkingPointsMemo | 3.6 | 3 | 7 | 0.9 |
| FireDogLake | 4.6 | 3 | 6 | 0.8 |
| Atrios/Eschaton | 5.8 | 4 | 7 | 0.9 |
| Crooks and Liars | 5.8 | 4 | 7 | 0.9 |
| Think Progress | 6.3 | 3 | 15 | 4.3 |
| Washington Monthly | 8.8 | 7 | 12 | 1.1 |
| Balloon Juice | 9.4 | 6 | 21 | 4.1 |
| Matt Yglesias | 10.9 | 7 | 24 | 4.7 |
| Digby | 11.4 | 9 | 15 | 1.8 |
| America Blog | 13.5 | 6 | 17 | 2.6 |
| Pandagon | 14.4 | 9 | 22 | 2.9 |
| Juan Cole | 15.1 | 8 | 22 | 3.9 |
| Talk Left | 16.3 | 12 | 19 | 1.8 |
| FiveThirtyEight | 17 | 8 | Unranked | 13.2 |
| Truthdig | 17.4 | 14 | 22 | 1.9 |
| Glen Greenwald | 17.4 | 8 | 27 | 6.5 |
| Ezra Klein | 19.4 | 10 | 42 | 10.3 |
| Shakespeare's Sister | 20 | 13 | 24 | 2.9 |
| Feministing | 20.1 | 10 | 36 | 7.9 |
| The Moderate Voice | 20.2 | 15 | 27 | 2.8 |
| Sadly, No! | 20.6 | 17 | 27 | 2.9 |
| Open Left | 21.8 | 15 | 47 | 5.8 |
| Crooked Timber | 23.5 | 19 | 27 | 2 |
| MyDD | 25.3 | 19 | 38 | 5.3 |

progressive variance occurs among Feministing, which launched a community platform that improved its rankings, and OpenLeft and MyDD, the two community sites that declined in popularity as their top authors joined larger blogs (see subsequent section).

Among conservative sites, Instapundit has slid down the rankings. A former top-five site, it is likely that some of this decline is due to the rise of Twitter. Glenn Reynolds, the site's purveyor, has long maintained a style of links-with-short-commentary, posting up to 20 entries a day, many of which are short enough to be tweeted instead. With no space for community comments, the sole purpose of the site has been to curate information for his large conservative audience. Reynolds himself makes slim use of Twitter, using an auto-post mechanism that repeats all his

*Table 2.2* Conservative rankings, 2009–2010

| Site | Average rank | Minimum rank | Maximum rank | Standard deviation |
|---|---|---|---|---|
| Hot Air | 1 | 1 | 2 | 0.2 |
| Michelle Malkin | 3.6 | 1 | 6 | 1.5 |
| Ace of Spades | 3.6 | 2 | 6 | 1.2 |
| Big Government | 4.5 | 2 | 16 | 5.2 |
| Newsbusters | 5.3 | 2 | 14 | 4 |
| American Thinker | 5.4 | 3 | 8 | 1.4 |
| LittleGreenFootballs | 8 | 3 | 15 | 3.7 |
| Volokh Conspiracy | 8.5 | 5 | 11 | 1.4 |
| TownHall | 9.4 | 3 | 20 | 5 |
| Ann Althouse | 10.1 | 7 | 17 | 2.8 |
| Gateway Pundit | 11.2 | 7 | 19 | 3.5 |
| Jihad Watch | 11.5 | 7 | 26 | 4.1 |
| Instapundit | 12 | 3 | 28 | 8.9 |
| Powerline | 12.3 | 10 | 22 | 2.5 |
| Patterico's Pontifications | 13.5 | 9 | 18 | 2.6 |
| Wizbang | 14.6 | 11 | 18 | 1.6 |
| Outside the Beltway | 15.2 | 8 | 21 | 4.2 |
| Jawa Report | 16.2 | 12 | 21 | 2.6 |
| Red State | 18 | 5 | 21 | 3.4 |
| Hugh Hewitt | 19.7 | 8 | 31 | 8.2 |
| Right Wing News | 19.8 | 10 | 33 | 5.8 |
| IMAO | 20.6 | 18 | 26 | 1.8 |
| Memeorandum | 21.8 | 11 | 36 | 8.4 |
| American Digest | 24.6 | 20 | 31 | 3.2 |

blog entries on the site. In the past few years, this style of blog-based curation has largely been replaced by twitter-based curation.

There are few new entrants to the BAI rankings, few major rank-order shifts and little variance at the top. This is in keeping with ongoing findings of systemic stability.

## Comparative stability

As part of the BAI ranking system, I produce a monthly 'combined BAI' top-50 list that offers an aggregate comparison of the top left – and right-wing blogs. Computing the mean rank of the average progressive and conservative blog provides a simple measure of the comparative strength of the two networks. If the left and right blog networks were at even strength (or if the rank-order were randomly assigned), we would expect the mean scores to be approximately 25. The wider the gap between these two scores, the greater the conservative/progressive deficit/advantage. In the first iteration of the BAI, from November 2007, the mean progressive rank was 23.5, while the mean conservative rank was 27.48. The four-point gap between the two was indicative of a moderate lead for the progressive blogosphere. In a previous study (Karpf 2009), I found that that gap grew to approximately ten points during the 2008 election season and remained at ten points in 2009 (progressive average rank 20.24, conservative average rank 30.29). The top progressive blogs were far more visited, linked to and commented upon than their conservative equivalents.[8]

Since Barack Obama took office in 2008, we have seen an upwelling of grassroots conservatism, particularly in the form of Internet-mediated Tea Party organisations. Many commentators have taken this to indicate a shrinking enthusiasm gap in the political blogosphere. Well-known conservative blogger/political consultant Patrick Ruffini offered boastful claims in 2009 and 2010 that conservative blogs had reached parity or even moved ahead of their progressive equivalents (Ruffini 2009, 2010). The BAI data tells a different story, however. Table 2.4 provides the average site ranks for 2010, the year in which Tea Party enthusiasm and mobilisation was at its peak. The rank-order gap between progressive and conservative blogs has moved from an average of ten ranks to an average of nine (Table 2.3) ranks.

What appears to be occurring here is that, even as conservative blogs have increased in traffic, progressive blogs *also* continue to build a larger audience. The community activity on DailyKos, FireDogLake, Huffington Post and other top progressive sites remains vibrant, as political progressives engage in spirited debate over how and when they should critique President Obama from the left. The conservative blogosphere has grown stronger, as Ruffini and others claim, but it hardly equals the large quasi-political associations of the progressive 'netroots'.[9] RedState.com, for instance, has increased from 50,000 page visits per day to 150,000 page visits per day, but that still pales in comparison to the 500,000 to 1,200,000 visits per day experienced by DailyKos. Andrew Breitbart's collection of sites, Biggovernment.com, bigjournalism.com, bighollywood.com and Bigpeace.com (collectively known as the bigs) are designed to be a conservative response to the Huffington Post, but their traffic is minimal by comparison. The heightened conservative activism embodied by the Tea Party has not translated into equivalent Internet-mediated communities-of-interest in the blogosphere.

*Table 2.3* Average site ranks in the combined BAI dataset, 2008 election season

| Date | ProgAvgRank | ConsAvgRank | Difference |
|---|---|---|---|
| November 2007 | 23.5 | 27.48 | P +3.98 |
| 24 August 2008 | 18.72 | 31.96 | P +13.24 |
| 21 September 2008 | 19.6 | 30.96 | P +11.06 |
| 28 September 2008 | 20.48 | 30.32 | P +9.84 |
| 5 October 2008 | 19.28 | 31.36 | P +12.08 |
| 12 October 2008 | 20.08 | 30.56 | P +10.48 |
| 19 October 2008 | 20.28 | 30.16 | P +9.88 |
| 26 October 2008 | 19.92 | 30.68 | P +10.76 |
| 2 November 2008 | 21.52 | 28.92 | P +7.4 |
| 9 November 2008 | 20.72 | 30.12 | P +9.4 |
| 16 November 2008 | 19.72 | 30.84 | P +11.12 |
| 23 November 2008 | 20.24 | 30.4 | P +10.16 |
| 30 November 2008 | 19.64 | 31.04 | P +11.4 |
| 7 December 2008 | 19.96 | 30.72 | P +10.76 |
| 14 December 2008 | 21.4 | 29.32 | P +7.92 |

*Table 2.4* Average site ranks in the combined BAI dataset, 2010

| Date | ProgAvgRank | ConsAvgRank | Difference |
|---|---|---|---|
| January 2010 | 20.04 | 30.52 | +10.48 |
| February 2010 | 20.36 | 30.24 | +9.88 |
| March 2010 | 20.64 | 29.88 | +9.24 |
| April 2010 | 19.72 | 30.96 | +11.24 |
| May 2010 | 20.72 | 29.92 | +9.20 |
| June 2010 | 21.68 | 28.8 | +7.12 |
| July 2010 | 20.4 | 30.32 | +9.92 |
| August 2010 | 20.72 | 29.96 | +9.24 |
| September 2010 | 21.56 | 28.96 | +7.40 |
| October 2010 | 21.72 | 28.96 | +7.24 |
| November 2010 | 21.2 | 29.8 | +8.6 |
| December 2010 | 20.6 | 30 | +9.40 |
| **2010 Average** | 20.78 | 29.86 | +9.08 |

*Note*: Wilcoxan Mann-Whitney Rank Sum Test produces a z-score of −5.4773, significant at the 0.0001 level.

An alternate explanation could be that the tea party activism has translated into a different cluster of the blogosphere. That explanation appears highly unlikely though. Zernike (2010) notes that top blogger Michelle Malkin played a key role in the initial round of Tea Party protests, hyping them on her blog and donating plates of pulled pork to support their 'porkulus' theme (in reference to Obama's stimulus package). Top bloggers in this cluster have been offered contributing roles on CNN and FoxNews and have actively supported the tea party's rhetoric. New Tea Party-supporting sites like Breitbart's 'bigs' are now included in the conservative BAI rankings, indicating that new blogs are not being ignored by the existing conservative cluster.

## Change

While the rankings in the elite blogosphere have remained relatively stable – both within-clusters and between-clusters – there have been substantial changes among those component blogs in the intervening years. Four themes highlight these changes: new architecture, author migration, professionalisation and consolidation.

In a 2008 paper, 'Understanding Blogspace', I introduced a typology of blog architecture. Like the BAI, the blogspace typology has some transparent limitations: it imposes a two-dimensional spatial logic onto multi-dimensional variations in blog architecture. Blogspace helps to clarify the differences between a *New York Times* blog, a community blog like DailyKos and an independent blog like ShoutingLoudly. These are differences not only of genre, but also of *architecture*. You can do different things on each site, and some sites are connected to offline authoritative sources, while others are not. Mapping blogs according to their architecture helps clarify our expectations and moves us away from assuming a single overarching Blogosphere which clearly does not exist.

Figure 2.1 provides a graphical depiction of blogspace – a four-quadrant chart in which we can spatially arrange political (or other) blogs on the basis of their structural attributes. The x-axis measures authorship – open versus closed. The defining feature that differentiates open – from closed-authorship blogs is the diary feature. Additional features can make a blog more or less open, however. Some blogs, such as Glenn Reynolds' historically popular Instapundit.com, do not allow for reader comments, leaving absolutely no room for voices other than the author's. Others, such as conservative hub blog HotAir.com, require user registration before commenting is allowed, but maintain a closed registration policy so that no new users can join the commenting community. On the other end of the spectrum, some open-authorship blogs include sophisticated reputation systems that allow users to gain authority and increased community exposure, while others enable diaries but provide few tools for increasing exposure to the best diaries.

| | **Closed authorship/ mobility ←** | **→ Open authorship/ mobility** |
|---|---|---|
| Personal → reputation | Independent blogs (FiveThirtyEight.com) | Community blogs (Dailykos.com) |
| Organizational reputation ↓ | Institutional blogs (news, campaign, or organizational) (Fivethirtyeight.blogs. nytimes.com) | 'Bridge blogs' (HuffingtonPost.com) |

*Figure 2.1* The blogspace typology

The y-axis highlights the reputational basis of the blog. While the original wave of blogs were universally counter-institutional – independent sites, a self-publishing outlet for individual bloggers – a second wave ported the software platform over to existing websites, or added a blog feature to a broader Web-based offering. Many interest groups and political campaigns, for instance, now include a blog on their website. Such blogs are designed to augment the organisation's broader mission, and their trustworthiness is based on a visitor's opinion of that institution, rather than starting from nothing. News blogs, campaign blogs and organisational blogs all form distinct genres, categorically differing from independent blogs because they are designed to augment the broader purpose of an existing institution. Internet-mediated news ventures also fit within this category. Though such organisations do not have an existing, offline reputation, they mimic the blog practices of such organisations and seek to augment their online presence and reputation through their blogging.

A fourth blog-type, called bridge blogs, also appears in the typology. Such blogs combine the reputation of a large media or political institution with open authorship platform. Such blogs are exceedingly rare, because combining institutional reputation and open authorship often proves to be a challenging combination, fraught with pitfalls. The Huffington Post provides a good example. HuffPo started as a blog and continues to provide a blogging platform for thousands of unpaid contributors. But it is also a news venue, having hired several reporters away from legacy media institutions like the *New York Times*. It is a media organisation, with reporters in the field. But it also features celebrity

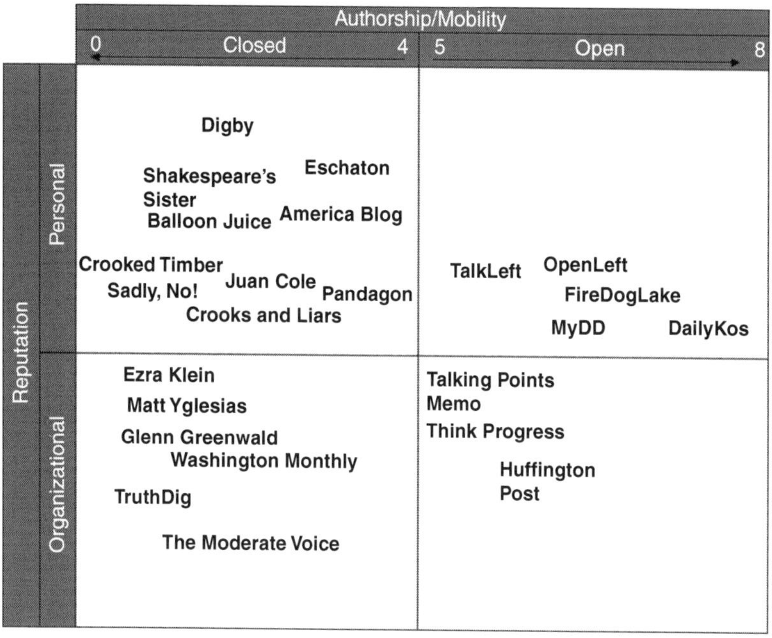


*Figure 2.2* Progressive blogs, by quadrant

blog posts and allows registered users to post their own content to the site. A new user's content is kept far away from the front page, however, and navigation proves somewhat difficult. *Talking Points Memo* employs a similar strategy, with a front page reserved for *TPM* staff reporters, and a separate 'Café' where registered users can congregate and post their own material. Media branding and user-generated content are a tricky mixture.

Overall, the progressive blog cluster continues to include more community and bridge blogs than the conservative blog cluster. Figures 2.2, 2.3 and 2.4 demonstrate this trend. Figures 2.2 and 2.3 place each blog cluster into the blogspace typology. Figure 2.4 highlights the top five sites in each cluster, placing them side-by-side, since these sites receive the lion's share of traffic, hyperlinks and comments.

## New architecture

Several blogs have migrated across the blogspace typology between 2008 and 2011, adding new supportive features and software architecture.

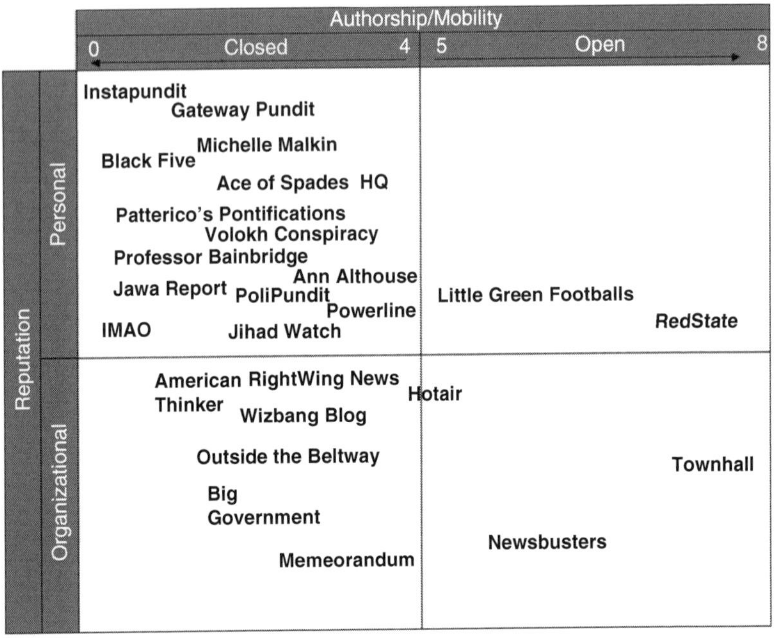


*Figure 2.3* Conservative blogs, by quadrant

The trends have universally been in the directions of greater community participation and greater institutional reputation – sites either remain fixed in the independent quadrant or migrate outward from it, no sites move towards the informal, independent blog type. Most notably on the right, the top conservative blog, HotAir.com has added a 'Green Room' section where registered users can now post diaries of their own. This moves Hotair along the x-axis of the typology, though the closed registration policy prevents it from being wholly in quadrant two or four, with sites such as RedState and TownHall. A new conservative visitor to the site cannot become a diarist, because registration is semi-permanently closed. Meanwhile, Andrew Breitbart's Big Government site is one of many new institutional blogs, seeking to provide a conservative response to liberal news bias.

On the left, the mid-tier blog Feministing.com conducted a fundraiser in 2009, raising enough money to support the rollout of a new community architecture, including user diaries. FireDogLake likewise undertook a site redesign, adding several authors (discussed in the 'author migration' subheading, below), a diary architecture and an action toolkit

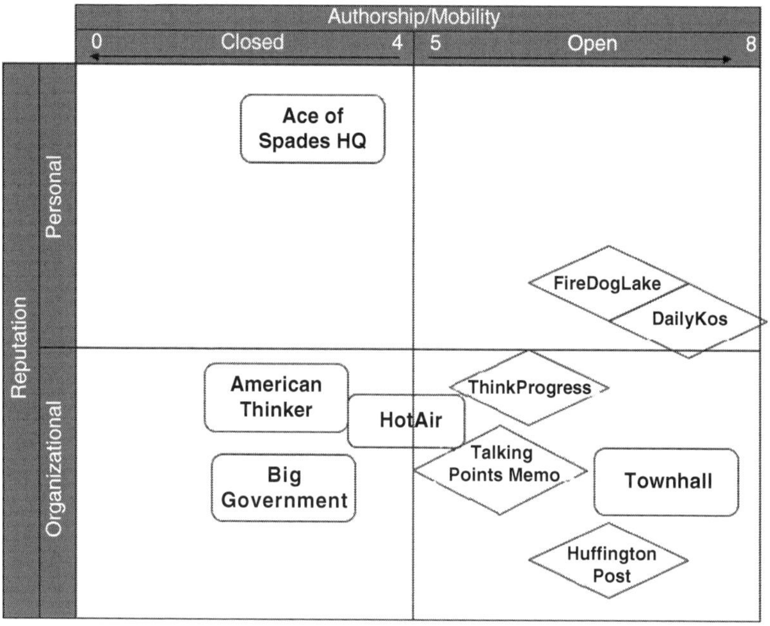


*Figure 2.4* Top five progressive (diamond) and conservative (rectangle) blogs

to support advocacy group-style online actions. Meanwhile DailyKos, already the most community-engaging site in the typology, spent over a year developing 'DK4', a new community platform that features tag clouds, a modified recommendation system and novel search functionalities. Markos Moulitsas has referred to DK4 as an attempt to make DailyKos the equivalent of blogspot (blogger.com) for political progressives. Bridge blogs ThinkProgress (the Center for American Progress's blog), HuffingtonPost and TalkingPointsMemo have all added features in the past two years, though these have been incremental in nature.

## Author migration

New site architecture has primarily cropped up amongst the very top blogs, evidence of a positive feedback loop. Higher advertising revenue at the top of the power law distribution supports further investment in cutting edge software support, further making these hub sites a go-to destination (Hindman 2008). A related trend, occurring through the lower and middle tiers of the BAI rankings, is author migration from site to site. On the right, Ed Morrisey, the author of Captain's Quarters (the tenth largest blog in 2007), joined the authorship at HotAir.com, sun setting his blog. Dozens of smaller bloggers have started adding content to Breitbart's BigGovernment and BigJournalism sites. On the left, independent blogger Ezra Klein accepted a position at the *Washington Post*, where his blog is now hosted. Matt Yglesias likewise has held several such positions at Think Progress, The American Prospect and other sites. Nate Silver, started out as a diarist on DailyKos, then launched an independent blog (FiveThirtyEight.com) that ranked as highly as eighth in 2009. Silver moved his blog to the *New York Times* in the summer of 2010. FireDogLake added several independent bloggers, including Marcy 'EmptyWheel' Wheeler, to its authorship group. Chris Bowers, one of the founders of the community blog OpenLeft.com, was hired by DailyKos in the summer of 2010 to run their online advocacy campaigns.

The general trend here suggests an unresolved 'ension between Hindman's (2008) 'missing middle' thesis and Yochai Benkler's (2006) 'networked information economy' thesis (further discussed below). Benkler suggests that information and participation can 'trickle up' through the blogosphere, allowing minor players to develop their reputations and eventually move into more established sites with larger audiences and stable pay (much as Open Source software developers participate in a reputation economy – Weber 2004). Hindman argues that 'there's not much room at the top' – that the power law structure of online traffic (reinforced by advertising dollars) further limits the space for efficacious political voice online (anyone can speak, but very few can be heard). Author migration around the mid-tier blogs suggests that both Hindman and Benkler may be correct, while operating at different levels of analysis. Mid-tier sites like OpenLeft *do* become victims of the power law traffic structure, eventually shutting down. But the authors of those sites gain reputation and move upward to bigger hubs (OpenLeft's founders now work for DailyKos and the MSNBC television news network). So it would seem that we have stability among power law hubs, limiting voices, but fluctuation among mid-tier sites that supports the trickling up of new voices.

## Blog professionalisation

Particularly among the institutional and bridge blogs, there has been an increasing professional quality to the sites in the BAI. This presents a set of tricky methodological issues: sites like Talking Points Memo and

Huffington Post have hired journalists away from major newspapers and news magazines. They are increasingly referred to as 'media sites' rather than blogs. The Daily Caller (unranked) and Breitbart's constellation of sites on the right are attempting to fill an equivalent niche. The institutional quadrant of the blogspace typology is filled with individual bloggers who are now essentially engaging in professional journalism, along with sites that function as online news outlets. Particularly in light of the ongoing newspaper crisis, with several newspapers facing bankruptcy or switching to online-only formats, the categorical distinction between institutional blogs and online 'newspapers' has grown vague – nearly indistinguishable. It would appear, in the short term, as though online newspapers are sites that currently or formerly have/had an ink-and-pulp equivalent. In discussions of the future of news and journalism, blogs are often referenced en masse as a threat to news gatherers, providing 'commentary, not original reporting' (Schudson and Downie 2009). As these institutional and bridge blogs continue to professionalise, this distinction rings hollow, indicating the extent to which all blogs simply cannot be treated as equal.

Similarly, FireDogLake, DailyKos and (the now defunct) OpenLeft have developed substantial online advocacy capacities, moving beyond blog-based activism to develop large e-mail lists. In so doing, they have hired staff and invested in software to behave as 'internet-mediated issue generalists' (Karpf 2012), similar to MoveOn.org. Indeed, there are several examples of progressive blogs working in coalition with progressive advocacy groups in the past two years. This appears to be an ongoing process, with community blogs professionalising and adding the features of more established online advocacy groups. The two-dimensional, spatial logic of the blogspace framework has always been a simplification. That simplification will continue to become more problematic as these community hub sites professionalise.

## Consolidation

OpenLeft.com shuttered its doors on 4 February 2011. On one level, the closure of the site is indicative of what Hindman has termed 'the missing middle' (2008). Fluctuating between ranks 13 and 23, OpenLeft didn't make enough money through online advertisements alone to sustain itself and had to engage in annual fundraisers to pay for its full-time bloggers and server space. The power law structure of the blogosphere means that the vast majority of online traffic flows to a handful of sites, meaning even the top 25 sites on the left don't receive that much revenue.

On another level however, OpenLeft is indicative of the networked information economy discussed by Benkler (2006). What killed OpenLeft wasn't a lack of funds – costs were low enough that it likely could have continued to close the gap through reader donations. Instead, it appears that OpenLeft was retired through success. Founded in 2007 by Chris Bowers and Matt Stoller, two front-page authors at MyDD.com, and Mike Lux, a long-time Democratic strategist, the site ran multiple political campaigns and earned wide respect amongst the political netroots (Karpf 2009). This led to reputational rewards and better job opportunities for the main authors. Stoller was hired in 2009 to work for Congressman Alan Grayson (and has since moved on to work for MSNBC since Grayson lost his re-election bid). Bowers, as previously mentioned, was hired by DailyKos in the summer of 2010. Lux consults with DailyKos and other organisations. The remaining authors who had joined the site – several of whom had taken positions with other Internet-mediated organisations – eventually decided that it had served its purpose. In a series of 'farewell' posts on the final day of the site, they declared a collective 'mission accomplished', with Lux noting, 'I have been a part of starting a great many organisations over the years, and I have always felt that there is a cycle to institutions, and that it is sometimes better to shut them down than to keep them alive too long.'[10]

To the extent that community sites – be they blogs or online advocacy groups – can be created, accomplish their goals and produce reputational rewards that move their leadership into more stable parts of the online ecology, the 'missing middle' proves to be less of a challenge to Benkler's 'trickle up' theory (2006) than researchers have previously expected.

## A wish list for better blog data collection

Two years of data collection produce some useful findings, as demonstrated above. As the Internet and the blogosphere continue to evolve, however, our tracking systems should as well. While the BAI serves as a nice tool for tracking blogs over time, it also has some underlying limitations. It is my intention to address these in the coming years through a revamped 'BAI 2.0'. This final section provides a bullet point list of expected modifications to the BAI. Researchers designing similar systems would be well advised to pursue similar design modifications.

## Cracks lurking in the BAI system

There are three ongoing issues with the BAI data collection scheme.

### Network centrality score over-stability

Bloggers rarely update their blogrolls. The persistence of LittleGreenFootballs in the conservative BAI ranks years after it publicly split from that cluster provides a telling example: the site is not commonly linked to by its conservative peers anymore, but it persists in many blogrolls out of laziness. The rare updating practices are part of the appeal in using blogrolls for cluster analysis. Active (in-text) hyperlinks mostly point to news sites. Passive (blogroll) hyperlinks point to ideological neighbours, which provide a clearer signal of a neighbourly tie between two members of a blog community. Scraping software like IssueCrawler cannot distinguish between passive and active hyperlinks, and this results in crawls that overestimate the role of news sites in blog networks (a link to a news site is indicative of a news source, a link to a fellow blogger is usually indicative of a *conversation*).

Nonetheless, one source of stability in the BAI rankings is that NCS ranks almost never change. The most central NCS sites of 2008 will be the most central NCS sites of 2010, even if their traffic, hyperlinks and comments were to crater. In the next iteration of the BAI, I plan to change the ranking algorithm to ignore the NCS ranks.

There are two arguments against such a change. First, network centrality *is* a source of authority, and it should continue to be weighed alongside the others. Using the NCS only to establish cluster boundaries thus would involve 'throwing out some data', which should make any good researcher cringe. Second, and with more practical consequences, it would artificially lower the rankings of some blogs that face known data-availability issues. There is no ideal solution to this problem – the vagaries and limitations in underlying blog data make systems like the BAI a messy endeavour.

### Data availability issues

There is no simple solution to this problem; it plagues all blog researchers. But the continuing professionalisation of the blogosphere creates increasing problems for public datasets. There is no solution, for instance, for attaining Site Traffic Scores for bloggers hosted by major media organisations. Glenn Greenwald, Ezra Klein, Nate Silver and Matt Yglesias do not use Sitemeter and operate within domains that receive substantially more traffic than their sole blogs. Alexa, Quantcast, Compete and Hitwise provide domain-level tracking data, so these blogs cannot receive Site Traffic Scores, even though we know them to be highly trafficked. A few blogs similarly are untracked by Technorati, though there is no systematic reason for this flaw.

For the BAI, there is no solution to this problem. As political blogs become more sophisticated and take on media organisation-like properties, the limits of public data will only increase. Researchers contemplating the design of BAI-like systems, particularly in cross-national or international contexts, should approach this issue with care. What Sitemeter, Alexa and Technorati equivalents will exist in (for instance) Denmark in 2014? We cannot know the answer today. Our tracking systems of tomorrow should be designed around newly available data sources.

### Unweighted comparative top 50 rankings

We know that these blog clusters display a power law distribution (Hindman 2008; Karpf 2008a). As such, a shift from rank three to rank two is representative of a much greater change than a shift from rank 46 to rank 45. The latter is essentially noise, the former deserves careful scrutiny. Yet the current means of comparing blog network strength (average rank) treats these rank order shifts as equal. Theoretically, the top conservative blogs could have moved up in the top 50, yet their average rank could remain unchanged if the bottom ones fell alongside (this has not actually occurred – conservatives continue to have two or three blogs in the top ten, and to include most of the blogs ranked 40–50). Converting cardinal data to ordinal rankings is an important form of data-loss, and it in turn limits the utility of the average rank comparative metric.

I have maintained the simple ranking structure so that the BAI would be user-friendly and its limitations transparent. Along with the growth of computational social science, however, it is now time to experiment with more sophisticated, weighted algorithms for the comparative index.

## Additional utilities to add

Along with these 'system cracks' – areas of self-critique that can be further optimised – changes to the media environment yield new opportunities for expanding the BAI collection mechanism.

- Twitter analysis: All of the elite bloggers now use Twitter. Many of them use it to actively drive traffic to their sites, posting links to new blog entries. This potentially offers an additional rank-ordered data source. At a minimum, total followers per blogger can be used as a measure of twitter-reach. More sophisticated measures, including multiple-author tracking for the larger sites, total tweets and retweets, are worth considering as well. Other chapters in this volume provide examples of the Twitter analysis tools that are quickly becoming available.
- Meme tracking: Advances in text analysis programs now make it possible to track memes as they spread through the blogosphere. This is a complicated issue when studying the full, global blogosphere (over 100 million sites), but is much simpler for identified elite clusters. Between 'Wordles' applied to tag clouds and bag-of-words tracking of blog posts, it becomes possible to not only track the rankings of the top blogs, but also *the topics that those blogs are discussing*. Doing so not only represents a substantial additional effort, but also immensely expands the value of the dataset to the research community.

## Conclusion

This chapter has been meant to highlight trends in the US political blogosphere based on the BAI dataset. The BAI is an intentionally simple data collection scheme. Keeping it simple has allowed me to collect several years of data at tremendously low cost. As that data has accrued, three important trends have become clear. The first trend is that the political blogosphere is, indeed, a very stable system. The second trend is the professionalisation, migration and consolidation that occur within this elite blogosphere. The third is the ongoing gap in readership and participation between top blogs on the left and the right.

The BAI dataset also opens up avenues for more complex research questions. The tension between Hindman's 'Missing Middle' thesis and Benkler's 'Networked Information Economy' thesis is long-standing in the literature. While data from the BAI does not provide a direct test of the theses, it does highlight appropriate case studies such as OpenLeft. Leverage in alternate research methods can then help us enrich and expand upon the dominant theories within the field.

The BAI dataset is openly available to the research community. Its strengths and limitations are transparent. Simple tools like this one are an asset, both to the researchers who create them and to the research community as a whole. Particularly around fast-developing digital fields like the changing blogosphere, simple data-aggregation tools like this one can be particularly valuable.

## Appendix: Elite conservative and progressive blogs

### Conservative blogs

HotAir – www.hotair.com
Michelle Malkin – www.michellemalkin.com
Ace of Spades – ace.mu.nu
Big Government – www.biggovernment.com
Newsbusters – www.newsbuster.org
American Thinker – www.americanthinker.com
LittleGreenFootballs – www.littlegreenfootballs.com
Volokh Conspiracy – www.volokh.com
Townhall – www.townhall.com
Ann Althouse – althouse.blogspot.com
Gateway Pundit – www.thegatewaypundit.com
Jihad Watch – www.jihadwatch.com
Instapundit – www.pjmedia.com/instapundit
Powerline – www.powerlineblog.com
Patterico's Pontifications – www.patterico.com
Wizbang – www.wizbangblog.com
Outside the Beltway – www.outsidethebeltway.com
Jawa Report – mypetjawa.mu.nu
Red State – www.redstate.com
Hugh Hewitt – www.hughhewitt.com
Right Wing News – www.rightwingnews.com
IMAO – www.imao.us
Memeorandum – www.memeorandum.com
American Digest – www.americandigest.org

### Progressive blogs

Huffington Post – www.huffingtonpost.com
DailyKos – www.dailykos.com
Talking Points Memo – www.talkingpointsmemo.com
FireDogLake – www.firedoglake.com
Atrios/Eschaton – www.eschatonblog.com
Crooks and Liars – www.crooksandliars.com
Think Progress – www.thinkprogress.org

Washington Monthly – www.washingtonmonthly.com
Balloon Juice – www.balloon-juice.com
Matt Yglesias – http://www.slate.com/authors.matthew_yglesias.html
Digby – www.digbysblog.blogspot.com
America Blog – www.americablog.com
Pandagon – www.pandagon.net
Juan Cole – www.juancole.com
Talk Left – www.talkleft.com
FiveThirtyEight – http://fivethirtyeight.blogs.nytimes.com
Truthdig – www.truthdig.com
Glen Greenwald – http://www.salon.com/news/opinion/glenn_greenwald/index.html
Ezra Klein – http://www.washingtonpost.com/blogs/wonkblog/
Shakespeare's Sister – www.shakesville.com
Feministing – www.feministing.com
The Moderate Voice – www.themoderatevoice.com
Sadly, No! – www.sadlyno.com
Open Left – www.openleft.com (now defunct)
Crooked Timber – www.crookedtimber.org
MyDD – www.mydd.com (now defunct)

## Notes

1. http://www.theatlantic.com/magazine/print/1969/12/learning-to-love-the-shallow-divisive-unreliable-new-media/8415/
2. www.blogosphereauthorityindex.com
3. This shunning was frequently evident in conservative political blog comment threads throughout the 2008 election season. Ron Paul supporters were referred to as 'Paultards' and often found their accounts blocked or deleted by bloggers who disliked them.
4. For more details on the construction of the BAI, consult Karpf (2008a) or contact the author directly.
5. Institutional blogs generally display problems in gathering site traffic data. Site traffic is primarily calculated with Sitemeter data, an opt-in system for sites to record unique visits per day. Blogs that do not use Sitemeter can be included through triangulation using the traffic rankings at Alexa.com, but Alexa rankings cover complete domain names rather than specific URLs. Thus a blog hosted by Slate or New Republic Online will be treated by Alexa as if it received all the traffic to the online news magazine's site. Similarly, bridge blogs systematically underperform in the network centrality rankings, and community blogs occasionally underperform in the comment rankings by enabling comments in unrecordable areas of the site.
6. Six additional entries for March to August 2011 are available online, but are not included in this study.

7. http://www.shoutingloudly.com/2009/11/30/lgf-quits-conservatism-snap-reaction/
8. Using a Wilcoxon-Mann-Whitney Rank Sum Test to test for non-parametric significance, these findings are significant at the 0.0001 level.
9. 'Netroots' is a portmanteau of 'Internet' and 'Grassroots', commonly used to describe online political activists.
10. http://openleft.com/diary/21610/thank-you-by-Mike-Lux

## References

Adamic, L. and Glance, N. (2005) 'The Political Blogosphere and the 2004 US Election: Divided They Blog'. Presented at Conference on Knowledge Discovery in Data. Available at: http://portal.acm.org/citation.cfm?doid=1134271.1134277, date accessed 28 May 2008.

Barzilai-Nahon, K. and Helmsley, J. (2011) 'Democracy.com: A Tale of Political Blogs and Content', 44th Hawaiian International Conference on System Sciences, Hawaii, January 2011.

Barzilai-Nahon, K., Helmsley, J., Walker, S. and Hussain, M. (2011) 'Fifteen Minutes of Fame: The Place of Blogs in the Life Cycle of Viral Political Information', *Policy & Internet*, 3 (1), 6–33.

Benkler, Y. (2006) *The Wealth of Networks: How Social Production Transforms Markets and Freedom* (New Haven, CT: Yale University Press).

Benkler, Y. and Shaw, A. (2010) 'A Tale of Two Blogopheres: Discursive Practices on the Left and Right', Berkman Center for Internet & Society. Available at: http://cyber.law.harvard.edu/publications/2010/Tale_Two_Blogospheres_Discursive_Practices_Left_Right

Davis, R. (2009) *Typing Politics* (New York: Oxford University Press).

Gil de Zúñiga, H., Puig-i-Abril, E. and Rojas, H. (2009) 'Weblogs, Traditional Sources Online and Political Participation: An Assessment of how the Internet is Changing the Political Environment', *New Media & Society*, 11 (4), 553–574.

Gil de Zuniga, H., Veenstra, A., Vraga, E. and Shah, D. (2010) 'Digital Democracy: Reimagining Pathways to Political Participation', *Journal of Information Technology and Politics*, 7 (1), 36–51.

Hindman, M. (2008) *The Myth of Digital Democracy* (Princeton, NJ: Princeton University Press).

Hindman, M., Tsioutsiouliklis, K. and Johnson, J. (2003) ' "Googlearchy": How a Few Heavily-Linked Sites Dominate Politics on the Web', paper presented at the Annual Meeting of the Midwest Political Science Association, Chicago, IL, 3–6 April.

Karpf, D. (2008a) 'Measuring Influence in the Political Blogosphere', *Politics and Technology Review*, George Washington University's Institute for Politics, Democracy, and the Internet, 33–41.

Karpf, D. (2008b) 'Understanding Blogspace', *Journal of Information Technology and Politics*, 5 (4), 369–385.

Karpf, D. (2009) 'Stability and Change in the Political Blogosphere in the 2008 Election', paper presentation at the Midwest Political Science Association Annual Meeting, Chicago, IL.

Karpf, D. (2012a) *The Move On Effect: The Unexpected Transformation of American Political Advocacy* (New York: Oxford University Press).
Karpf, D. (2012b) 'Social Science Research Methods in Internet Time', *Information, Communication and Society*, 15 (5), 639–661.
Lawrence, E., Sides, J. and Farrell, H. (2010) 'Self-Segregation or Deliberation? Blog Readership, Participation and Polarization in American Politics', *Perspectives on Politics*, 8 (1), 141–157.
McKenna, L. and Pole, A. (2004) 'Do Blogs Matter? Weblogs in American Politics', paper presentation at 2004 Annual Meeting of the American Political Science Association, Chicago, IL, 2 September.
Perlmutter, D. (2008) *Blog Wars* (New York: Oxford University Press).
Pole, A. (2009) *Blogging the Political: Politics and Participation in a Networked Society* (New York: Routledge Press).
Ruffini, P. (2009) 'Rising Rightroots and Declining Netroots Now at Parity (or Better)', Blog Post, 17 September 2009. Available at: http://www.thenextright.com/patrick-ruffini/rising-rightroots-and-declining-netroots-now-at-parity-or-better, date accessed 16 October 2009.
Ruffini, P. (2010) 'Why the Right Is Winning Online in 2010', blog post, *TheNextRight.com*. 28 September 2010. Available at: http://thenextright.com/patrick-ruffini/why-the-right-is-winning-online-in-2010
Schudson, M. and Downie, L Jr. (2009) 'The Reconstruction of American Journalism', *Columbia Journalism Review*. Available at: http://www.cjr.org/reconstruction/the_reconstruction_of_american.php?page=all
Wallsten, K. (2007) 'Political Blogs: Transmission Belts, Soapboxes, Mobilizers, or Conversation Starters?', *Journal of Information Technology and Politics*, 4 (3), 19–40.
Wallsten, K. (2008) 'Agenda Setting and the Blogosphere: An Analysis of the Relationship Between Mainstream Media and Political Blogs', *Review of Policy Research*, 24 (6), 567–587.
Wallsten, K. (2011) 'Drudge's World? The Drudge Report's Influence on Media Coverage." Paper presented at the annual meeting of the Southwestern Political Science Association. Las Vegas, NV. March 16-19, 2011.
Weber, S. (2004) *The Success of Open Source* (Cambridge, MA: Harvard University Press).
Zernike, K. (2010) *Boiling Mad* (New York: MacMillan).

# 3

# Analysing YouTube Audience Reactions and Discussions: A Network Approach

*Mike Thelwall*

The video-sharing site YouTube is one of the most popular websites in the world according to the search tool Alexa.com. It is a social phenomenon, allowing individuals to create and share media content with millions of other users worldwide. It also serves as an important new information source for a myriad of mainstream and specialised interests, housing as it does a vast array of videos on various topics. In addition to its visual component, YouTube also facilitates discussion by allowing individuals to comment on the videos they have seen. This allows researchers to investigate audience reactions to the topics covered.

In this chapter, we discuss the methodological and ethical challenges that are involved in studying YouTube in general, as well as conduct a pilot study of the comments made on a video of a speech by Barack Obama. We do so using a new software application – Webometric Analyst – that has been developed by the author (and is freely available at http://lexiurl.wlv.ac.uk). Webometric Analyst downloads comments on videos and public information about commenters such as their age, sex and geographic location. Using these data, the software creates a series of network diagrams mapping the relationships between the commenters. These networks allow us to more systematically describe the debate surrounding the video and the response of the audience. Our results show that YouTube data has value in providing a new means of measuring public responses to local or international events or issues; however, our ultimate conclusion is that for issues that are not native to YouTube it is best used as part of a mixed-method strategy, or restricted to pilot studies.

## YouTube as a new tool for measuring public opinion?

Much of the analysis of YouTube has focused on its video content; however, it also provides an important potential new source of evidence about global public opinion (Paek et al. 2010). Many YouTube videos have a list of comments attached to them, which have been left by viewers. Since these comments are public and displayed on the open Web they are available to be researched by those seeking insights into societal responses to the events depicted in the videos or the topics represented in them. A key advantage in using YouTube data as compared with other more traditional sources of public opinion such as interviews or surveys lies in the speed with which it can capture responses and its 'real-time' quality. In addition, the responses are already in the public domain which means they have fewer ethical issues associated with their collection and analysis. Finally, the method of data collection is non-obtrusive and therefore does not impose on people by requesting their time to complete a survey or an interview.

From the perspective of politics, investigating the comments left on certain videos may give fast and highly valuable insights into public opinion. For example, YouTube videos are now a standard part of political campaigning in many countries and an analysis of the comments on a particular campaign video may reveal which aspects of the message are most responded to. Similarly, it may be possible to get 'real-time' insights into political events that are captured on film, such as the UK riots of 2011 from the comments posted to online videos of the riots. In the former case and some other cases such as the Neda murder in Iran (see Mortensen 2011), the London tram racist in Britain (BBC News 2011) and the Fitna anti-Muslim video (van Zoonen et al. 2011) the message may be inherently video-based and hence natural to investigate via YouTube.

This chapter provides a demonstration of the utility of YouTube comment data for social scientists through the application of a new publicly available Web-based data collection and analysis tool – the Webometric Analyst software. YouTube automatically delivers information about comments and commenters on a particular video. The Webometric Analyst tool captures these data and re-presents them as a series of networks surrounding the videos. Here we examine the response to a speech of Barack Obama based upon the comments left by viewers. A network approach is useful in revealing overall patterns in the commenter population and the wider public reaction that may not be evident from reading each post individually. In particular, it allows us to profile more basic features such as who is most interested in the video and how demographically diverse the population of commenters are. It also allows us to understand the population in a dynamic manner by revealing the extent of interaction between commenters, as well as the tone or nature of that interaction – is it friendly or antagonistic?

The chapter is organised into three basic sections. First, we seek to profile some of the key methodological challenges that researchers face when studying YouTube in general and, particularly, in relation to its comment data. Second, we present the Webometric Analyst software and show how it can be used to describe to describe those networks that are developed through the comment facility of YouTube. Finally, we demonstrate the utility of the new software and YouTube comment data for measuring public responses to important events by applying it to the comments generated by the video of a speech given by Barack Obama in Egypt.

## Methodological challenges and opportunities in studying YouTube

Any Internet-based research method that seeks to describe parameters of interest in a population that contains a significant number of individuals who are not online faces the problem of sample bias. Although access is widening within most countries, Internet users are still not fully representative of the general population. For example, in the United States in February 2012 (Pew Internet 2012) it seems that while there is now approximate gender equality in Internet use with males only 2 per cent more likely to report access than females (81 per cent compared to 79 per cent), black and Hispanic citizens were about 12 per cent underrepresented (71 per cent use the Internet compared to 83 per cent for whites) and the most educated and youngest were almost twice as prevalent as the least educated and those over 65. For an international study this demographic bias will be exacerbated by the cross-country differences in the proportion of the population that is online. For instance, if a much higher proportion of South Koreans are online compared to Senegalese, then any sample will heavily over represent South Koreans compared to Senegalese.

From a traditional social science perspective clearly the problem of sample bias places significant limits on the value of YouTube data as a means of measuring opinion for most populations of interest. Posters of video and commenters are self-selected and their motivations are unknown. Anyone with Internet access can upload or view a YouTube video and then leave a comment afterwards. This immediately skews the sample towards people that use the Internet and who are prepared to watch YouTube videos. Thus, unless the subjects of the study are those using and commenting on YouTube videos, the results of any study are unlikely to truly measure wider public opinion or response to an event.

The problem of self-selection in YouTube analyses extends beyond sample bias to the topic of research itself. To a large extent, the researcher is dependent on the posters of the material and commenters in selecting their subjects of study. For instance, an investigation of attitudes towards immigration during an election campaign using YouTube would require relevant material was first uploaded, and then that sufficient comments were posted on the material to allow for a meaningful examination of attitudes. This dependency means that YouTube material is generally more suitable for exploratory analyses rather for in-depth investigations of a predefined topic of interest to social scientists

Despite the problem of selection bias, it is clear that analyses of YouTube can still be useful on pilot study grounds or as part of a multi-method approach. Indeed in some cases online data sources like YouTube may be the only way in which it is possible to study a phenomenon for practical reasons. In such cases, the biases would have to be accepted as an unavoidable limitation if one wanted to study the phenomenon in question. This acceptance is not without precedent in social science research. The now widely practiced method of snowball sampling, for instance, accepts it is inherently biased around a small cluster of individuals. Also interview-based research and focus groups typically use sample sizes that too small to make meaningful statistical inferences about the population of interest.

YouTube comment data also has some advantages over other types of opinion data that are gathered using more established methods. One key benefit is that it allows for unobtrusive data collection in the sense that individuals are not directly contacted for their opinions but offer them voluntarily on a publicly accessible platform. This more 'remote' or indirect aspect of data collection means that respondents are entirely free to express their concerns in the way that they like, unconstrained by any interviewer or questionnaire. Of course, the lack of interviewer interaction or pre-set survey questions also means that the researcher must do more to infer the meaning of the comments and the motivation of the commenter. Unlike with interviews or questionnaires the researcher cannot control the interaction to ensure that specific topics of interest are adequately covered. YouTube commenters may also deliberately and systematically hide their motives, potentially misleading investigators. Perhaps the most extreme example of this is trolling whereby individuals deliberately provoke others with hostile commentary in order to start an argument rather than to genuinely engage in debate (Herring et al. 2002). Researchers need to remain alert to the presence of this type of deliberate bias when interpreting in the tone or sentiment of the online debate.

## Ethical considerations in using YouTube data

As with all research involving human subjects, studying YouTube raises ethical concerns. The issues raised, however, are arguably less significant than those arising from other more conventional modes of data collection. This is due largely to its unobtrusiveness as a method of data generation. Much of YouTube's content is explicitly placed by its 'authors' in the public domain and does not require their permission to be viewed. Thus, while material may not be posted for research purposes, it serves as an open archive or documentary resource that anyone can access (Wilkinson and Thelwall 2011). Given this openness, it seems somewhat unreasonable for someone to claim an expectation of privacy for their comments or to complain after the fact that it had been used for a purpose that they did not intend.

Despite this openness, there is of course a need for researchers to exercise discretion when personally identifying individuals in the course of their research. Thus, while it is not normally required to seek permission of authors to analyse their public comments or videos, it is good practice to protect the authors' identities when writing up research for publication. It is possible that an individual's privacy may be compromised if their opinions or behaviours gain attention after being re-published in a different format (Nissenbaum 2009). By way of example, one could cite a case whereby an individual posted a video about their gender-change experience to YouTube that was subsequently used by a researcher in work that enters the public domain through a television documentary or book. This could have a potentially devastating effect on the person concerned if they had forgotten to delete the video and were now living comfortably with their new gender identity. While this might be a rare occurrence, it demonstrates that a 'best practice' rule in using YouTube data is to ensure that video authors and commenters remain anonymous, unless they are already high profile media figures. This should extend to disguising their comments or video names if these would be searchable so that their identity could not be discovered indirectly in this way.

## Appropriate uses of YouTube data

Drawing these considerations together, we argue that despite the inherent limitations and restrictions currently in place regarding the collection and YouTube data, it nevertheless can play a valuable role for certain types of social science analysis. These are:

- When YouTube *itself* is the object of study. As the third most visited website in the world for many years (Alexa 2012), YouTube itself is a valid object of study. This applies not only to YouTube as a whole but also to any issue where YouTube has played a significant role, such as election campaigns (Gueorguieva 2008) or a health campaign (Lazzara 2010).
- As a *pilot study* to gain an immediate insight into an issue. The results can be used to help shape the main study that follows by identifying key topics for interview or survey questions. For example, a project studying reactions to gay marriage might begin by analysing comments on YouTube videos of gay weddings and use these insights to design interviews and surveys as the main project instruments.
- As a component within a wider study involving *methods triangulation*, whereby different methods are used to draw out and develop richer insights into an issue would otherwise be possible. Analysis of reactions to a YouTube video about assisted suicide, for example, could allow for a deeper exploration of the emotions and sensitivities of audience responses when presented with visual stimuli on the topic rather than simply discussing or reading about the topic.
- When *no alternative* is available. Some phenomena may be impossible or impractical to study with offline methods, leaving online methods as the only realistic option. This may apply to phenomena that are difficult to access because they are geographically remote such as lesbian parenting in rural communities. Or because they deal with controversial topics such as illegal or criminal activities, mental illness (Lewis et al. 2011), or other sensitive topics such as obesity (Yoo and Kim 2012). In some cases, these topics may have been under-researched in the past partly because of the difficulty in gaining useful data.
- As part of *methods training*. The novel limitations of YouTube projects, as with many Internet studies, can be useful for methods training

because the many limitations provide scope for students or trainees to learn and demonstrate an understanding of good methodological practice.

In the section that follows, we illustrate the above points by providing a step by step guide to conducting a systematic analysis of YouTube comment data using the Webometric Analyst software.

## Data collection and sampling on YouTube: Using Webometric Analyst

The first stage of most empirical analyses is to identify the cases for analysis. This may include the entire population but generally involves the selection of a sample of representative cases to be studied. In the case of YouTube, both approaches are possible. If, for instance, the study focuses on campaign videos posted by political parties during an election then the analysis could most likely include the entire population. In most situations, however, it is not possible or practical to study the population of relevant videos and a more selective approach is needed. For example, if one were investigating reactions to the UK riots of 2011 then one would need to limit the scope of the study in some way and develop rules for inclusion. One simple way this can be done is by searching the YouTube website with a series of logical queries or terms. The search would return a list of riot-related videos that the researcher could then manually filter to ensure topic relevance. Brief annotations justifying the reasons for inclusion and exclusion of the videos could be supplied to ensure maximum transparency of the selection process. This initial list can be randomly sampled if the initial number of cases is too large for manual filtering. While this approach will inevitably lead to some slippage in its coverage of the wider population of interest, it does provide a more systematic and replicable basis for ongoing analysis than relying on ad hoc and opportunistic browsing. Of course, it is important to bear in mind that even if one uses identical search terms across two sets of analysis, the contents of YouTube change rapidly, making it unlikely that the results of any two studies will remain the same over time.

## Running Webometric Analyst

The program Webometric Analyst can help with producing lists of videos to be analysed because it has the facility to submit queries to YouTube and save the results as a plain text file that can be added to spreadsheet or word processor for analysis (see Thelwall et al. 2012 for further details). This can be done in a few simple steps that we outline below:

(1) Download Webometric Analyst from http://lexiurl.wlv.ac.uk to your computer.
(2) Start Webometric Analyst, select the classic interface from the start-up Wizard and click OK.
(3) Select the YouTube tab from near the top of the screen to get to the main set of YouTube functions.
(4) Create a plain text file by using Windows Notepad for example that contains your queries, one per line.
(5) Click on the *Search for Videos Matching Each Query in File* button, select your plain text file and wait for the program to finish.

Once completed, these five steps will create a set of additional plain text files, one of which will be a list of all videos matching each search query in the original plain text file (created in step 4). This can be copied into a spreadsheet in order to be read more easily. A word processor document can also be used. Unwanted videos may be filtered out by marking them with a text highlighter or deleting them from the spreadsheet. This filtering can be based on the titles of the videos, or viewing the videos if the titles are not enough to make a decision.

Finally, we need to give each YouTube video a unique identifier. This is assigned using the URL address and the specifically the 11 characters immediately following the ?v= part. For example the video with URL http://www.YouTube.com/watch?v=F7rsrO3kEe4 has identifier F7rsrO3kEe4 and the video with URL http://www.YouTube.com/watch?v=jz0Z5_h_CtY&feature=related has identifier jz0Z5_h_CtY.

## Downloading the comments and information about the commenters

Once the list of video identifiers has been created then the complete set of comments associated with each video are downloaded by the software for the subsequent analysis. YouTube allows up to 1000 of the most recent comments on a video to be viewed on its website (in batches of 50) although most videos have fewer comments than this and some do not allow commenting. The process of downloading the information is fully automated but is quite slow. Indeed, it may take up to half an hour per video. To reduce the time involved in this process, if the number of videos returned by a search is large then a random sample of the videos should be drawn prior to downloading. To download the comments and commenter information, first complete steps 1 to 3 listed in the previous section. Then:

(1) Create a plain text file (using Windows Notepad) that contains the identifiers of the videos, one per line. Put this file in a new empty folder on your computer because Webometric Analyst will create many new files in this folder.
(2) Click on the *Get Commenter Networks* button, select your plain text file and wait for the program to finish.

Once the program has finished running a large number of new files will appear in the folder with the original plain text list of identifiers. The files contain numbers to identify all files associated with each video. For example, the files associated with the eighth video identifier in your file will contain the number eight in their filename. The key file needed is the one for each video with a name that ends in Comments.txt. This contains a list of all comments, plus information about the commenters.

## Data analysis: Identifying the key topics of comments

Once they are downloaded, the comments on each video are ready for analysis. Although the sections below describe more complex network-based types of analyses using the Webometric Analyst software we recommend beginning with some basic description of the content of the comments. There are a number of methods that have been developed for systematic analysis of textual data. We profile three of the most widely used below – content analysis, grounded theory and discourse analysis – and show how they can be applied to YouTube comment data.

Content analysis (Neuendorf 2002) of YouTube comments is a fairly straightforward process that involves coding the text of the comments into a set of pre-defined categories relevant to the research question.[1] These categories generally focus on the substantive topics covered by the comments, as well as the tone or sentiment of the comment. New categories can be added as required. The end result is a quantitative measure of the frequency of mentions of certain topics and the overall balance of the tone of the texts as positive or negative. In the context of YouTube comment analysis, therefore, findings might be that 80 per cent of the comments on a video of the Chancellor's budget speech were negative, and 30 per cent of those negative comments mentioned alcohol price increases.

If the analysis is substantial rather than for a pilot study then it is good practice to use more than one coder for the categories and to assess the extent to which the codes given by the different people are consistent. Inter-coder consistency can be assessed with a relevant statistic, such as Cohen's kappa. For more information about coding texts into categories, please see a standard content analysis textbook. If there are hundreds of comments then a random sample of 100–200 could be coded rather than the full set since coding can be quite time consuming.

A grounded theory (Charmaz 2006) approach differs from content analysis in that it does not generally involve applying pre-defined classes but instead codes text or comments in an unrestricted way at first. This is useful when one is working on a topic which has very little existing theory that can be applied to it, or a clearly defined conceptual framework. The categories are subsequently clustered together with theory being built up from the clusters. In addition, grounded theory typically uses purposive rather than a random sampling. This involves purposefully selecting new videos or comments to code in order to fill gaps or a 'quota' in clusters of interest and to test any theories developed.

Finally, a discourse analysis (Stubbs 1983) of comments is useful in drawing out the underlying structure, dynamics and meaning of a text through an in-depth analysis of its recurrent themes and the language used. It is also useful for analysis of the commentary and commentators' interaction. So a typical question it might seek to address what techniques are typically used by commenters to refute arguments of others? Or what are the rhetorical devices and values that are typically used to voice support or opposition towards a particular video.

## Data analysis: Interpreting comments as a network

Although analysing YouTube comments as a list can give insights into the topics discussed, it may not clearly reveal the nature of any discussion between commenters, especially if an approach other than discourse analysis is taken. Given that YouTube comments can either be posted as separate entities or as replies to previous comments it is possible to take a structural approach to understanding the discussion surrounding the videos posted. Analysing comments as a whole in the form of a network analysis can capture the entirety of the discussion relating a video's comments and reveal underlying patterns in those discussions. Through Webometric Analyst we can draw a network diagram of the comments on a video. In the following section, we outline how the information downloaded from YouTube can be used by Webometric Analyst to create networks for each video – the *ReplyTo network* (not currently available, but can be manually drawn), the *Subscriptions* and *Subscriptions in common network*. The nodes are as above. Lines (not arrows) between users are drawn to indicate that two users have common channel subscriptions in YouTube. The thickness of a line between two users is proportional to the number of common channel subscriptions that they have. In each diagram, the nodes (circles) represent individual commenters and arrows between nodes represent replies from one commenter to another. Node sizes are also proportional to the number of comments made by the commenter.

Following the approach set out above for extracting comments as a list, the Webometric Analyst facility *Get Commenter Networks* is used for construction of the networks. This facility downloads the comments and information about the commenters for a set of videos. The following information is extracted for each video in the submitted list.

- A list of all comments made to the video, up to a maximum of 1000. If there are more than 1000 comments then the most recent 1000 are selected.
- The username of each commenter and their list of subscriptions in YouTube.

**ReplyTo network**

The ReplyTo network provides the main overview of the network of comments attached to a video. It shows commenters that either replied to other comments or received a reply to one of their comments. This network can be viewed in software like Pajek, UCINET, NodeXL, Gethi or Webometric Analyst. To view the ReplyTo network of a video in Webometric Analyst, follow the following instructions.

(1) Use the steps in the section above (downloading the comments and information about the commenters) to create the ReplyTo network. It will be in a file with name ending in ReplyTo or ReplyTo.net (it may not be available due to YouTube changes).
(2) Start Webometric Analyst, select the classic interface from the start-up Wizard and click OK.
(3) Select *Draw Network* from the *File* menu. A new window will open showing a small network diagram.

(4) In the new window, select *Load Pajek Graph*... from the *File* menu and select the ReplyTo file. The network should then be drawn.
(5) The network may need to be rearranged to show the pattern more clearly. For example, the nodes can be moved by clicking on them and then dragging them. Visit the Webometric Analyst website (http://lexiurl.wlv.ac.uk) for more ideas about how to rearrange the network.
(6) Click on a node to produce a list of all comments written by the user in addition to all replies sent to the user.

This network can be used to visually explore the overall structure. In particular, it can be used to identify the following features of the discussions.

- The usernames of the individuals comment the most – those with the largest nodes.
- The overall structure: for example, it could be a small set of isolated exchanges, mainly one large discussion, or dominated by a few prolific commenters.
- Pairs of commenters that have particularly extensive exchanges of comments (visualised as thick arrows in the network diagram).

Some Social Network Analysis (SNA) statistics about the network, including a list of the individuals sending the most comments (have the highest out-degree in SNA jargon) or receiving the most comments (have the highest indegree) can be obtained from the network diagram in Webometric Analyst by selecting *calculate centrality statistics from loaded network* from the *Stats* menu of the network drawing window.

## Sentiment analysis of networks

ReplyTo networks can also be annotated by the sentiment analysis program developed by the author – SentiStrength (Thelwall et al. 2012). Through this software, it is possible to analyse the strength of positive and negative sentiment in social Web texts. This program can be used to colour an arrow black if the replies represented by the arrow are predominantly negative and red if they are predominantly positive. Instructions are available for this in the YouTube page of the Webometric Analyst website. Essentially, the program SentiStrength has to be downloaded and then the menu option YouTube *Networks – Calculate sentiment of all comments to colour network arrows* must be selected from SentiStrength's

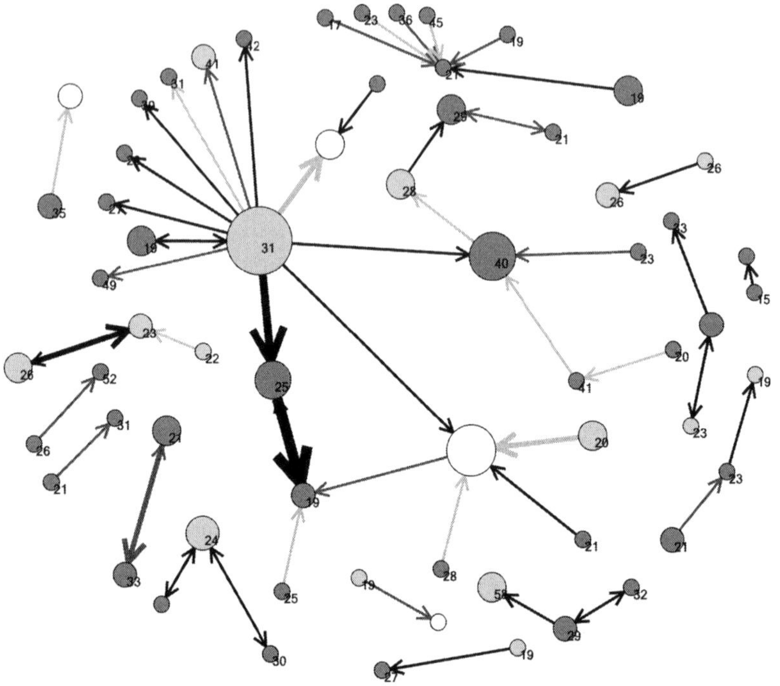

*Figure 3.1* Reply network from the Wolverhampton Riots video
*Note*: Numbers are ages; nodes are dark for male, light for female and white for unknown. Predominantly negative comments are represented by black arrows and positive by grey arrows.

*Sentiment Strength Analysis* menu and the program pointed to the location of the YouTube networks. Figure 3.1 is an example of a reply network for a YouTube video with relatively few comments.

Figure 3.1 illustrates a reply network for the Wolverhampton riots of summer 2011. These riots were part of a wave of rioting in the United Kingdom that began with the death of Mark Duggan on 4 August 2011 in Tottenham, London, and spread to many other cities in the United Kingdom. During the riots, social media were blamed for some of the coordination of activities. This particularly affected the BlackBerry Messenger (BBM) service, but Facebook was also mentioned in court cases, indicating the wider influence of social media. During the riots, participants, bystanders, news media, the police and surveillance cameras took numerous photographs and videos. Some of these were subsequently published online, providing both a record of some of the events and an opportunity for participants and interested others to view specific events and discuss them with strangers, acquaintances or friends. Figure 3.1 is based on a single YouTube video of part of one of the riots. The comments left on the video were not made during the riots themselves and can be seen as expressing the reactions of those members of the public who viewed the video after the event. The frequency of the black and red arrows present indicates that the event was still seen as controversial. Content analysis of the comments would clearly yield deeper insights into these observations.

### Subscription networks

When analysing the discussions in a comment network it may be useful to investigate whether the commenters know each other or have beliefs or interests in common. While it is impossible to get definitive answers to these questions, some light can be shed on them using the subscriber relationships in YouTube.

In order to leave a comment on a YouTube video, a person must join the YouTube site. Members get their own home page and have the option to harness some social networking features, such as the ability to subscribe to the videos of other members. Hence, one way to look for an indication that two YouTube commenters know each other is to see if one subscribes to the videos of the other. Of course, two people can be offline friends without being registered as YouTube subscribers, but if two people are YouTube subscribers then this gives good evidence that they at least know of each other. In addition to looking at whether there is a direct connection between two individuals through the subscription facility of YouTube, it is also possible to check for connections between individuals by looking at whether they have subscriptions in common. If users do have a high degree of overlap in their subscriptions then this seem to be a useful indicator of the degree of a similarity of interests.

Information about the existence of commenter connections can be shown by Webometric Analyst's subscription networks. Information about the existence of commenter common interests can be shown by Webometric Analyst's subscriptions in common networks. In each network, nodes represent commenters and arrows or lines between nodes represent the type of connection. To see these networks, follow the instructions below:

(1) Use the steps in the section above on downloading the comments and information about the commenters) to create the networks.

These networks will be in files with names ending in Subscriptions.net and SubscriptionsInCommon.net.
(2) Start Webometric Analyst, select the classic interface from the start-up Wizard and click OK.
(3) Select *Draw Network* from the *File* menu. A new window will open showing a small network diagram.
(4) In the new window, select *Load Pajek Graph*... from the *File* menu and select one of the above files to investigate. The network should then be drawn.
(5) The nodes in the network may need to be rearranged to show the connections more clearly.

In summary, Webometric Analyst provides for a number of ways of examining the structure of the discussion networks that take place on YouTube. In all networks, the nodes in the network are users that commented on the video. The size of each node is proportional to the number of comments left on the video by the commenter. The three main representations of the discussion are as follows:

- *ReplyTo network*. Arrows between users are drawn to indicate that one user replied to comments by another user. The thickness of an arrow is proportional to the number of replies made.
- *Subscription network*. Arrows are drawn between users to indicate that one user subscribes to the channel of the other. Subscription in YouTube is a non-symmetrical relationship that allows one user to quickly access the videos produced by the other.
- *Subscriptions in common network*. Lines (not arrows) between users are drawn to indicate that two users have common channel subscriptions in YouTube. The thickness of a line between two users is proportional to the number of common channel subscriptions that they have.

## Pilot study of a video of a 2009 Obama speech in Egypt

This section provides a brief demonstration of the methods described above and utility of the Webometric Analyst software through a pilot study of a prominent political video posted on YouTube – 'Obama In Egypt On US-Muslim Tensions-Full Speech' (YouTube identifier ANk9qydfGe4). The video contains a high profile speech given by Barack Obama in Cairo, Egypt on 4 June 2009 with the apparent aim of explaining US foreign policy in the region to an Arab audience (Khatib et al. 2012). The research question for this analysis is very broad: How did the world react to this speech? Given that this is pilot study, we provide some 'topline' results in this chapter rather than an in-depth analysis of the networks created. This includes a basic content analysis of a random sample of the comments on the video and a network analysis demonstrating the 'ReplyTo' and 'Subscription' structure of the comments.

In terms of nationality, the majority of the 291 commenters that declared a location were from the United States (58 per cent), with the second largest contingent coming from the United Kingdom (10 per cent). Only 15 per cent of the commenters declared an origin in a country with a majority Muslim population, with Egypt (7 per cent) forming the largest contingent within this group of 16 countries. Since the talk was apparently directed at citizens of the Middle East, the low number of responses from this region is surprising. A possible reason is that the talk was primarily delivered to the mass media of the Middle East and so YouTube is not the natural forum to discuss it. Moreover, YouTube does not get a significant proportion of its users from the Middle East and the commenter demographics partially reflect this. An important implication of these statistics is that the analysis of the comments is likely to reflect a predominantly US perspective on the talks.

## Content analysis results

Tables 3.1 and 3.2 report the results of two basic content analyses carried out by one coder for two different dimensions. Given it was a pilot study, additional coders were not considered necessary. The first dimension coded is the sentiment of the comment, that is, whether the attitude of the commenter towards the speech or Obama is positive or negative (Table 3.1). This shows majority opposition to it from those that expressed an opinion.

Table 3.2 reports the main topics of the comments, perhaps reflecting the majority US location of the commenters, a quarter discussed or evaluated Obama or the speech itself rather than engaging with the issue raised or discussing something else. The second most popular topic was an explicit discussion of religion, perhaps reflecting the focus of the speech itself, which explicitly discussed Islam. Also discussed were geopolitical issues, such as the role of religion in war and wars in the Middle East. A small percentage of comments (12 per cent) merely insulted or praised a previous commenter without explicitly discussing another topic.

*Table 3.1* Sentiment of comments on the Obama in Egypt YouTube video

| **Attitude** | **Description** | **Frequency** |
|---|---|---|
| Anti-Obama | Commenter expresses opposition to, or disagreement with, Obama, US policies in the Middle East or the arguments made in the speech. | 25 |
| Neutral | Commenter expresses neutrality or an undecided attitude towards Obama, US policies in the Middle East or the arguments made in the speech. | 0 |
| Pro-Obama | Commenter expresses support of, or agreement with, Obama, US policies in Middle East or the arguments made in the speech. | 17 |
| Unclear | The text does not reveal an attitude towards Obama, US policies in the Middle East or the arguments made in the speech, or the attitude is ambiguous. | 58 |

*Note*: Table based on a manual coding of 100 randomly selected comments (overall N of 648).

*Table 3.2* Topics of comments on the Obama in Egypt YouTube video

| **Topic** | **Description** | **Frequency** |
|---|---|---|
| Obama or Obama's speech | Comment discusses the speech itself or Obama himself rather than the topic or contents of the speech. | 25 |
| Religion | Comment focuses on religion but not explicitly in the context of war or US foreign policy. | 22 |
| Insult or praise commenter | Comment is directed at a previous commenter with praise or insults rather than discussing a substantive topic. | 12 |
| Religion and war | Comment focuses on religion in the context of war or war in the context of religion, such as the propensity of different religions to be involved in violent actions. | 10 |
| Iraq/Afghanistan/ Palestine/ US power in the Middle East | Comment focuses on war or US military power in the Middle East but not directly relating it to religion. | 7 |
| History | Comment discusses the history of the Middle East. | 4 |
| Other | Comment does not fit into the above categories (one was Spam, the other discussed Egypt). | 2 |
| Unclear | The context of the comment was unclear because it was a reply to another comment or too short to give an unambiguous interpretation. | 18 |

## ReplyTo network analysis

After examining the basic content of the comments we turn to probe its underlying structure using the network analysis techniques of Webometric Analyst. The results for the ReplyTo network analysis are shown in Figure 3.2. Here we see that there was a core debate taking place among a few significant debaters but there were also a number of

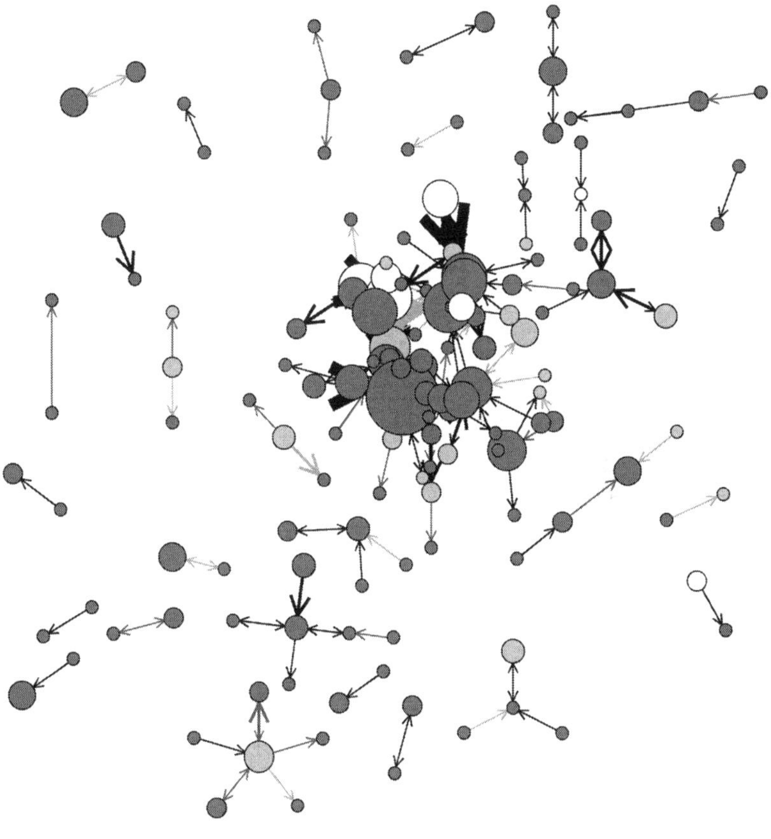

*Figure 3.2* ReplyTo Network from the Obama in Egypt video

*Note*: Nodes represent commenters making and receiving at least one reply. User names and ages have been removed (the first for anonymity, the second to avoid obscuring the network shape). Negative comments are dark arrows, positive are light arrows. Node sizes and arrow widths are proportional to the number of comments posted. Nodes are dark for male, light for female and white for unknown.

*Table 3.3* Centrality statistics for the top ten users in the ReplyTo Network for the Obama in Egypt video

| User | Number of other users replying to this user (indegree Binary) | Number of other users this user replied to (outdegree Binary) | Number of other users this user interacted with (degree Binary) |
|---|---|---|---|
| A | 7 | 6 | 9 |
| B | 6 | 5 | 6 |
| C | 5 | 6 | 6 |
| D | 4 | 6 | 6 |
| E | 5 | 0 | 5 |
| F | 3 | 4 | 5 |
| G | 4 | 4 | 4 |
| H | 4 | 0 | 4 |
| I | 3 | 3 | 4 |
| J | 3 | 2 | 3 |

other small exchanges. The usernames have been removed but these can be seen in the original version and so can be recorded by the researcher.

In addition to providing a visual depiction of the network, we are also able to extract some statistics on the nodes and thus individual commenters' status and importance vis-à-vis one another. We utilise three main types of centrality statistic for commenters which are shown in Table 3.3. Although this has been anonymised, this type of table can be used to find the most influential users in the network. Of interest are F and E, both of which have not replied to any other users but have received five and four replies, respectively. The most central user, A, was a man from California who argued strongly against Obama by making claims such as that Obama is 50 per cent Muslim by birth. In contrast, B was a Muslim, also from California, who argued that terrorism is against the teachings of Islam. Both engaged in quite heated debates with people of opposing beliefs.

## Subscription network analysis

The network of replies includes clusters of discussions which seem to be mainly antagonistic, but is there any evidence of a systematic attempt to influence the debate? The friend (and to a lesser extent, the subscriber network can reveal evidence of connections between commenters – although these connections may have formed as a result

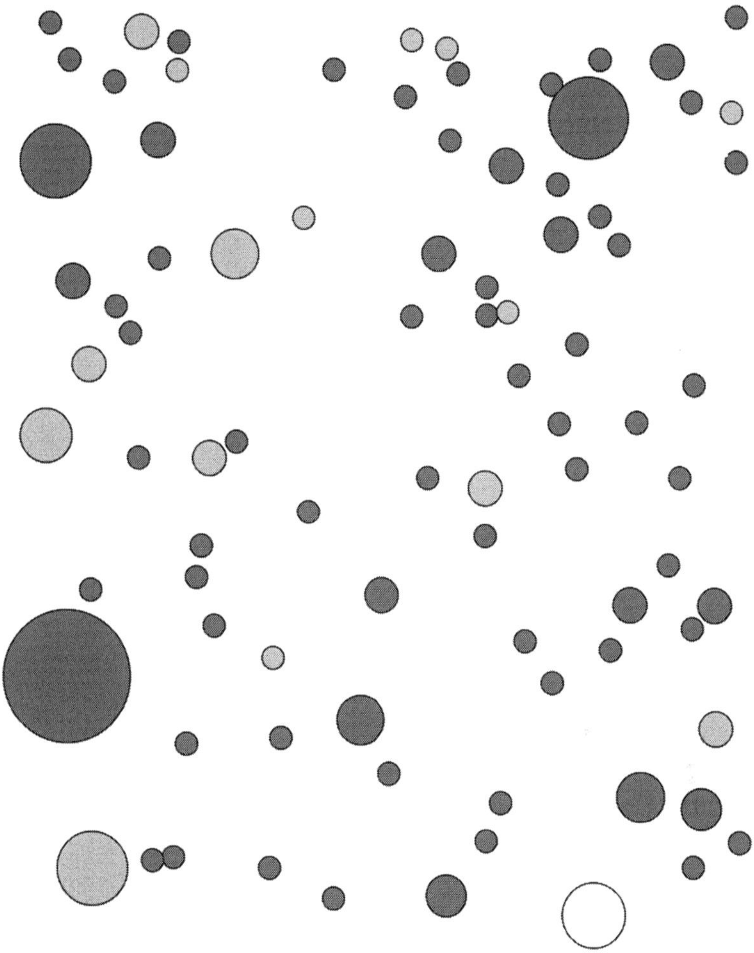

*Figure 3.3* Friend network from the Obama in Egypt video

*Note*: Users are represented by circles. Friend connections would be represented by lines between nodes but none of the commenters are Friends. Node sizes are proportional to the number of comments posted. Nodes are dark for male, light for female and white for unknown.

of the comments or may have pre-existed the comments. Figure 3.3 is the Friend network (no longer available in YouTube) and the Subscriber network is identical (not shown). There are no Friend or subscriber connections between commenters so it seems possible that they are all unknown to each other.

Figure 3.4 shows the Friends in common connections. In this diagram, there is a line between two commenters if they are both Friends with one or more common YouTube members. In contrast to Figure 3.3 and 3.4 shows that most of the commenters have some kind of connection with at least one other commenter through a shared Friend. Examining

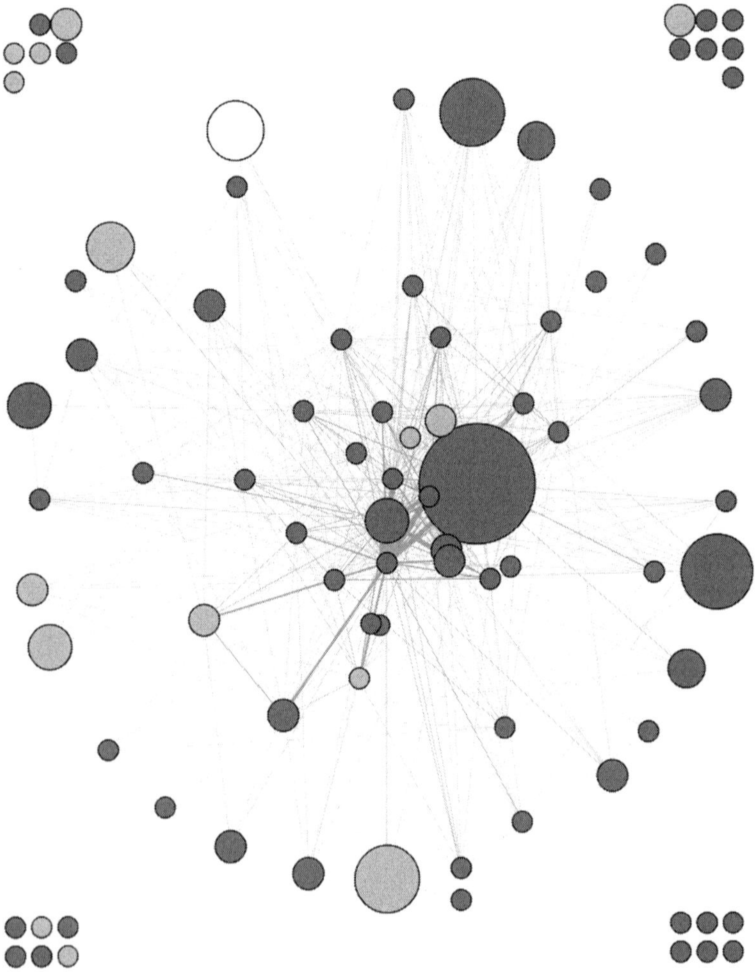

*Figure 3.4* Friends in common network from the Obama in Egypt video

*Note*: Node sizes are proportional to the number of comments posted. Line widths are proportional to the numbers of friends in common. Nodes are dark for male, light for female and white for unknown.

the file ending in FriendsInCommon.ArrowInfo.txt reveals who these common Friends are. For instance, the most central commenter, A in Table 3.3, has the same Friend in common with two other commenters. This Friend appears to be a right-wing US male whose YouTube account has been terminated due to repeated community guidelines violations. This Friend in common suggests that A and the other two with this Friend in common share a similar political outlook and presumably visit similar YouTube pages for discussions. Commenter B also has a Friend in common with two other commenters, although a different Friend in each case. One of the Friends in common has an explicitly Muslim profile, suggesting this connection, but the other has a profile in Arabic that does not focus on religion – suggesting a possible real-world connection. Other commenters have more extensive Friends in common connections. For example, one has this kind of connection with 38 other commenters based upon a variety of types of common Friends, including Friends based upon media channels. In this case, the Friendships may primarily reflect extensive and partially similar uses of YouTube to the other commenters.

To summarise, this pilot study has provided several key pieces of information on the audience of commenters for a prominent and politically significant YouTube video and thus provided some insight into how the world reacted to Obama's Egypt speech. First, we find the commenters are predominantly young American men. Most commenters seem to be strangers to each other but to have common interests with at least one other commenter. There does not seem to be any systematic attempt by groups to influence the arguments in YouTube but a few commenters have engaged in systematic debates with several other commenters (or at least exchanged several comments with them using the YouTube *Reply To* button). The focus of the commenters is predominantly on the speech itself but they also talk about Obama, religion and conflict in the Middle East more generally. Based on the evidence gathered here, there is no strong evidence that Obama's speech has worked in the sense of influencing the intended target audience. However, it has arguably given space for some individual Muslims such as commenter B, to argue their case.

## Conclusions

The chapter has described and applied some of the new methods being developed to analyse YouTube data and particularly the comments surrounding the videos it contains. The methods have been used to conduct a simple content analysis and also a series of network analyses. We have shown how to extract the necessary information from YouTube using the Webometric Analyst software and to draw network diagrams. The pilot study of the 'Obama in Egypt' video reported above took approximately four hours to complete, including the content analysis and the network diagram. More information about the techniques is also available on the software website (http://lexiurl.wlv.ac.uk).

In terms of the types of substantive conclusions that can be from an analysis of YouTube commentary, the work performed here has shown that it is relatively easy to systematically identify the topics of interest for commenters on YouTube videos through basic content analysis. It is also possible to discover who the most significant contributors to the discussion in demographic terms and to measure their connectedness with other commenters. This latter information can help us to understand what drives the discussions about the video and also the extent of bias present in the data. Armed with this information it then becomes possible to make some cautious extrapolations from the data to address research questions that deal with offline issues. In general, however, our study leads us to recommend that YouTube commentary is best deployed to investigate research questions where the audience for the online video channel are the primary object of study. It can also serve as a useful means to conduct a pilot study on a topic of general interest, but should be triangulated with data drawn from other sources. It also provides a means of training social scientists in approaches to analysis of YouTube data. From an ethical perspective, we have noted that there are advantages to investigating YouTube video comments since they are already in the public domain and do not raise privacy concerns. Nevertheless, researchers should avoid drawing attention to people or their comments by publishing their identities or comments in academic publications.

As a final note, we seek to draw the reader's attention to the range of other methods that are available to analyse YouTube video content and networks. These methods can provide a more detailed picture of the individual commenters and the overall patterns of exchanges between pairs of commenters to better understand how the debates form, continue and resolve. An example of this is the type of more detailed analysis can be found in the Fitna video in YouTube by van Zoonen et al. (2011). For our part, we hope that the work set out here has laid some foundations for those keen to gain deeper and more systematic insights into the audience for this new type of digital information source.

## Note

1. Examples of content analysis style categorisations of YouTube videos can be found in the reference section of a recent article by Kousha et al. (2012).

## References

Alexa. (2012) YouTube.com site info, available at: http://www.alexa.com/siteinfo/YouTube.com, date accessed 9 April 2012.

BBC News. (2011) 'Croydon-to-Wimbledon Racist Tram Rant Accused in Court', available at: http://www.bbc.co.uk/news/uk-england-london-15933829, date accessed 11 April 2012.

Charmaz, K.C. (2006) *Constructing Grounded Theory: A Practical Guide Through Qualitative Analysis* (London: Sage).

Gueorguieva, V. (2008) 'Voters, MySpace, and *YouTube*: The Impact of Alternative Communication Channels on the 2006 Election Cycle and Beyond', *Social Science Computer Review*, 26 (3), 288–300.

Herring, S., Job-Sluder, K., Scheckler, R. and Barab, S. (2002) 'Searching for Safety Online: Managing "Trolling" in a Feminist Forum', *The Information Society: An International Journal*, 18 (5), 371–384.

Khatib, L., Dutton, W. and Thelwall, M. (2012) 'Public Diplomacy 2.0: An Exploratory Case Study of the US Digital Outreach Team', *Middle East Journal*, 66 (3), 453–472.

Kousha, K., Thelwall, M. and Abdoli, M. (2012) 'The Role of Online Videos in Research Communication: A Content Analysis of *YouTube* Videos Cited in Academic Publications', *Journal of the American Society for Information Science and Technology*, 63 (9), 1710–1727.

Lazzara, D.L. (2010) '*YouTube* Courtship: The Private ins and Public outs of Chris and Nickas', in C. Pullen and M. Cooper (eds.), *LGBT Identity and Online New Media* (New York, NY: Routledge), pp. 51–61.

Lewis, S.P., Heath, N.L., St Denis, J.M. and Noble, R. (2011) 'The Scope of Nonsuicidal Self-injury on *YouTube*', *Pediatrics*, 127 (3), e552–e557.

Mortensen, M. (2011) 'When Citizen Photojournalism sets the News Agenda: Neda Agha Soltan as a Web 2.0 Icon of Post-election Unrest in Iran', *Global Media and Communication*, 7 (1), 4–16.

Neuendorf, K. (2002) *The Content Analysis Guidebook* (London: Sage).

Nissenbaum, H. (2009) *Privacy in Context: Technology, Policy and the Integrity of Social Life* (Stanford, CA: Stanford University Press).

Paek, H.J., Kim, K. and Hove, T. (2010) 'Content Analysis of Antismoking Videos on *YouTube*: Message Sensation Value, Message Appeals, and their Relationships with Viewer Responses', *Health Education Research*, 25 (6), 1085–1099.

Pew Internet (2012) 'Who's Online: Internet User Demographics', available at: http://pewinternet.org/Static-Pages/Trend-Data/Whos-Online.aspx, date accessed 11 April 2012.

Stubbs, M. (1983) *Discourse Analysis: The Sociolinguistic Analysis of Natural Language* (Oxford: Basil Blackwell).

Thelwall, M., Buckley, K. and Paltoglou, G. (2012) 'Sentiment Strength Detection for the Social Web', *Journal of the American Society for Information Science and Technology*, 63 (1), 163–173.

Thelwall, M., Sud, P. and Vis, F. (2012) 'Commenting on *YouTube* videos: From Guatemalan Rock to El Big Bang', *Journal of the American Society for Information Science and Technology*, 63 (3), 616–629.

van Zoonen, L., Mihelj, S. and Vis, F. (2011) '*YouTube* Interactions Between Agonism, Antagonism and Dialogue: Video Responses to the Anti-Islam Film Fitna', *New Media and Society*, 13 (8), 1283–1300.

Wilkinson, D. and Thelwall, M. (2011) 'Researching Personal Information on the Public Web: Methods and Ethics', *Social Science Computer Review*, 29 (4), 387–401.

Yoo, J.H. and Kim, J. (2012) 'Obesity in the New Media: A Content Analysis of Obesity Videos on *YouTube*', *Health Communication*, 27 (1), 86–97.

# Part II

# Contents and Interactions

# 4

# Social Data Analytics Tool: A Demonstrative Case Study of Methodology and Software

*Abid Hussain, Ravi Vatrapu, Daniel Hardt and Zeshan Ali Jaffari*

This chapter presents a methodology and software tool for the analysis of Facebook data. In particular, it describes and demonstrates the analytical framework and computational aspects of the Social Data Analytics Tool (SODATO). SODATO fetches, stores, analyses and visualises data from Facebook walls. The method has been previously applied to the US elections of 2008 (Robertson 2011; Robertson et al. 2010a, 2010b). Here, we replicate and extend the analysis to Danish elections in 2011. Our substantive research question is to measure the extent to which Facebook walls function as online public spheres. To do so, we extract the Facebook walls of three prominent candidates in the 2011 Danish general election. Our findings show overlapping online public spheres and how different types of individuals inhabit these overlapping public spheres and how they provide structure and interpretive information for others.

The chapter proceeds as follows. First, we present the theoretical framework of the analysis and outline the concept of online public

---

We thank Scott Robertson for his contribution to the early phase of this work presented at the Digital Methods Workshop at the University of Manchester, UK, and for inspiration.

This work was partially supported by the International Workshop on Social Media Analytics (IWSMA) 2012 grant to the second author from the Danish Ministry of Science, Technology and Innovation under the Third International Network Programme. Any opinions, findings, interpretations, conclusions or recommendations expressed in this paper are those of its authors and do not represent the views of the Danish Ministry of Science, Technology and Innovation.

spheres in general, and how it can be used to interpret the new social space of Facebook walls. We then provide a discussion of the methodology used by profiling the Social Data Analytics Tool[1] (SODATO) and the two main types of data it collects from Facebook walls – social graphs and social texts. We then present the findings of our social graph and social text analysis from the Danish elections of 2011 to understand how far Facebook functioned as a public sphere. The chapter concludes with a discussion of the conceptual, methodological and analytical challenges in empirical studies of political participation and deliberation in new social media spaces such as Facebook.

## Theoretical framework: The public sphere

The notion of a public sphere, as its most renowned proponent Habermas (1991) noted is 'a domain of our social life in which such a thing as public opinion can be formed' (398). According to Habermas, the public sphere is a mediating space between the private realm of the civil society and the sphere of public authority represented by the state. Figure 4.1 presents a schematic of Habermas' public sphere.

Building on this definition we have argued elsewhere that

> [a] public sphere is a democratic space where public interests, opinions, agendas and problems are formed, transformed, and exchanged by citizens' proactive participation. The relationship between citizens engaged in public discourse and communication is the critical feature of a public sphere. Critical rationality, equality, freedom of expression, and dissemination are the necessary conditions for the proper structuring and functioning of a Habermasian public sphere.
>
> (Vatrapu et al. 2008)

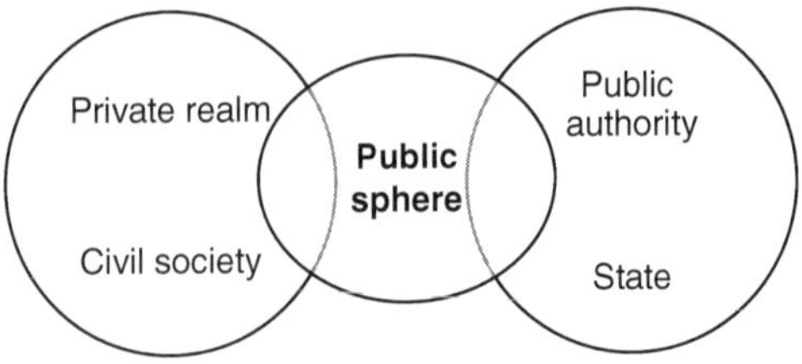


*Figure 4.1* Schematic of a Habermasian Public Sphere
*Source*: Vatrapu et al. (2008).

## Online public spheres

Habermas' original formulation of the public sphere has been critiqued for its limited scope and exclusion of key social groups such as women (Fraser 1992), as well as its failure to include a wider range of media platforms (Calhoun 1993). Subsequent work has sought to widen its applicability and also extend it to encompass communication through the medium of film, television and now the Internet (Dahlberg 2001; Vatrapu et al. 2008; Robertson and Vatrapu 2010; Shirky 2011). In this chapter, we seek to understand Facebook as a social networking platform in general and the Facebook pages of a political candidate in particular as an online public sphere (Robertson and Vatrapu 2010; Robertson et al. 2010b).

In earlier work, Robertson and colleagues divided the attributes of Facebook into three main components (Robertson et al. 2010b). Table 4.1 below provides a summary of this work by distinguishing the key sociological, technological and political functions of Facebook as

*Table 4.1* Public sphere characteristics of a Facebook in particular and social media in general

| Function | Features |
|---|---|
| Sociological functions | Dissemination<br>Opinion<br>Activism<br>Advocacy<br>Social relations (weak & strong ties) |
| Technological features | List of friends<br>Linear threaded discussion forum (Wall)<br>Status updates<br>News postings<br>Information sharing (links, photos, videos)<br>User comments<br>Groups<br>Affiliations<br>Un-moderated vs. Moderated<br>Open door vs. Registration |
| Public sphere characteristics | Freedom of expression<br>Participation<br>Interaction<br>Rationality<br>Emotionality<br>Authority<br>Democratic |

an online public sphere. In brief, they argued that Facebook is a socio-technical system that supports the sociological processes of activism, advocacy, opinion formation, sentiment expression, dissemination of ideas, creation and maintenance of social ties. These sociological functions are supported by Facebook's technological infrastructure, technical architecture and in particular features such online groups, status updates, pages, access controls, community management functionalities. Taken together, the technological features supported by Facebook and the sociological processes that are facilitated by it result in the emergence of an online public sphere where such a thing as public opinion can be formed.

## Facebook and Facebook walls as online public spheres

Here we expand on the understanding of Facebook and Facebook walls in particular as a form of an online public sphere. Civil society actors are increasingly using the medium of the Internet to document and share social and physical reality, with these practices occurring predominantly if not wholly through new social media tools such as Facebook. The documentation and dissemination of events and inter-subjective perspectives on objective events that these tools allow open up a window on what was once an exclusive province of professional occupations such as journalism, marketing and public administration. In particular, prior to the advent of the Internet, access to mass media channels such as the print media, public television and radio, network television, broadcast radio and cable television was highly restricted. The rapid diffusion of low-cost audio-video devices such as mobile phones, webcams, digital voice recorders and computers, combined with increasingly cheap Internet hosting and sharing services such as Facebook has empowered civil society actors with the capabilities to record and share their lives as well as their realities. The implications of this for everyday social and political life are clearly profound. In essence as one seasoned commentator on the Internet revolution has termed it, the technology has created a new 'architecture for participation' (O'Reilly 2005) that carries with it a radical expansion in the scale and nature of political discussion and participation. In relation to the public sphere qualities named above we can see that it has expanded opportunities for freedom of expression, discussion and deliberation of topics, organisation of activities ranging from petitions to protests and formation of communities.

While Facebook in general clearly has a claim to status of an online public sphere, it can also be seen to be made of a series of sub-public spheres in the shape of its wall facility. Walls provide a new and more informal but public means for citizens to enter the engage in political debate and discussion with politicians themselves and others citizens. As socio-technical systems, they provide opportunities for meaning-making and action-taking with regard to politics and public life. Engagement on Facebook walls can range from interactions under normal conditions to activities during extra-ordinary events such as the recent Arab Spring. Facebook walls also provide opportunities for the expression and experience of emotions in politics and public life. We think that this aspect of emotional experience is a crucial addition to Habermas' original conception of the public sphere.

Having presented the case for considering Facebook and particularly its walls as online public spheres, we outline below our empirical strategy for analysing the extent to which these new social arenas actually equate to a Habermasian ideal. In particular, we examine how individuals use these Walls to relate to, interact with and understand individual politicians during an election campaign. We do so analytically using two main types of data – social graphs of users of Facebook walls and social text of the Facebook wall. These measures are central to understanding Facebook walls as a public sphere in that they characterise the social graph and the social text. The social graph is a structural characterisation of an online public sphere in that it identifies the actors involved, the activities they participate in, the actions they perform and the artefacts they create. Social text is a discursive characterisation of online public spheres in terms of the topics discussed, the key words mentioned, pronouns used and sentiments expressed.

The data are collected and analysed using a new purpose-built software application Social Data Analytics Tool (SODATO). This allows us to examine public interactions on the Facebook walls of politicians by extracting several core pieces of information. These include the overarching categories of breadth of engagement (how many Facebook walls do individuals participate) and depth of engagement (how frequently do individuals participate) and specific analytical issues such as modes of address (measured use of first person, second person and third person pronouns), the expression of emotion (positive, negative and neutral sentiment), the use of resources such as web pages and YouTube videos, verbosity and extent of participation. In the case of modes of address and expression of emotion, we examine how they evolve over time. We outline more specifically how this is done below.

## Using SODATO for social data analysis

The growth of social media use in society is generating large quantities of new digital information about individuals, organisations and institutions that is now commonly labelled 'Big Data'. Social media analytics is a term we use here to refer to the collection, storage, analysis and reporting of these new data (Vatrapu 2013). This chapter introduces and applies Social Data Analytics Tool (SODATO) a new tool developed by the authors specifically to conduct social media analytics (see Appendix for a technical description and the tool can be accessed at http://cssl.cbs.dk/software/sodato/). Here we apply it to the case of one specific social media channel – the Facebook walls of three key politicians during the Danish general elections 2011. We provide more contextual details on the election and the candidates in our discussion of the data below.

Social media analytics can be undertaken in two main ways – '*Social Graph Analytics*' and '*Social Text Analytics*' (Vatrapu 2013). Social graph analytics is concerned with the structure of the relationships emerging from social media use. It focuses on identifying the actors involved, the activities they undertake and the artefacts they create and interact with. Social text analytics is more concerned with the substantive nature of the interactions, it focuses on the topics discussed and how they are discussed. What keywords appear? What pronouns are used? How far are negative or positive sentiments expressed? These two types of data, we argue, can provide measures of the extent to which the Facebook Walls are serving as online public spheres in that:

- The graphical or structural data allow us to map *the breadth* of the public sphere by reporting the overall number of posts made, which of the three walls received most posts and whether they linked out to other sources of information. In addition to looking at the posts in the aggregate we also can look at them individually and map cross-linkage across walls. Was the posting entirely independent such that individuals only posted to one wall or did they post more widely on two or three walls?
- The social text data allow us to examine *the depth* of the engagement taking place through the Facebook walls and thus whether walls are acting as an online public space. In particular we look at three key aspects of the posts – their length, their focus in terms of the use of pronouns in the posts – categorising them as inward (use of 'I') or outward (use of 'you' and 'they'); and the direction of sentiment positive or negative.

While we do not claim that these data can definitively demonstrate that an online public sphere is emerging from Danes' use of Facebook, it is argued that they provide us with some helpful cues. Specifically, through documenting the overall frequency of posts, and the amount of cross-posting between candidate's walls, we can see how public these spaces were in terms of how widely Danish society was engaged with them. If a high proportion of Danish citizens are posting to the walls then this makes it more likely that they approximate a public sphere. The provision of links would indicate the extent to which the Walls were being used to refer readers either to additional information or other users, thereby turning the Walls into more networked and arguably more diverse and outward looking public spheres. In terms of the extent of cross-posting, we would argue that the more of this that is found to be taking place then the better it is for the public sphere in that it indicates individuals are not remaining in their 'silos' of conversation but engaging in a wider and possibly creating a more diverse debate. The social text data collected in terms of the length, focus and sentiment of the posts made during the election offers some insight into the quality of the discussions taking place and particularly how substantive and consensual or conflictual they were. In particular, the pronouns allow us to assess if there a move from more inward looking and self-referential discussion (use of first and third person) to a more genuine 'debate' and engagement with 'other' (use of second-person)? Through the analysis of the direction of the sentiment we can measure the amount of positive and negative discussion occurring. If a public sphere is developing we should see a converging or consensus in sentiment emerging, as a more deliberative and less polarised discourse develops.

## Analysis

The core data extracted by SODATO were the Facebook wall posts, comments and likes for three prominent Danish politicians over a 24-month period (1 October 2009 to 15 September 2011). These data were then linked with unique keys for Facebook wall id and poster ids. This meant that we could track the extent to which individuals appeared in all three Walls or just one or two. We also aggregated individual data by politician so we had a record of all their posts/status updates and comments.

For the social graph analysis we compiled a list of unique posters to the three Facebook walls being studied. In order to count the links and videos we combined all the links from the free text of the posts and comments as well as dedicated link type of posts. String matching database queries were applied to count number of total links and links to particular Web host, for example *YouTube*. For the social text analysis, we calculated the number of words within each post used by defining word boundaries through the use of space separator character. First, we parsed the text to identify the pronouns used and then applied analysis to identify how positive or negative it was to the candidate, toward politics? For this task, we created a sentiment analysis tool specific to our project. The sentiment analyser was originally built for and trained on the Danish language user reviews collected from the Internet (Hardt and Wulff 2012) and then applied to the Facebook corpus of this chapter. The analyser classifies texts into three categories: Positive, Negative and Neutral. The posts were divided into monthly time slices, giving 13 slices for each of the three candidates across the period of September 2010 to September 2011. Each post in the time period was labelled with a sentiment of positive, negative or neutral by the sentiment analysis tool. Then for each month, the ratio of Positive to Negative postings was automatically computed. For one candidate, Pia there was very little activity until November 2010, so we use 11 time slices for this candidate.

## Case for analysis: The Danish election of 2011

The Danish general election was held on 15 September 2011 for a total of 179 seats in the Danish parliament. The election saw widespread use of social media channels. Danish politicians and political parties have adopted social media channels for political communication as well as for election campaigns strategy (Dyrby and Jensen 2013). According to Socialbakers,[2] a social media analytics firm, Denmark's Facebook adoption as of February 2013 is at 54.63 per cent of the general population with 2,995,800 Facebook accounts registered. The use of social media channels by politicians was also quite widespread[3] with all major political parties and candidates communicating and campaigning on their Facebook walls. Given these 'majority' rates of adoption then one can argue that Facebook at least has the potential to approximate an online public sphere.

For our purposes, we focused on three particular arenas within Facebook – the walls of three Danish politicians: the incumbent prime minister (Lars Løkke Rasmussen),[4] the opposition prime ministerial candidate (Helle Thorning-Schmidt),[5] and an influential right-wing policy-maker and outside supporter of the incumbent government (Pia Kjærsgaard).[6] The posts on their walls were collected for the year leading up to the election in September 2011, from 1 October 2009 to

15 September 2011. These individuals are all highly prominent politicians and among the most popular in the country based on their poll ratings.

In summary, therefore, to conduct our social graph and social text analysis of Facebook walls as a new online public sphere we gathered the following key information:

- total number of posts and total for each candidate wall;
- total number of individual posters as a percentage of Danish VAP;
- average number of posts per poster;
- average number of links included in the post overall and by candidate wall;
- cross-posting – number of individual posting on one, two or all three walls;
- average length of post overall and by candidate wall;
- average number of inward/outward pronouns by candidate wall by month over one year;
- average number of positive and negative posts by candidate wall by month over one year.

## Results

In this section we present the results from our descriptive case study of the Facebook walls of three candidates during the Danish general elections 2011. We organise the results according to our two types of data – the network or structural aspect of the posts (social graph data) and the content of the posts analysed (social text data).

### Social graph analytics: Breadth of engagement

Through these data we analyse the walls as online public spheres in our first key dimension of the breadth of user engagement. We measure this in terms of the overall volume or amount of posting taking place and the extent to which these posts were creating a wider network of interaction. We examine this interaction through first looking at the extent to which hyperlinks are present within the posts and second with regard to the extent of cross-posting by individuals across the three walls.

*Frequency of posting*

Across the two year period studied (1 October 2009–15 September 2011) a total of 162,646 posts were made across all three walls were made.

These were made by a total of 25,987 individuals. The voting age population (VAP) of Denmark[7] for the 2011 election was 4,374,759 with 3,579,675 voters exercising their franchise for a VAP turnout of 81.8 per cent. Individual posters on the Facebook walls of the three Facebook candidates, therefore, constitute only 0.73 per cent of the VAP turn-out and 0.59 per cent of the Danish VAP. The average number of posts per user was six although this statistic masks the fact that the 'default' position was a single post, with over half (55 per cent) of those posting (13,115) posted only once. Moving up the scale to posters who made between two and ten posts, around a third fewer people fulfilled this criteria (9629). A much smaller proportion (1378) has posted between 11–100 times. Finally, in the high frequency or 'super-poster' category we find 180 users who posted between 101 and 150 times. Once we look in more depth at the results by candidate we can see that Lars had the most popular wall with 84,008 posts recorded (52 per cent) during the study. Second was Helle with 60,642 posts (37 per cent) and Pia was third with 17,996 posts (11 per cent). Despite the unrepresentative nature of the posters in terms of their overall size in comparison to the population this distribution broadly follows the popularity of the candidates.

Overall then this evidence shows that the Facebook walls of three major Danish politicians did not approximate the public sphere in terms of the scope and wider engagement of Danish society. However, our data analysis is of active participation on Facebook posts and does not account for passive engagement of viewers in terms of sporadic visits or 'active lurking' (Takahashi et al. 2003). A more comprehensive analysis of the entire online ecosystem that included campaign and news websites, discussion forums and other social media tools would yield higher rates of public engagement and thus a stronger case for an online public sphere.

*Links embedded in post*

In terms of the links embedded in the posts a total of 7,885 links were found across all the posts. This constituted an average of 0.05 links per post. Figure 4.2 presents a distribution of the top ten most frequent websites domains in the links.

Links were most commonly made to other Facebook users and other social media such as YouTube. The other sites listed are to Danish mainstream media channels ranging from television channels (DR and TV2), newspapers (Jyllands-Posten and Politiken) to tabloids (Extrabladet and BT). The distribution of the top ten domains is consistent with the media

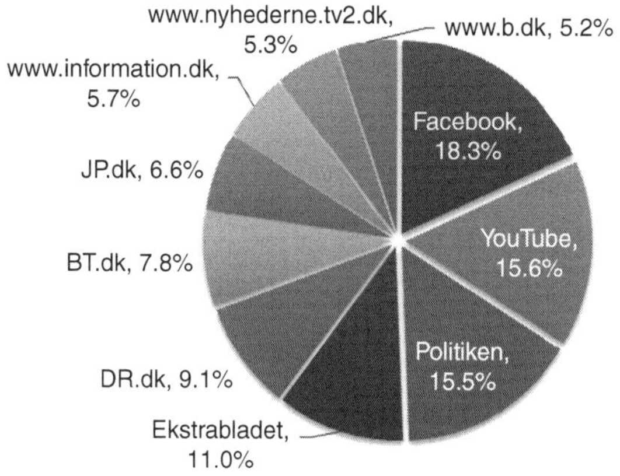


*Figure 4.2* Distribution of links to top ten domains

ecosystem of Denmark (Jan Damsgaard, Personal Communication). These results suggest that despite being a very small sector of the Danish public, information sharing was taking place. Breaking the results down by candidate we find the number posts with links was 4.85 per cent, this was highest for candidate Lars and lowest for candidate Pia.

*Cross-posting*

There were a total of 25,987 unique posters in the data corpus. Of this total the vast majority (22,740) posted on only one wall (Pia: 2157, Lars: 9315 and Helle: 11,268). A much smaller proportion, around one in 20 individuals (1439) posted at least once on two Facebook walls (*Pia+Helle: 242, Helle+Lars: 1071* and *Lars+Pia: 495*). Finally, a very small number of users posted at least once on all three Facebook walls. The largest number of wall-crossing users was *1071* for the *Helle* and *Lars* combination; *495* and *242* used crossed the partisan barrier to post on both *Pia*'s Facebook wall and on one or both of the other politicians' walls of Lars and Helle respectively. From a public sphere perspective, the results suggest a 'partisan sphere' (Vatrapu et al. 2008) rather than inclusive public space of individuals engaging on multiple platforms and considering multiple-view points. Figure 4.3 presents the wall-crossing results. Such figures do not suggest a wide breadth of engagement and are not strongly supportive of the emergence of a public sphere on Facebook in the election in that they suggest little cross-party debate was occurring with individuals using the technology to engage with other points of view. Within this small sub-population

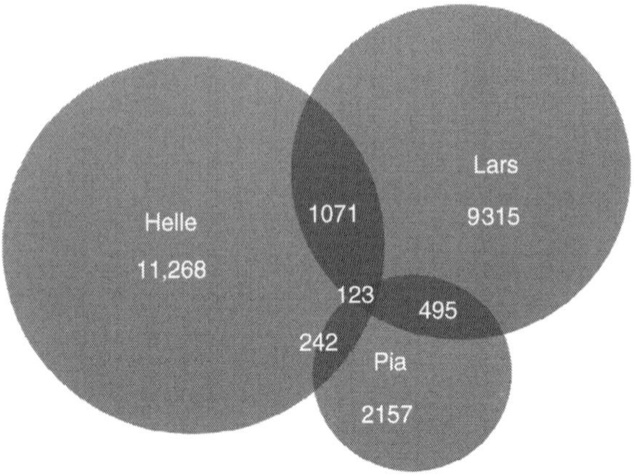


*Figure 4.3* Overview of Facebook wall crossing

of the Danish public, most people focused on one candidate and did not seek to engage with supporters of other candidates.

## Social text analytics: Depth of engagement

Here we switched our focus to examine the content of the posts rather than their structure and examined the Facebook walls on our second key public sphere dimension – the depth of engagement occurring. In particular, we looked at the length of the posts, their focus in terms of whether they were 'self' versus 'other' focused and sentiment.

### *Length of posts*

Posts were measured by the number of words they contained. The average length of a post was 39.91. Overall the number of words indicates that posts were not extensive in terms of being long statements of opinion but possibly more short responses and conversational in nature.

As a general finding it was interesting that on average the longest posts were posted by those individuals that posted across all three walls, while those posting to only one wall had shorter entries. In addition these individuals posted for a longer time period. The average length of time measured in number of days between the first and last posting for those posting across all three walls was longer than those posting only to two or one wall. These results indicate a relationship between the breadth of engagement and depth of engagement. In other words, those posters that chose to cross the partisan boundaries contributed with longer posts and for a longer time-period.

*Focus of posts: Use of pronouns*

To further examine the content and nature of the online discussion taking place on candidate walls we analysed the focus of the posts by measuring the use of pronouns as modes of address. These data are used to examine the expectations for an online public sphere with regard to engagement with others. Specifically, we looked at how far the discussion on a candidate's Facebook wall moves from a more inward position of engagement that is directed to the self, to a more outward one directed to the candidate and then on to one that is directed to others, either to persuade or oppose. These variables capture the extent on inward versus outwardly focused discussion and level of personalisation around the candidate. SODATO was used to extract the number of occurrences of first person, second person and third person pronouns in each posting. The pronouns counted are:

- First person 'jeg' (I), 'vi' (we), 'mig' (me)
- Second person 'du' (you) 'dig' (you – accusative)
- Third person 'han' (he) 'hun' (she) 'ham' (him) 'hende' (her) 'dem' (them)

The pronoun 'de' was ignored because it can be used to refer to a third person pronoun and is also used as a plural article, with the plural article appearing far more frequently. Following the categorisation of Robertson et al. (2010a) with regard to the deictic direction of the pronouns we classify the first person as inwardly directed, while second and third person are outward. A distinction is made between outward pronouns that are direct or accusative and those that are more passive and refer to 'other' in a more neutral or referential way. In essence this division captures the extent to which posts were interactive or engaging in dialogue (use of second person) versus being more discrete opinion statements by users (use of first person and third person). As noted above for a vibrant public sphere to be in operation we would expect a mix of all three but a stronger emphasis on second person pronouns.

The results show that overall users were more likely to use first person throughout the course of study and least likely to use the third person and this held for all discussion across all three Walls. In terms of the public sphere, the use of the accusative stayed relatively constant as well although this differed across candidates, with more direct engagement rising in Lars' site but falling in Pia's. This indicates that levels of debate

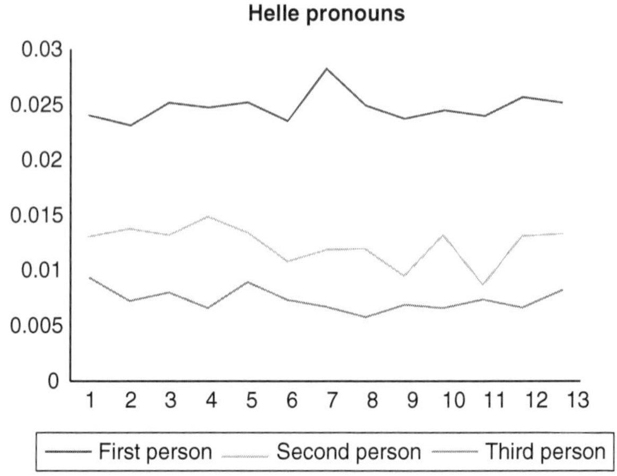


*Figure 4.4* Distribution of pronouns on Helle's *Facebook* wall

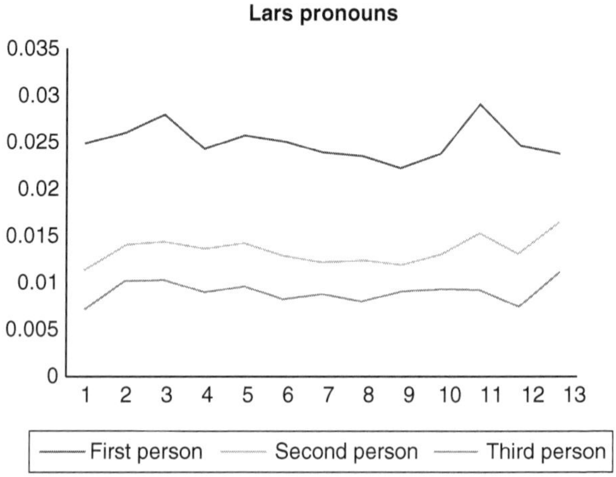


*Figure 4.5* Distribution of pronouns on Lars' *Facebook* wall

were increasing for the former but decreasing for the latter. Figures 4.4, 4.5 and 4.6 present the results.

## Sentiment of posts

The final type of data extracted from the text of the posts was the direction of the sentiment. This was used to test the expectations of

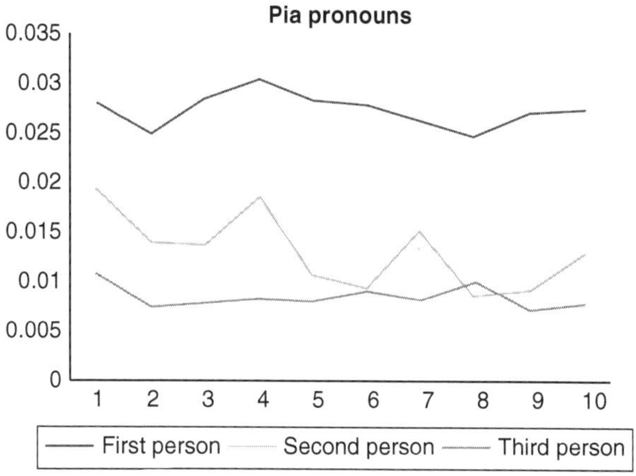


*Figure 4.6* Distribution of pronouns on Pia's *Facebook* wall

convergence that follow from an emergent online public sphere. Following earlier work by Robertson (2011, 2–3) which examined sentiments of posts on the Facebook walls of Obama, McCain and Clinton for the US presidential election 2008, it was proposed that the amount of positive and negative sentiment on the Walls would become more balanced as the participants widened their focus beyond their preferred candidate and moved from defending their stance to recognising the position of rival candidates and being willing to engage in debate. This process was seen as linked to the development of the public sphere in that this would entail a move from more negative to more positive sentiments which would allow for more deliberative and less polarised debate. To measure sentiment each post in the period was automatically labelled with a sentiment of Positive, Negative or Neutral (for methodological details, see Hardt and Wulff 2012). Then for each month, the ratio of Positive to Negative postings was computed.

The overall results show that across all postings there were many more negative than positive sentiments expressed. However, there was also a shift over time in that positive sentiments did increase as negative decreased. This convergence was replicated across each individual candidate's Wall. Thus for Helle, the ratio of positive to negative posts rose from 0.33 in September 2010 to 0.43 in September 2011; For Lars the ratio rose from 0.21 to 0.48 and or Pia, the ratio rose from 0.41 in November 2010 (where significant activity began on her site) to 0.55 in September 2011. Figures 4.7, 4.8 and 4.9 present the results.

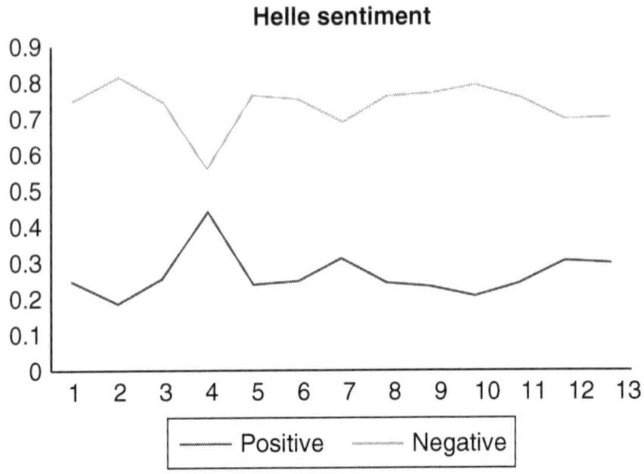


*Figure 4.7* Sentiment over time on Helle's *Facebook* wall

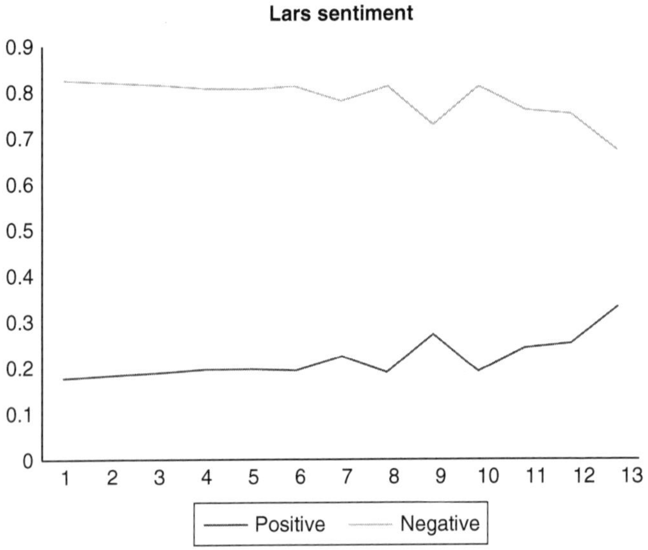


*Figure 4.8* Sentiment over time on Lars' *Facebook* wall

## Discussion

In this chapter we have sought to explore whether the notion of a public sphere can be applied to online social platforms such as Facebook walls. Taking three case studies of prominent Danish politicians we have extracted and analysed a range of structural and textual data using a

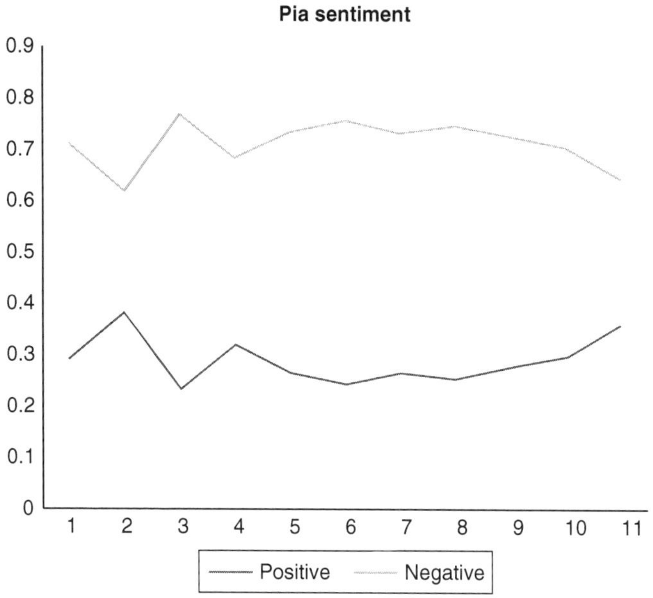


*Figure 4.9* Sentiment over time on Pia's *Facebook* wall

new tool developed specifically for the systematic collection, storage and analysis of social media data – SODATO. This has allowed us to examine the walls as public spheres in two specific dimensions – breadth and depth of engagement. The first we examined through structural information about the frequency of posts, extent of cross-posting and use of hyperlinks. The second we examined through evidence about the quality of the posts themselves in terms of their length, focus and sentiment.

Drawing the evidence gathered together our main conclusions is that the Facebook walls of Danish politicians in 2010 did not constitute an online public sphere in the Habermasian sense of inclusiveness and representation of the wider public. Postings were limited to a very small proportion of the population, most of whom posted only once during the course of the election. In addition, analysis of the content of the posts as measured through the use of pronouns provided little evidence of the idealised communicative discourse that a public sphere would support. Use of personal pronouns dominated and there was no move toward a more outward engagement with others and interactive type of debate. Evidence regarding the sentiment of the posts provided more grounds for optimism, with positive postings increasing over time and negative postings decreasing. By way of follow up it would be useful to examine posts' sentiment on a week-by-week or even day-by-day basis and see whether this correlates with weekly or daily polling data. Does the more general tone of debate in society become more positive overall as the election becomes closer and thus Facebook is reflecting this wider shift in sentiment, or perhaps it provides a contrast in that it is fostering a more positive debate than is occurring offline?

Despite the limited support we found for an emergent online public sphere it is clear that the walls served as an outlet for some citizens to express themselves in quite extensive ways with evidence of a reciprocal impact of the breadth and depth of engagement. The more widely people engaged in online debate in terms of crossing partisan lines the more time and effort they took to communicate their ideas (as measured through length of the post). One idea for future work that follows from this finding is to use the posting data to define a distance metric between parties' walls. It would be interesting to see to what extent the distance metric corresponds to the left – right ordering, or perhaps other ways of thinking about political distance between parties. For example, from the Venn diagram on cross posting (Figure 4.2), it seemed to show that Venstre was between Social Democrats (SD) and Danish Folk Party (DFF) as one would expect. Although SD and DFF might be considered closer to each other in that they both have a populist appeal to working class voters that Venstre does not have.

More generally these results should be interpreted from the wider standpoint that Facebook walls represent only one 'slice' of the wider digital media ecosystem. It is inevitable that they under-represent the extent of online political engagement occurring in Danish society.

## Appendix

To fetch the relevant social graph and social text data from the three Facebook walls we examined and conduct analysis we used a custom-built Social Data Analytics Tool – SODATO. SODATO utilises Facebook open source API named as Graph API. SODATO is a combination of Web as well as Windows-based console applications that run in batches to fetch data and prepare data for analysis. The Web part of the tool is developed using HTML, JavaScript, Microsoft ASP.NET and C#. Console applications are developed using C#. Microsoft SQL Server is used for data storage and data pre-processing for social graph analytics and social

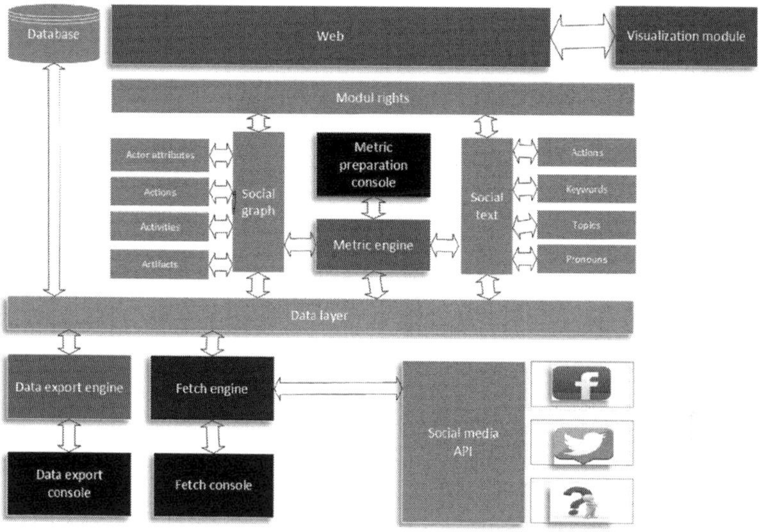


*Figure 4.A1* Schematic of the technical architecture of SODATO

text analytics. A schematic of the technical architecture of SODATO is presented in Figure 4.A1.

## Notes

1. http://cssl.cbs.dk/software/sodato
2. http://www.socialbakers.com/Facebook-statistics/denmark
3. http://www.valg-2011.dk/
4. https://www.Facebook.com/larsloekke
5. https://www.Facebook.com/hellethorningschmidt
6. https://www.facebook.com/pages/Pia-Kj%C3%A6rsgaard/33510214383
7. http://www.idea.int/vt/countryview.cfm?id=63

## References


Calhoun, C. (1993) *Habermas and the Public Sphere* (MIT Press).

Dahlberg, L. (2001) 'Computer-mediated Communication and the Public Sphere: A Critical Analysis', *Journal of Computer-Mediated Communication*, 7, 27.

Dyrby, S. and Jensen, T.B. (2012) 'Exploring Affordances of Facebook as a Social Media Platform in Political Campaigning',*ECIS 2013 Completed Research Paper 40*, http://aisel.aisnet.org/ecis2013_cr/40.

Fraser, N. (1992) 'Rethinking the Public Sphere: A Contribution to the Critique of Actually Existing Democracy', in C. Calhoun (ed.), *Habermas and the Public Sphere* (Cambridge: MIT Press), pp. 109–142.

Habermas, J. (1991) 'The Public Sphere', in C. Mukerji and M. Schudson (eds.), *Rethinking Popular Culture: Contemporary Perspectives in Cultural Studies* (Berkeley: University of California Press), pp. 398–404.

Hardt, D. and Wulff, J. (2012) 'What is the Meaning of 5*'s? An Investigation of the Expression and Rating of Sentiment', *Empirical Methods on Natural Language Processing: Proceedings of the Conference on Natural Language Processing,* pp. 319–326.

O'Reilly, T. (2005) 'Web 2.0: compact definition', *Message posted to http://radar. oreilly. com/archives/2005/10/web_20_compact_definition. html*

Robertson, S. (2011) 'Changes in referents and emotions over time in election-related social networking dialog', 44th Hawaii International Conference on System Sciences (HICSS), IEEE, pp. 1–9.

Robertson, S. and Vatrapu, R. (2010) 'Digital Government', in B. Cronin (ed.), *Annual Review of Information Science and Technology, American Society for Information Science and Technology*, 44 (1), pp. 317–364.

Robertson, S., Vatrapu, R. and Medina, R. (2010a) 'Off the Wall Political Discourse: Facebook use in the 2008 U.S. Presidential Election', *Information Polity,* 15, 11–31.

Robertson, S., Vatrapu, R. and Medina, R. (2010b) 'Online Video "Friends" Social Networking: Overlapping Online Public Spheres in the 2008 U.S. Presidential Election', *Journal of Information Technology and Politics,* 7, 182–201.

Shirky, C. (2011) 'The Political Power of Social Media Technology, the Public Sphere, and Political Change', *Foreign Affairs,* 90 (1), 28–41.

Takahashi, M., Fujimoto, M. and Yamasaki, N. (2003) 'The Active Lurker: Influence of an In-house Online Community on its Outside Environment', Proceedings of the 2003 international ACM SIGGROUP conference on Supporting group work, ACM, 1–10.

Vatrapu, R. (2013) 'Understanding Social Business', in K.B. Akhilesh (ed.), *Emerging Dimensions of Technology Management* (New Delhi: Springer), pp. 147–158.

Vatrapu, R., Robertson, S. and Dissanayake, W. (2008) 'Are Political Weblogs Public Spheres or Partisan Spheres?' *International Reports on Socio-Informatics,* 5, 7–26.

# 5

# Opportunities and Challenges of Analysing Twitter Content: A Comparison of the Occupation Movements in Spain, Greece and the United States

*Gema García-Albacete and Yannis Theocharis*

The year 2011 could well be remembered as a year marking the rebirth of protest politics on a global scale. Hundreds of thousands participated in protests against authoritarian regimes in what became known as the 'Arab Spring' while, in the Western world, large-scale protest campaigns shook European capitals like Madrid and Athens for months, inspiring thereafter thousands to occupy central squares in more than 200 American cities. The extensive use of digital media for organisation and mobilisation was a distinctive feature of the protest events and elicited much commentary and speculation about the political effectiveness and democratising potential of the Internet.

The role of the Internet in mobilising citizens politically, and particularly the potential of the information transmitted through diverse online social networks, has preoccupied social scientists for more than a decade (Castells 2001; Norris 2002; Rainie and Wellman 2012). Given their wide use and relevance in recent events, democracy and media

The authors are deeply grateful to Jan van Deth for his support and ideas and to Will Lowe for making our data management and coding procedure so easy. We also want to thank Nikos Karavias, Florian Zielbauer and Anne Weber for their research assistance. The authors also want to acknowledge the financial support provided by the Mannheim Centre for European Social Research (MZES) and the Chair of Political Science and International Comparative Social Research at the University of Mannheim.

scholars have increasingly emphasised the role of information technologies: on the one hand for either facilitating democratisation and promoting transition in young and developing democracies (Oates et al. 2006; Howard 2010) or prohibiting it (Morozov 2011), and on the other for consolidating and stabilising commitment, as well as strengthening participation in already established democracies (Barber 2004; Mattes and Bratton 2007; Dalton 2008; Shirky 2011). At the same time, social movement scholarship has been increasingly interested in how digital media contribute to protest events and has argued that the Internet can help activists diversify their engagement repertoires, move beyond previous spatial and temporal confines and organise and coordinate participation in protest events more effectively (McCaughey and Ayers 2003; van de Donk et al. 2004; van Laer and van Aelst 2010; Bennett and Segerberg 2012).

This chapter focuses on the methodological challenges posed by developments in the new media domain, specifically those triggered by the arrival of Web 2.0 applications such as social networking sites (SNS), microblogging and video-sharing sites. We focus on Twitter, which, being the most widely used microblogging site,[1] and thus a valuable source for acquiring information about protest events, can allow us to examine protest movements' dynamics, goals and motivations through following citizens' political discussions and online actions. In doing so, we examine the content distributed by users online and the opportunities it provides for addressing questions regarding the protesters' demands, information distribution, political tactics and the organisation of protest activity. Moving beyond the many benefits of using SNS for political engagement, by now widely discussed in the literature (Anduiza et al. 2012; Coleman and Shane 2012), we concentrate on the opportunities they provide for political behaviour research, aiming to answer the following question: Does information distributed via Twitter help us understand social and political protest better?

With this objective in mind, we explore tweeted content and build indicators that allow us to compare the use of Twitter for political mobilisation by different movements. Specifically, we monitored the 'indignant citizens' of Spain and Greece, and the US-based 'Occupy Wall Street' (OWS) movement from their early beginnings. Using tweets as the unit of analysis, this chapter presents the development of a coding scheme that can be adapted to the focal points of different case studies and used to systematically answer questions such as: What is the purpose of the tweet?; are there political issues mentioned in it, and if so which? Is there a particular repertoire of political actions mostly promoted through tweeting? What are the twitterers' sentiments towards the movements and how are the latter being evaluated?

Furthermore, building on previous work on using Twitter to 'listen' to audiences, the chapter proposes the construction of an exhaustive list of indicators from diverse pieces of information contained in Twitter metadata with the aim of observing in detail the mediation processes involved and how they related to the given protest ecology. We therefore construct indicators related to: link direction (where do the links posted lead to?) (see also Bennett and Segerberg 2011); media sources mostly linked (if tweets link to media sources, are these mainstream or alternative media?) (Chew and Eysenbach 2010); type of twitterer (who sends the tweet?) (Boyd and Ellison 2007); and type and direction of the tweet (is it a retweet? to whom is it directed?).

After a brief introduction to the structure of Twitter, our cases and the methodology, we illustrate the usefulness of these indicators by presenting differences and similarities in Twitter use in the three movements. The concluding section discusses the challenges posed by analysing this source of information, reflects on the opportunities and limitations it offers for political behaviour and communication scholars and suggests other potential uses of this type of information to understand citizens' political involvement.

## Twitter's microblogging structure

Twitter, like so many other Web 2.0 platforms, levitates in an environment of affordances and 'informational exuberance' (Chadwick 2012),[2] also referred to as a 'polymedia' environment to designate the numerous communicative opportunities that 'function as an "integrated structure" within which each individual medium is defined in relational terms in the context of all other media' (Madianou and Miller 2013, 2). It lies at the crossroads of SNS and blogs and belongs to a relatively new form of communication tools known as 'microblogging' platforms. Microblogs can be understood as 'a form of blogging that lets you write brief text updates about your life on the go and send them to friends and interested observers via text messaging, instant messaging, email or the web' (Java et al. 2007, 56). Like blogs and SNS, Twitter interactions take place in real time allowing users from across the world to post, target to specific others and exchange written and multimedia content through private and public messages. These messages, known as 'tweets', are organised chronologically and in columns on each user's account, and their content is often categorised using hashtags (#). What differentiates

Twitter from both popular SNS, such as Facebook, MySpace, Google+ and MeetUp, and blogging platforms, such as WordPress and Blogger, is the message length. Rather than allowing for long-winded posts in which users can extensively express themselves and exchange detailed information, Twitter promotes instead faster and 'lighter' communication by restricting users to a 140-character limit, thus encouraging very short posts. Although this method of exchanging viewpoints and information has been found to increase individuals' awareness of broader viewpoints, some have argued that it lowers users' investment of time and thought in content creation (Java et al. 2007), while others found that it restricts their ability to engage in meaningful conversation (Yardi and Boyd 2010). Finally, unlike most other social media, Twitter has an asymmetric follower structure. This means that if user A is 'following' user B, user B does not have to follow back user A. This differentiates Twitter from other SNS making it less prone to capturing pre-existing ties, but enforcing instead bi-directionality (Takhteyev et al. 2012). This, as Takhteyev and colleagues observe, makes Twitter more akin to blogs where the costs (technically and socially) of establishing a unidirectional tie by becoming a reader is similarly low; yet, 'unlike the weak ties between bloggers and their readers, which most often stay invisible, Twitter ties can be easily observed and analyzed' (2012, 74).

Contrary to the 'members-only' access to profiles that SNS such as Facebook permit, with the exception of a small number of 'protected' accounts almost anyone can access Twitter content (regardless of whether one is registered or not) – not only through websites, but also through mobile devices[3] and tablets via a range of applications. Through them, Twitter users (sometimes called 'tweeps') can post several visible updates in a single day, thus increasing the speed and interactivity with which content is created and distributed. Twitter messages can subsequently be instantly retweeted by other users and therefore accessed by a larger number of people that belong to different social circles.[4] The ease of passing on such information is demonstrated in a recent study by Kwak and colleagues who found that 'any retweeted tweet is to reach an average of 1000 users no matter what the number of followers is of the original tweet. Once retweeted, a tweet gets retweeted almost instantly on next hops, signifying fast diffusion of information after the first retweet' (2010, 591). Yet, recent research has shown that Twitter communities tend to form around global or local 'high centres', that is, popular individuals, celebrities and organisations (Gruzd et al. 2011; Theocharis 2013). The organisation 'Invisible Children', which gained prominence in the media through its social-media-based *KONY 2012* campaign,[5] made the most of the platform's community-building properties by encouraging celebrity Twitter users like Oprah Winfrey, Justin Bieber, Alex Baldwin and even Barack Obama to endorse the campaign and post about its new video.

Twitter was quickly picked up by Internet users. As of April 2007, shortly after its launch, it counted around 94,000 users (Java et al. 2007), a figure that rose to 19 million in April 2010 (Waters and Williams 2011). In the following two years, the platform saw a sharp rise in users as, according to the company's statistics, Twitter surpassed 500 million users in April 2012 (Dugan 2012) becoming the eighth most visited website on the Internet by September 2012. Twitter generates over 400 million tweets daily (D'Orazio 2012). Demographic-wise, according to the Pew Internet and American Life Project, some 15 per cent of online adults in the United States use Twitter as of February 2012 with 8 per cent doing so on a typical day (Smith and Brenner 2012). There is no digital divide with regard to gender and ethnicity (in fact, African-Americans and Hispanics use Twitter at higher rates than white), but use among young people aged 18–29 is nearly double to that of users aged 30–49. There is also a clear divide between residents of urban and suburban (which are significantly more likely to use Twitter) and rural areas.

## Twitter's opportunities as a source of information for political behaviour researchers

Topics of discussion on Twitter range from daily life updates and personal interests to links to current events and news stories. In fact, a recent study by Kwak and colleagues (2010) has shown that more than 85 per cent of popular topics mentioned on Twitter are headline news, while Chew and Eysenbach (2010) found that news websites were the links most commonly shared among users. Twitter rose to prominence not only as news disseminator but also as a 'tool for democratisation' during the victory of the Iranian President Mahmoud Ahmadinejad in the 2009 disputed Iranian presidential election (Leyne 2010), although the extent to which it has benefited democracy has since been a subject of heated debate between academics, pundits and public commentators (Esfandiari 2010; Howard 2010; Morozov 2011; Farrell 2012). Research has shown that social media, blogs and microblogs such as Twitter can be an important tool for information exchange when access to mainstream news and other communication media is restricted or blocked (Howard 2010; Castells 2012).

Facebook and Twitter, along with other forms of interpersonal communication, have been used heavily for information exchange and protest organisation during the Egyptian protests that led to the resignation of President Hosni Mubarak (Papacharissi and de Fatima Oliveira 2012; Tufekci and Wilson 2012). In the same vein, another study by Lotan and colleagues (2011), focusing on online information flows during the Egyptian and Tunisian uprisings, found that Twitter supports distributed conversation among different kinds of participants (ranging from journalists and bloggers to activists at the protest battlefield and interested online bystanders), shaping a dynamic information network which itself constitutes a peculiar kind of alternative press.

Tweeted messages provide unusually rich information regarding the context, content, and dynamics of political action, and we are slowly gaining a limited insight into how it benefits political organisation, cooperation and participation (Bennett and Segerberg 2011; Theocharis 2013). Social media use has also been found to increase bonding and bridging social capital while it also has small but positive effects on civic engagement and participation (Valenzuela et al. 2009; Boyd and Ellison 2007; although not all research reported positive effects, cf. Dimitrova et al. 2011). Social media has also been found to contribute to other forms of engagement with politics. Attention to social media for campaign information, for example, was significant during the 2008 US presidential campaign, when 27 per cent of adults younger than 30 reported to have obtained campaign information from SNS – compared to 4 per cent of adults aged 30–39 and only 1 per cent older than 40 (Smith and Rainie 2008). Additionally, exploring the effects of Twitter on political conversation, Yardi and Boyd (2010) found that discussion between like-minded individuals strengthened group identity and that people were more likely to interact with others who shared the same views as they did. However, contrary to the much discussed (and worrying) alleged effect of 'echo chambers' voiced by Sunstein (2008), they were in fact also actively engaged with those with whom they disagree.

Conversely to their prominence in the public sphere and in providing information and organisational tools for events across the world, social media can also be a rich information source for researchers, particularly given that its content is public. As pointed out by Farrell (2012, 36), 'if personal interactions on the Internet can be systematically captured in a way that offline transactions cannot, then we can for the first time begin to observe and make reasonable inferences'. Referring to data collected through such processes as 'Big Data', Margetts and colleagues indeed also argue that, on the policy level, this information 'can be used to match policy to preferences, match services to what citizens are willing – and are not willing – to do, in terms of managing their own affairs' (2012, 13).

However, its potential for understanding public opinion, informational dynamics and even individuals' preferences and behaviours is only starting to be explored – and has raised a number of controversial methodological questions (Boyd and Crawford 2012). For example, the 'Sentimeter Index' has been recently used to accurately forecast electoral results in the United States by analysing up to 40 million of tweets (Social-Media Observatory 2012; see also Tumasjan et al. 2010 for the German election). Others have analysed the connection between online networks, social contagion and collective dynamics such as recruitment patterns (González-Bailón et al. 2011), while a study published by the *Guardian* explored how riot rumours spread on Twitter during the 2011 UK riots (Richards and Lewis 2011).

Using content analysis to explore tweeted content during social movement mobilisations remains a relatively underdeveloped approach for researchers (but see Bennett and Segerberg 2011) due to the inherent difficulties in following mobilisations from their very beginning but also for the preference to use automated data analyses for big amounts of data. Building, thus, on previous studies on the dynamics, sentiments and aggregate measures collected through Twitter information, we contribute to the methodological discussion proposing the adoption of 'a closer look' at the content provided in 140 characters in order to understand, describe and examine citizens' political mobilisation in a comparative perspective across – in this case three – social movements.

We argue that Twitter is a source of information that allows studying political protest from yet a new perspective which can be truly valuable for the study of political behaviour. Since the wave of political unrest in the 1960s, behavioural research has approached protest activities from different perspectives. Social movement research has used protest event analysis to understand the patterns of different aggregates of protest; for example, regarding numbers of participants, claims and forms of protests across time, themes and territory. Furthermore, social movement scholars have studied how political opportunities structures shape social movements and influence their outcome (Kriesi 1995; McAdam 1996; Tarrow 1996). Survey-based research has been extensively used to study the population's attitudes towards protest groups as well as respondents' potential and actual participation in protest activities. This kind of research informs us about the socio-demographic, attitudinal and other individual characteristics of the respondents as correlates for participation in different forms (Barnes, Kaase et al. 1979; Inglehart 1990; Jennings and van Deth 1990; Norris 2002). These perspectives place emphasis on values, attitudes, recruitment and resources as the most important predictors of protest participation. From a rational-choice perspective, several researchers focused on cost and benefits evaluating individuals who chose to take part or abstain from protest activities (Finkel et al. 1989; Muller and Opp 1986; Opp and Hartmann 1989).

We understand Twitter as a tool that can provide additional information for both behavioural and social movements research. Survey research uses retrospective questions on participation but provides limited information regarding individuals' decision to participate in one specific mode of action or the effects of contextual factors on one's decisions. Protest activities have a sporadic character that is – or was – difficult to tackle 'in situ'. Researchers of social movements have used participant observation and followed protest movements in case studies asking participants for their motivations (Walgrave and Rucht 2010). However, concentrating on those who are politically active in a protest overlooks the opinion or opposition of those who decide not to participate. Collecting and analysing real time and publicly available messages exchanged on Twitter can now offer us a better sense of the context in which decisions and mobilisations take place and a clearer outlook on the discussions, aims and perspectives of both participants and non-participants.

## Studying social movements on Twitter: *Indignados*, *Aganaktismenoi* and Occupy Wall Street

The 15M movement in Spain got its name from the first demonstration organised on 15 May 2011 in several Spanish cities. Once the demonstration was over in Madrid a large number of participants decided to continue the protest by means of a peaceful sit-in. Following evictions and violent clashes with the police, more than 3000 people gathered together again on the 16 of May in Madrid's main square.[6] The clashes between the police and the peaceful sit-ins resulted in setting up tents, the 'acampadas' (or occupations) in Madrid and Barcelona that spread to several cities in Spain with the initial aim to stay in the squares until the 22 May, the day when the local election was to be held. However, the movement lasted much longer and, although with a different structure, continues to operate at the time of this writing. This movement was followed with high interest and was positively evaluated by the majority of the Spanish population (Centro de Investigaciones Sociológicas 2011).[7] On their part, in Greece, anti-austerity protesters organised by the 'Direct Democracy Now' movement – also known as *Aganaktismenoi* or the 'Indignant Citizens Movement' – started demonstrating in major cities across Greece on 29 May 2011. Contrary to the wave of protests that took place in Greece in 2010, and similarly to the protests organised in Spain, this wave of demonstrations had an apartisan and peaceful character, although several clashes with the police occurred. It lasted until the beginning of August. Inspired by the movements in western Europe and the Middle East, a similar mobilisation began on 17 September 2011 in Zuccotti Park, located in New York City's Wall Street financial district. Participants sought to express their outrage towards the levels of inequality, financial speculation, unregulated financial institutions and corporate class greed. The Canadian activist group Adbusters placed the first seeds for the mobilisation calling, on 2 February 2011, for protests similar to those in the Middle East and later creating the *OccupyWallStreet* domain through which subsequent calls for mobilisation would be posted.

Several characteristics of these three movements signal similarities in their causes, tactics and aims. In all three cases the key demands were explicitly related to the economic crisis, the bankers' power and their influence over governmental decisions. The three movements also shared the main aspects of their organisation and protest tactics. They prided themselves of being non-violent, apartisan movements that, allegedly, lacked any hierarchy and officially rejected nominal leaders. To achieve their goals, protesters from all three movements acted on consensus-based decisions made in general assemblies, following a direct democracy model (Castells 2012). They demanded the need for citizens' direct political action. In addition to the occupation of main squares, the three movements organised numerous events such as rallies, demonstrations, sit-ins or the occupation or blockage of symbolic political and economic buildings such as parliaments and banks. They also developed a transnational connection through new media platforms, shared common slogans and made explicit statements of mutual support and solidarity.

However, each of these three movements put the emphasis on slightly different issues. The Greek movement burst as a reaction against the bailout by the European Union and the binding budget cuts imposed by the so-called 'troika' (the European Commission, the International Monetary Fund and the European Central Bank), while citizens also reacted against corruption of political elites. The Spanish movement started with the demand for a 'Real Democracy Now', the slogan 'they do not represent us' referring to the two main political parties. Concerns for the precarious situation of young people, a group particularly badly hit by unemployment, was also one of the main issues raised in Spain. In *OccupyWallStreet* (OWS) the slogan 'We are the 99 per cent' summarised the movement's main claim in connection with economic inequalities and the perceived disproportionate influence of corporations on the government.

Contextual factors also marked differences between the movements. Simply extracting fragments of content from complex communication processes that involve many actors, technologies and aims without considering local and national peculiarities would be unwise. Exploring in greater detail the use of Twitter in the collective action context that emerges from each mobilisation allows us to understand more than the function of a simple and continuous flow of messages; we can learn more especially regarding the movements' use of new media for improving organisational tactics, the organising agents, the content of the online discussions and the connection of the discourse with people's stance and demands, the mobilisation strategies and so on. To better understand the similarities and differences among the movements, we examine and interpret the information distributed in Twitter that directly referred to these mobilisation aspects.

We started monitoring the Spanish and Greek movements only a few days after the first demonstration in Madrid, although we could only systematically retrieve tweeted information from the 5th of June onwards. For the purposes of this chapter we decided to present and examine the information distributed via Twitter during two weeks, until the 19 June 2011. That is to say, during the peak of the *Indignados* and *Aganaktismenoi* protest activities in Spain and Greece respectively. We captured and archived the content of tweets along with the hashtags, usernames, dates, time-stamps and other miscellaneous bits of information such as the platform a tweeted message was sent from (for example, android device, iPhone, Tweetdeck). Consistently with the spontaneous and diverse character of the movements, the first weeks a plethora of diverse hashtags were used to organise and discuss the events. We traced a number of those hashtags that were evolving around the protests activities (for example, #acampadasol, #indignados, #spanishrevolution, #aganaktismenoi), but in order to come up with a manageable amount of information we focus on the hashtags that resulted more consistently and widely used across time: the #15M hashtag for the Spanish movement and the #greekrevolution hashtag for the Greek case.

*Table 5.1* Number of tweets collected by period and by country

| Country | From | To | Hashtag | Total tweets in period | Random sample |
|---|---|---|---|---|---|
| Spain | 5 June 2011 | 19 June 2011 | #15M | 80,074 | 2,000 |
| Greece | 5 June 2011 | 19 June 2011 | #greekrevolution | 19,784 | 2,000 |
| The United States | 2 October 2011 | 16 October 2011 | #occupywallstreet | 342,479 | 2,000 |

Regarding *OccupyWallStreet*, we focus on the most prominent tag used during the period of the mobilisations: #OccupyWallStreet.[8] As others have pointed out, it is important to note that cutting through the Twitter stream provides us with access to just a slice of a collective action's mediation process. As Bennett and Segerberg observe, 'depending on where one cuts into a Twitter stream, then, one may find different actors and different kinds of activity going on, from rallying in the midst of a demonstration, to debriefing and planning for next events at later stages' (2011, 2020). In order to analyse a time span that can be considered equivalent (in the sense of movement development) to those of the Spanish and Greek movements, in what follows we use the information distributed under the #OccupyWallStreet hashtag during two weeks after the movement started, between the 2 and 16 October. The overall database offers us a total of 442,337 units, of which 18 per cent belong to the Spanish movement, 4.4 per cent to the movement in Greece and 77 per cent refer to Occupy Wall Street (see Table 5.1).[9]

## Dealing with the 140-character barrier

In an exploratory fashion, we wanted to get as much information as possible aiming to tackle a central question: what were the main uses of Twitter for political mobilisation? This question includes a broad range of topics. To explore the information available we conducted a content analysis. Given the large size of our dataset and our qualitative approach we started by drawing a simple random sample of 2000 tweets for each of the #15m, #greekrevolution and #OccupyWallStreet datasets. The process used to select our sample was simple random sampling procedure without replacement assigning equal probabilities to be selected to all individual elements of the complete dataset (Groves et al.

2004, 99).[10] Therefore we are working with a more manageable sample of a total 6000 cases. After drawing the sample, the authors separately scanned the content of 60 tweets from the United States, Greek and Spanish datasets (30 for each case), attempting to list the distinct categories that linked the content of the tweet to our general axes of interest: the use of digital media for political action. After sharing and discussing the results we repeated the procedure three times, examining in total 90 tweets each. The English speaking tweets were examined simultaneously in order to assure validity and comparability of each category with the Spanish and Greek datasets.

As this chapter will show, 140 characters can include large amounts and diverse types of information. Below we describe the development of a coding scheme that allows exploring in detail the characteristics of each protest movement. We first present the indicators built automatically from each tweet and that are directly available from the metadata. In a second step, we describe the categories and codes developed to address two types of questions. Our main interest as political behaviour researchers is to answer the question: what can users' messages tell us about the characteristics of the protests movements, the participants or their mobilisation tactics? Second, and given the plethora of opinion articles written about the movements, we are interested in the rich discourse that followed the events' media coverage, the significant media attention they attracted, and the constant stream of information produced on Twitter in cases of such intense social and political developments (Lotan et al. 2011; Papacharissi and de Fatima Oliveira 2012; Tufekci and Wilson 2012; Rainie et al. 2012). For this reason, we explored which types (if any) of discourse were communicated through Twitter, and which hyperlinks were most predominant.

## Information automatically retrieved from tweets

Before describing the substantive categories resulting from a first qualitative approach, there are three pieces of information that we consider relevant to understanding citizens' use of Twitter and that can be coded automatically from any tweet. These are whether the tweet includes a link (which can be easily identified by searching for 'http'), whether it is an original tweet or the re-distribution of someone else's message (the tweet includes the 'retweet' (RT) abbreviation) and whether the tweet is directed to a specific user or just to the general public (identified by the use of '@'and the username). These indicators already provide valuable information regarding the way Twitter was used. As Table 5.2

*Table 5.2* Information automatically retrieved from the tweets

| | | Spain | Greece | The United States | Total |
|---|---|---|---|---|---|
| Retweeted | Yes (%) | 61.4 | 51.9 | 67.4 | 60.2 |
| Sent to another user | Yes (%) | 68.6 | 59.3 | 71.0 | 66.3 |
| Contained link | Yes (%) | 49.6 | 49.8 | 45.9 | 48.4 |
| Total (N) | | 1,999 | 2,001 | 1,999 | 5,999 |

shows, 48.4 per cent of all tweets contain a link to another web page, which implies a broad use of Twitter for sharing information. The large circulation of information is also visible when looking at the number of tweets that were not original pieces of information but dissemination of information written by others: 60.2 per cent of all the tweets were retweets. Finally, 66.3 per cent of all the tweets were directed to another user, which we interpret as an indicator not only for the existence of information exchange, but also for targeted communication and possibly discussion.

Considering these three indicators as measures of the extent to which information was distributed, shared and discussed, we can immediately observe some differences between the three movements (Table 5.2). To start with, the number of non-retweeted, 'original' tweets was larger in Greece, while the number of retweets was almost 10 per cent lower than in Spain and 15 per cent less than in the United States. The frequency of tweets sent to another user is also lower in Greece. Taken together these features may indicate that tweeting in Greece took a less conversational form than in Spain or the United States, with more emphasis placed on stating personal views. Finally, the frequency of tweets that were used to distribute information including a link was similar among the three movements.

## Identifying political attributes in tweets

To identify political attributes in the tweets sent and the type of media linked or discourse distributed, we developed several categories. The codebook and specific instructions for the coders were built by the authors according to the research interests referred to above, and after the simultaneous coding of English, Spanish and Greek tweets in order to assure the equivalence and validity of each category across the three movements. A summary of all the categories developed can be consulted in Table 5.3, but most of them are presented below.[11] The three distinct

*Table 5.3* Summary of categories and codes

| Category | Possible codes (only one code can be selected for each category) |
|---|---|
| Retweets | – Yes<br>– No |
| Link inclusion | – Yes<br>– No |
| Directed to another user | – Yes<br>– No |
| Purpose | – Political statement<br>– Moral support<br>– Humour<br>– Live protest action reporting<br>– Call for action<br>– Organisational issues<br>– Movement-related hashtags only<br>– Reporting news about the movement<br>– Reporting news related to the general movement's causes<br>– Information about a future event<br>– Information about the movement (no news reporting)<br>– Political conversation<br>– Information about the crisis<br>– Reference to sister movement<br>– I don't know how to classify it<br>– (Vague) cannot be classified |
| Language | – English<br>– Spanish<br>– Greek<br>– Other |
| Topic | – Protest acts and the movement<br>– Capitalism/crisis<br>– Media criticism<br>– Occupation visit<br>– Resentment of political elite<br>– Government inefficiency to address citizens' problems<br>– Cannot be classified<br>– Other political topic |
| Political Issues | – Inequality<br>– Economic mismanagement (government or corporate)<br>– Negative comment on the role of media<br>– Positive comment on the role of media<br>– Political violence<br>– Education/pension<br>– Employment<br>– Institutional reforms |

| | |
|---|---|
| | – Corruption<br>– Lack of representation<br>– Austerity measures<br>– Several political issues<br>– None<br>– Cannot be classified<br>– Other |
| Link destination | – News media: link led to a news media source<br>– Mainstream<br>– Alternative<br>– Unclear<br>– Picture<br>– Video<br>– Blog<br>– NGO<br>– Movement website<br>– Other organisation website<br>– Petition<br>– Social media post<br>– Picture or video on social media<br>– Map<br>– No longer available<br>– No link included<br>– Other |
| Tweet origin | – Individual citizen<br>– Citizen-blogger<br>– Professional blogger<br>– Journalist<br>– News agency<br>– Politician<br>– Protected account<br>– Organisational group of the movement<br>– Other organisation (for example, Amnesty International and teachers union)<br>– Other<br>– Account no longer exists |
| Movement's evaluation | – Positive<br>– Negative<br>– Neutral<br>– Unclear |
| Reference to any form of political action | – Street action<br>– Demonstration<br>– Occupation<br>– Action to prevent evictions<br>– Petitions<br>– Contacting public officials/politicians<br>– Vote |

*Table 5.3* (Continued)

| Category | Possible codes (only one code can be selected for each category) |
|---|---|
| | – Assembly<br>– Donation<br>– Abstention<br>– Virtual action<br>– No reference to political action<br>– Physical participation in the movement (if the type of action is unclear)<br>– Other (please add) __________<br>– None |

databases were entered into coding software developed at the University of Mannheim specifically for the purposes of the study by a text-analysis expert computer scientist. For the data coding we recruited Spanish, Greek and English-speaking student assistants.[12]

Given that the dataset contains information in three languages, the first training and reliability check was performed involving both the coders and the authors using data in the English language from the OWS dataset. The first stage involved training the coders according to the codebook prepared by the authors and discussion of the categories. The second stage involved the individual codification of 30 tweets and common discussion of the categories selected by all coders. This process was repeated again reaching an average agreement rate in the second round of between 65 and 80 per cent in all the categories.[13] Once this stage was finished, the same procedure and reliability tests were performed between pairs (one author and one coder) for the Spanish and Greek datasets. In this part of the training again each pair coded 60 tweets from the Spanish or Greek dataset. After coding the first 30 tweets each pair discussed the results for clarifications. We then coded another 30 tweets and the percentages of agreement rose to more than 80 per cent in almost all categories.[14]

## Purpose of the tweet

In this category, we were concerned with the general use of Twitter as a method for political communication. We thus introduced various different categories that may apply to a tweeted message. The challenge was how to deal with the very common cases in which a tweet that did not 'shout' its use but included a link that may have led to making a better judgement as to what it refers to, or cases in which the title of a newspaper/online news article was mentioned without any further elaboration. We regarded this information crucial for understanding the protest's wider composition and the specific protest theme that the information was embedded in. Indeed such links often revealed the organisations involved, diverse information channels, sources and SNS contributing to understanding the narrative (or part of it) behind an 'unrecognisable' tweet. In such cases, therefore, we looked at what is linked: posted links were clicked and followed with the aim of figuring out what the tweet referred to. This approach applies and extends to the following category: 'political issues'. The list of purposes identified and the frequency by which we encountered them can be seen in Table 5.4.

*Table 5.4* Purpose of the tweet (column percentages)

| | Spain | Greece | The United States | Total |
|---|---|---|---|---|
| Political statement | **29.8** | 0.8 | 6.4 | **12.8** |
| Reporting news about the movement | **18.1** | **26.9** | **13.6** | **19.2** |
| Conversation (if nothing else applies) | **10.1** | **32** | **31.8** | **24.4** |
| Article about the movement (not reporting news, editorial) | **9.1** | 2.6 | 6.7 | 6.3 |
| Reporting news about the movement's causes | 6.2 | 3.9 | 4.3 | 4.8 |
| Live action protest reporting | 4.1 | **9.2** | **8.5** | **7.2** |
| Moral support | 4 | 2.4 | **6.9** | 4.5 |
| Call for action | 3.4 | 6.2 | 3.3 | 4.2 |
| Information about a future event | 3.3 | 0.9 | 3.1 | 2.5 |
| Reference to sister movement | 1.8 | 1.6 | 2.2 | 1.9 |
| Organisational issues | 1.8 | 1.7 | 1.2 | 1.6 |
| Humour | 1.6 | **6.4** | 4 | 3.9 |
| Information about the crisis | 1 | 4.1 | 1.2 | 2 |
| Movement-related hashtags only | 0.3 | 0.7 | 1.2 | 0.7 |
| Vague, cannot be classified | 5.4 | 0.6 | 4 | 3.5 |
| I don't know how to classify it | 0.1 | 0 | 1.5 | 0.6 |
| Total (N) | 1,865 | 1,637 | 1,880 | 5,382 |

*Note*: Bold numbers represent the four main purposes for which tweets were used in each country or for the pooled dataset.

Some of the codes are not necessary exclusive. For instance, there were some tweets that contained political statements or moral support for the movement which were written in a humoristic manner. Since our main interest in this project is to identify political aspects in the use of Twitter, coders were instructed to only use some general categories such as 'Humour' if the tweet included nothing more than a joke or irony. Therefore, in the example of a political statement phrased in a humoristic way, the option 'political statement' was preferred. Some other instructions and decision rules were communicated to the coders such as the difference between call for action and information about a future event; in this case the former encourages mobilisation while the later does not.

As can be observed in Table 5.4, the two main uses in all countries were distribution of information (19 per cent of all the tweets in the pooled sample and up to 30 per cent if we add all the options that imply the distribution of articles about the movement, information about the crisis or reporting news) and expression of political statements or conversations (37 per cent of the pooled sample).[15] The use of twitter for organisation and coordination issues of the movement in general (for example, logistical communication among protesters on the ground), or specific protests in particular was lower than expected (1.6 per cent of the pooled sample). This was unanticipated given the extant literature's attention on how informational goods communicated through social media platforms could improve organisation and coordination of protest activity (Bimber et al. 2009; Shirky 2011). In addition to the most relevant uses discussed in the literature, we also identified other, less frequent manifestations. For example tweets whose sole purpose was humoristic are particularly observable in Greece (6.4 per cent). Another function was the provision of moral support to the movement, or tweets referring to sister movements. It was not possible to classify some tweets due to the lack of context – although this was observed in less than 4.1 per cent of all tweets. Overall these findings show that Twitter was less of a networking *agent*, that is, an organising mechanism within the protest, and more of a *window* into the protest space, revealing certain contextual features in which the protests were embedded (Bennett and Segerberg 2011).

## Political issues mentioned

This category refers to the political issues mentioned in the tweets. As introduced above, the three movements engaged in mobilisations for common but also for different reasons. Issues regarding unemployment and non-representation were, for example, more prevalent in the Spanish mobilisations. In Greece the issue of corruption was predominant along with that of distrusting the media, while in the United States, police violence and the negative role of mainstream media when referring to the *OccupyWallStreet* mobilisations were highlighted (Castells 2012).

As can be observed in Table 5.5, our coding scheme had identified 11 main political issues. However, the first important question refers to the number of tweets that actually included references to political issues. Table 5.5 shows that this was the case for half of tweets in our sample (50 per cent in the pooled sample did not include any reference to political issues). Furthermore, there are some differences among the three countries: *OccupyWallStreet* was the movement with the highest percentage of tweets with explicit references to political issues, followed by the 15M Spanish movement and then the 'Greek Revolution' movement. Furthermore, an important percentage of tweets discussed or mentioned

*Table 5.5* Political issues mentioned in the tweets (column percentages)

| | **Spain** | **Greece** | **The United States** | **Total** |
|---|---|---|---|---|
| Economic mismanagement (government or corporations) | 2.9 | 2.9 | **8.5** | **4.8** |
| Police violence | **6.7** | **4.2** | 3.4 | **4.8** |
| Negative comment on media | 3.6 | 3.1 | 4.5 | 3.8 |
| Economic inequality | 1 | 0.6 | **8.8** | 3.6 |
| Austerity measures | 0.8 | **9.6** | 0.1 | 3.2 |
| Lack of representation | 2 | **4.5** | 2 | 2.8 |
| Employment | 1.3 | 1.3 | 4 | 2.2 |
| Institutional reforms | 1.7 | 1.9 | 2.1 | 1.9 |
| Corruption | 1.4 | 1.3 | 1.5 | 1.4 |
| Positive comment on media | 0.2 | 0.4 | 1 | 0.6 |
| Education/pensions | 0.4 | 0.3 | 0.5 | 0.4 |
| Other political issue | **16.6** | 0.3 | **10.2** | **9.4** |
| Several political issues | **9** | 3.5 | 5.7 | **6.2** |
| No explicit mention to political issues | **45.4** | **65.2** | **40.1** | **49.6** |
| Cannot be classified | 6.9 | 0.9 | 7.6 | 5.3 |
| Total (N) | 1,865 | 1,637 | 1,880 | 5,382 |

*Note*: Bold numbers represent the four main political issues mentioned in each country or in the pooled dataset.

several political issues that were not identified due to the format of our coding scheme but were given entrance to our analysis through a separate 'notes' section in which each coder could list them if they were not mentioned. This is particularly the case in the Spanish movement where almost 17 per cent of the tweets referred to other political issues not included in the list, such as immigrants' rights, mortgages and housing evictions, and so on. Out of the issues identified in *OccupyWallStreet*, economic issues (including inequality and economic or government mismanagement) were the most predominant. In Greece, unsurprisingly given the nature of the protests, there is also an important number of references to austerity measures and to the lack of representation. Negative comments about the media and complaints about police violence were common in all three cases (for a contextual analysis see Castells 2012). Other issues that we expected to be prominent in the Greek and Spanish movements, corruption and institutional reforms, were curiously not that often discussed on Twitter which raises questions about how representative of the movement participants our slice of tweets was, how consistent the rhetoric of the movement was, and what the aims that the movement was truly associated with were.

## Political actions mentioned

This category responds to our interest in examining the types of political action that were mainly promoted by Twitterers. Studies have so far stressed the potential of social media for political mobilisation and particularly, the reduction of costs and the diversification of political acts as consequences of online engagement (van Laer and van Aelst 2010). Notwithstanding these claims, we expect that all three movements used Twitter to promote a diverse repertory of low- and high-cost actions. Given the distinct characteristics of the three movements, we also expect a preference for specific political activities over others among movements. Table 5.4 already showed that part of the information distributed via Twitter referred to future political events and calls for actions. In order to better understand how Twitter was used for promoting political actions, we also examined whether each message included references to specific political action repertoires. Granted that recent political science literature has argued about the expanding repertoire of citizens' participation (see, for example, Micheletti and McFarland 2010), we also wanted to identify 'new' or 'creative' forms of action. To capture the entire repertoire of political actions, coders were trained

*Table 5.6* Political actions mentioned (column percentages)

| | Spain | Greece | The United States | Total |
|---|---|---|---|---|
| Street action | **28.3** | **23.7** | **23.7** | **25.3** |
| Occupation | **6.4** | 0.3 | **18.6** | **8.8** |
| Virtual action | **3.2** | **4** | **2.6** | **3.2** |
| Assembly | **2.4** | **4.3** | 0.4 | **2.3** |
| Other | 1.9 | 0.1 | **2.1** | 1.4 |
| Voting | 1.2 | 0.9 | 0.9 | 1 |
| Contacting politicians/public officials | 1 | 1.9 | 0.1 | 1 |
| Prevent evictions | 0.8 | 0 | 1.2 | 0.7 |
| Donation | 0.1 | 0.1 | 0.7 | 0.3 |
| Petition | 0.3 | 0.2 | 0.2 | 0.2 |
| Abstention | 0.2 | 0 | 0 | 0.1 |
| No explicit reference to a political action | **54.4** | **64.6** | **49.5** | **55.8** |
| Total (N) | 1,865 | 1,637 | 1,880 | 5,382 |

*Note*: Bold numbers represent the political actions more frequently mentioned in each country or in the pooled dataset.

to openly identify and, if needed, add 'new' forms of participation they would come across. Table 5.6 shows that between 35 per cent (Greece) and 49 per cent (the United States) of the tweets indeed made reference to at least one political action.

Not surprisingly, the large majority of tweets refer to street protest activities (see Table 5.6). This category can be merged with occupations, since the two types of activities cannot always be easily distinguished in some of the tweets. The next most frequently mentioned action in the three countries was, however, a low-cost type of action: virtual participation.[16] Other types of actions identified included participation in assemblies, voting (or calls for abstention), the organisation of groups to prevent evictions, signing petitions, contacting politicians, or donating money. The comparison across countries shows similar patterns, the only two differences being the larger diversification of political actions in the United States and Spain and the higher frequency of tweets that mentioned political actions in the latter two countries in comparison to Greece. Furthermore, the 'open' approach to this category allowed identifying other forms of political action as diverse as calls to withdraw money and close accounts from banks (mainly, but not only, in the United States), contacting bankers and shareholders (instead of politicians), hacking institutional and corporate websites, a particularly high-cost action, promoting legal actions or proposing loots, and some references to the need of more referenda.

## Evaluation of the movement

In this category we tried to identify the attitude of Twitter users towards the movement. It examines whether direct support or disapproval/condemnation of the movement was explicit in the tweet. Four options were offered to the coder:

- *Positive*: was used when the tweet openly declares positive feelings towards the movement. Obvious cases with unclear wording that nevertheless indicated support for the movement (for example, an Occupy camp participant's reporting on what happens around her) were also taken as declaration of support;
- *Negative*: was used for unambiguously negative comment or critic about the movement goals, functioning and so on;
- *Neutral*: was used when a tweet did not include judgment of the movement;
- *Unclear*: was offered to the coders when the sentiment could not be identified with certainty.

Whether the user sending the tweet has a positive or negative attitude towards the movement is probably the most difficult piece of information we tried to gather. The reason is that a unique tweet, without its context, might just provide information and not include any attitudes. A better approach could be to examine a larger number of tweets sent by the same user. Our results confirm this difficulty: 23 per cent of the tweets fall in the option neutral and 8 per cent are unclear (see Figure 5.1). Still, we think this indicator can give us a sense of supporting or opposing views regarding a movement on the aggregate level. We observed that a majority of tweets implied a positive evaluation of the movement in Spain and the United States but not in Greece. Furthermore, if we look at the percentage of tweets that had a negative connotation, we see that this is larger in the United States (12 per cent). We interpret the fact that both more clearly positive or negative messages could be identified in the United States as a signal of the higher polarisation regarding the OWS movement in comparison with Spain or Greece. This interpretation is consistent with poll findings. According to a Pew Institute survey (2011), 44 per cent of the population supported

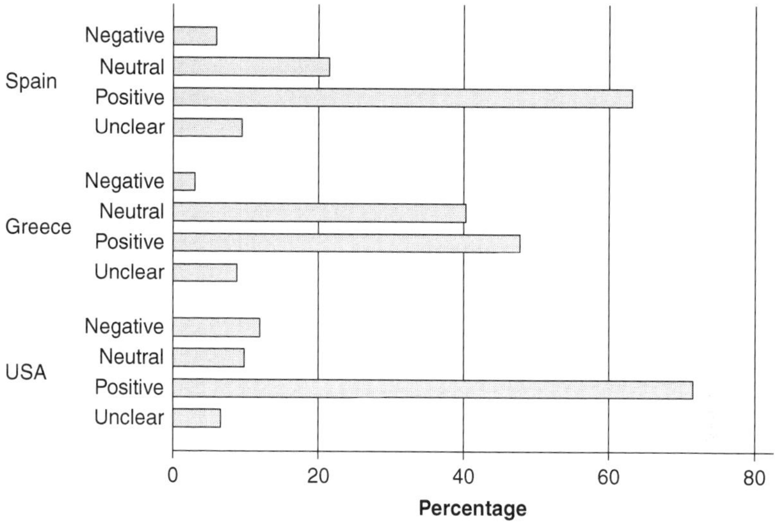


*Figure 5.1* Evaluation of the movement

the *OccupyWallStreet* movement but 39 per cent opposed it while when it came to the movement's tactics 49 per cent disagreed and only 29 per cent agreed. As discussed above, the large majority of the Spanish and Greek population supported the movement (Calvo et al. 2011; Public Issue 2011).

## Distribution of information on twitter

### Where does the link lead to?

As we showed previously, almost half of all the tweets in our sample include a link, therefore, most of the information is not necessarily included in the body of the message but rather, the tweet is used as a platform to distribute and share information. For this reason we also examined the type of information that was linked to each tweet. Table 5.7 shows that the most frequent information distributed differs across countries in those tweets that included a link. While in Spain the larger percentage of links directed users to mainstream news media, we found that in Greece the mainstream media were marginalised, and taken over by a clear preference for alternative news media. This chimes well with recent findings from the Eurobarometer (2011) which shows that Greek citizens are the most distrustful among Europeans

*Table 5.7* Types of information distributed in tweets via hyperlinks (column percentages)

| | Spain | Greece | The United States | Total |
|---|---|---|---|---|
| Mainstream news media | **30.4** | 8.6 | **17** | **19.3** |
| Video | **16.1** | **16.6** | **21.7** | **18.2** |
| Picture | **13.7** | **18.6** | **17.1** | **16.3** |
| Alternative news media | 5.2 | **24.8** | 9 | **12.5** |
| Blog | **11.2** | 9.6 | **10.4** | **10.5** |
| No longer available | 11 | **11.3** | 6.4 | 9.5 |
| Social media post (for example, Facebook) | 2.8 | 4.9 | 4 | 3.9 |
| Movement website | 3.2 | 2.4 | 3.4 | 3 |
| Other organization website (for example, private company) | 2.8 | 1.3 | 4.1 | 2.8 |
| News media (of unclear type) | 1.4 | 1.5 | 3.1 | 2 |
| Maps | 0.8 | 0 | 0.6 | 0.5 |
| Petition | 0.2 | 0 | 0.8 | 0.4 |
| Warehouse protest site | 0 | 0 | 0.7 | 0.2 |
| Total (N) | 917 | 781 | 847 | 2545 |

*Note*: Bold numbers represent the types of information more frequently distributed in each country or in the pooled dataset.

when it comes to mainstream media, including TV, radio and to a lesser extent the Internet. In the OccupyWallStreet case, the frequency with which links lead to mainstream or alternative media is similar. In the United States, links are more often used to distribute videos or pictures (mainly of protest events) which can perhaps be related to the intense reporting by amateur media users and professional journalists regarding outbreaks of police violence and its intensive visual mediation (Castells 2012). This percentage is also important in Greece and Spain which stresses the importance of distributing visual content that was perhaps unavailable through mainstream media. In addition, approximately 10 per cent of the tweets included a link redirecting users to blogs. Given the time lapse between the collection of information and the coding, approximately 10 per cent of all links referred to websites that were no longer available online and therefore could not be classified. In addition, other options linked to petitions, social media posts, maps and 'warehouse protest sites' (Earl and Kimport 2011). These findings suggest that linking may be used differently across mobilisations, even when these are under the same umbrella of grievances, indignation and demands.

### Who sends the tweet?

This category was concerned with the person or group of persons that had sent the tweet. To identify that, the coder had to click on the user name and get redirected to the profile where there is often a clickable link or sufficient information to identify the nature of the user – or at least the nature that the user puts forward as 'real'; a factor which reduces our certainty about the accuracy of our findings. The type of users identified were: individual citizen, citizen-blogger (that is, individual citizens that hold a regular blog – usually linked to their own Twitter profile – and therefore are more active on the Internet and prone to distribute and discuss information online), individual journalist, news agency, other organisation (such as a private company or an NGO), organisational group of the movement and politician. As Table 5.8 shows, the large majority of users referring to the movements on Twitter were individual citizens. This result reflects the aim of the three movements to avoid being linked to a specific organisation or political group and their emphasis in projecting themselves as a group of individual citizens with common aims regarding economic and political issues but with a comprehensive approach regarding a diversity of views, values or ideologies. In Greece, there is also an important number of what we call 'citizen-bloggers'. In addition, we identified journalists that tweeted in their individual capacity, but also tweets from news agencies. These last two categories are again more frequent in Greece which coincides with previous findings presenting the Greek blogosphere as

*Table 5.8* Type of sender (column percentages)

| | Spain | Greece | The United States | Total |
|---|---|---|---|---|
| Individual citizen | **75.1** | **41.3** | **81.9** | **67.2** |
| Account doesn't exist anymore | **11.2** | 12.9 | **8.8** | **10.9** |
| Citizen-blogger | 1.3 | **23.3** | 0.9 | **7.8** |
| Individual journalist | **3.3** | **10.1** | 1 | 4.6 |
| Other organisation | **3.3** | 1.7 | **4.3** | 3.2 |
| News agency | 2.8 | 3.7 | 1.9 | 2.7 |
| Organisational group of the movement | 1.3 | 6.6 | 0.4 | 2.6 |
| Protected account | 1.4 | 0.3 | 0.9 | 0.9 |
| Politician | 0.3 | 0.2 | 0 | 0.1 |
| Total | 1,865 | 1,637 | 1,88 | 5,382 |

*Note*: Bold numbers represent the type of users more frequently identified in each country or in the pooled dataset.

particularly active and restless when it comes to political mobilisation (Tsaliki 2010). A third group refers to some group formed around the movement usually responsible for coordination and organisation, more frequent in Greece. In addition, other organisations, social groups and private companies also addressed the movements. Finally, the percentage of politicians or political parties that relate to the movements is residual but noticeable in Spain, which could be explained by the closeness to the local elections at the time of the protest, and Greece. Our findings confirm similar explorations (Lotan et al. 2011) in showing that the Twitter flow in political mobilisations consists of a dynamic information network with diverse sets of participants.

## In what language is the tweet written?

Finally, the data reflects the internationalisation, or rather transnationalisation, of the three movements and the interrelationships among them through the diverse use of languages. For this reason, and also with the aim of controlling whether some tweets could not be coded due to the language used, the coders were instructed to also code the language in which the tweet was written. The options were restricted to the three native languages in which the tweets were coded (English, Greek and Spanish) and the option 'other language'. What we found is that around 95 per cent of the OWS and 15M movements were written in the native language. However, the Greek database included 48 per cent of tweets that were written in a language other than Greek. Most of those were written in English (34 per cent of the sample) and some in Spanish (15 per cent).[17] We interpret the diversity of languages used in Greece as a combination of trying to distribute the information and events going on in Greece as widely as possible and the frequent exchanges between the Greek and Spanish movements since they overlapped in time. Furthermore, it can be an indication of solidarity to the people of the country that has monopolised international media more than any other – at least as far as the European financial crisis is concerned.

## Conclusions

Scholars have emphasised the importance of social media as organising agents in protest events (Shirky 2011; Rainie and Wellman 2012; Bennett and Segerberg 2012), while the overall impact of new media technologies has ignited an animated discussion about the Internet's real effect on contentious politics (Gladwell 2010; Morozov 2011; Shirky

2011; Castells 2012). Recognising the vast potential that this new source of information offers to political behaviour researchers, this chapter argues for a more systematic way of understanding organisational and mobilisation content distributed by social media, especially Twitter, proposing an exhaustive way of analysing the large number of diverse information and meta-information that we can harvest from this media.

This chapter has proposed the construction of indicators directed to understanding the use of Twitter for political mobilisation, but also the aims, characteristics and tactics of social movements as reflected and communicated through the media. Twitter reveals diverse clues about protest events (such as the type of information distributed, political issues discussed, type of users that distribute the information, general purpose of the tweets and so on) that allow us to get a clearer picture of the entire protest dynamic, very often in real time, from the protesters themselves. Illustrating the potential of the information shared in Twitter comparing the 'indignant citizens' of Spain and Greece, and the US-based 'OccupyWallStreet' contexts, we saw similarities and differences across the movements. Among other things, the main usage of Twitter for information exchange was a common feature in the three countries. But the tweeted output of the *Aganaktismenoi* movement differs in several characteristics from the *Indignados* or Occupy Wall Street. Twitter was used to a lower extent for political discussion in Greece, while the type of users was also different, accompanied with a preference for distribution of information from alternative rather than mainstream news media.

We believe the qualitative approach used here could be easily adapted to different research questions from across behavioural sciences. Furthermore, it represents only a first step to the detailed analysis of social media information to understand political mobilisation and discussion. The descriptive information presented in this chapter can be further developed in several ways. First, once the indicators have been built, we can combine them to address more specific questions. For instance, if we were to be interested in whether microblogging tools such as Twitter actually permit meaningful political discussions among citizens, then combining those tweets that contain references to political issues, are directed to someone, and were sent by individual citizens, could give us a good answer. A second way in which this study could be further expanded is by using the coding scheme developed and the examination of the sample of tweets, as a basis to build an automatic text analysis procedure to examine the entire dataset. This approach would allow, among other things, the possibility to capture changes in the dynamics of the movements by enlarging the time span analysed or examining and comparing online peaks in action with the respective activity offline. A third potential development could focus on supplementing Twitter information with other data sources. For instance, one could examine whether Facebook – with its capacity for longer messages – allows for more meaningful and elaborated political debate than Twitter and complements what is lost in the 140 characters. Or the mobilisation potential of Facebook as a platform that lacks the rapidity of Twitter, yet allows for better community building due to different and more diverse built-in features. Another possibility is to combine extracted social media information with other sources of information – for example, interviews – in order to address questions that remain controversial, such as whether online mobilisation implies offline engagement with the movement's events.

A multi-method approach would also help addressing the potential limitations of basing our research on the information available on Twitter. An obvious limitation is the lack of representativeness of Twitter users. Twitter users are a very particular sub-set of the population and there is also an important difference between 'active' users and those that are just 'listeners' (Boyd and Crawford 2012, 669). We can only speculate regarding the representativeness of our results. Yet, there are two reasons why we think representativeness is not an important threat to our findings: the profile of Twitter users is probably very similar to the majority of participants in the three social movements analysed – young and educated; and the important role of technological tools such as Twitter in the development and spread of the movements could also imply that the information distributed with this tool offers a good reflection of the movements' characteristics. But even in this case, researchers should keep in mind that those that voice their concerns in social media are not even necessarily representative of the participants of the movements, their supporters or of those who oppose a concrete movement.

Summing up, social media offers a quality and quantity of information unprecedented in the study of political behaviour and social movements. We believe they are now an indispensable source of information for researchers aiming to understand the dynamics of protest movements and individuals' decisions to participate politically. Social networking platforms such as Twitter provide 'real time' data regarding the emergence and functioning of social protest which is particularly valuable given the sporadic character of protest political actions. It also provides extant information regarding the information distributed, demands, contextual characteristics and the interrelationships between movements. But this source of information also poses new challenges to researchers that should be kept in mind. Overcoming those difficulties will require a multi-method approach that combines information distributed online with other methodological approaches depending on the specific questions researchers have in mind.

## Notes

1. Other microblogging sites include Tumblr, FriendFeed and Quaiku.
2. The term 'Web 2.0' is derived from O'Reilly Media's Web 2.0 Conference. Tim O'Reilly, in his article 'What Is Web 2.0?' defines Web 2.0 as an upgraded computer-programming model that has enabled a set of participatory websites built on lightweight server-based applications that move rich data across platforms (Mandiberg 2012).
3. Twitter usage is highly correlated with the use of mobile technologies and especially smartphones. According to a recent report by the Pew Internet and American Life Project, in the United States 'one in five smartphone owners (20 per cent) are Twitter users with 13 per cent using the service on a typical day' (Rainie and Smith 2012).
4. For an analysis of Twitter's community-building capacities by fostering connections between different groups of people see Gruzd et al. 2011).
5. The KONY 2012 campaign, organised by the Invisible Children charity, was presented as an attempt to make famous and stop a war criminal by means of an online video. On 12 March, the magazine TIME declared it the 'most viral video in history' and the own organisation states that the experience resulted in 3.7 million people supporting their efforts (see http://invisiblechildren.com/kony/).
6. *El País*, 17 May 2011. See also the report by Calvo et al. (2011) for more information about the movements' composition.
7. According to a Metroscopia survey conducted in June, 66 per cent of the respondents expressed sympathy with the movement while 81 per cent agreed that the motivations for protesting were right (Calvo et al. 2011; Castells 2012).
8. Slight variations of each hashtag due to the use (or not) of capitals are also included in the database.
9. The large difference in the frequency of Tweets across the movements could just be the result of their size. For example, if we would expect the number of Tweets to reflect the population of each country we should find that 13 per cent come from Spain, 3 per cent from Greece and 84 per cent from the United States. This implies that Greek and Spanish movements are over-represented in 2 and 5 per cent, respectively, but overall the percentages are very similar to each country's population.
10. In practice, random numbers were applied directly to all the tweets in the list. We then selected those tweets with random numbers between 1 and 2000. We used the simple random sample procedure without replacement. That is to say, since by chance the same element can be chosen more than

once, we did not select it twice into the sample. Instead, we kept selecting until we had 2000 distinct elements.

11. A clear elaboration of the subcategories and the instructions provided to the coders is available in the codebook. In the interest of space, the codebook is not presented here but can be made available upon request.
12. As discussed below, tweets in the sample were not always written in the main language of the movement (Greek, Spanish or English). Particularly, the Greek database included 48 per cent of tweets in a language other than Greek. Those written in English (34 per cent of the sample) were also analysed, the rest were considered missing cases. For this reason, Tables 5.4–5.8 do not sum 6000 units but 5.382.
13. Specifically, the average agreement was of 65 per cent for the categories Action, Evaluation and Purpose. Regarding Action the low reliability was due to the ambiguous usage of some of the categories such as demonstrations, rallies or sit-ins. To increase the reliability we decided to merge these categories in the more general one street action. Evaluation of the movement (whether the tweet showed some clear support or opposition to the movement) turned out to be the most difficult category since many tweets were not explicit enough. For this reason an additional coding option 'unclear' was proposed to the coders so that they would not have to interpret incomplete information. The third category with lower agreement was the purpose of the tweet due to the large number of possible categories (up to 16 different possible values). Some of these values implied small differences so the resulting analyses are run on broader categories. All other categories had higher percentages of agreement, like 75 per cent for the type of link included or 80 per cent regarding the topic of the Tweet.
14. The actual percentages of agreement were as follows. For the Greek dataset the agreement between pairs was of 94 per cent for the type of action, 94 per cent the type of sender, 83 per cent the evaluation of the movement (note that the reliability is much higher here in comparison to the English-speaking tweets after including the option 'unclear' to the coders), 84 per cent for purpose, 84 per cent topic, 78 per cent issue and 94 per cent the link target type. The same information for the Spanish dataset is: 87 per cent action, 94 per cent sender type, 87 per cent evaluation, 90 per cent purpose, 87 per cent topic, 83 per cent issue, 97 per cent link target type.
15. The finding that in Greece the most frequent purpose of the tweets was 'Conversation' could seem contradictory with the expectation – and overall interpretation – that tweeting in Greece took a less conversational form than in Spain or the United States (see also Table 5.2). To clarify this issue we examined if those tweets were actually directed to someone else, implying political discussion, or not. To do so we analysed whether those tweets coded as 'conversation' were directed to a specific user – including @user – finding that indeed most of those tweets where directed to someone in Spain (81 per cent) and the United States (69.7 per cent), but that percentage is significantly smaller in Greece (47 per cent). This implies that more than half of the 26 per cent tweets coded as conversation in the Greek movement were an individual expression of opinions or preferences but did not have the intention of discussing issues with other users.
16. By 'virtual action', we refer to any political activity that is realised online.

17. All our coders had a good knowledge of English and they were instructed to also code tweets in other languages in which they felt comfortable with.

## References


Anduiza, E., Jensen, M.J. and Jorba, L. (eds.) (2012) *Digital Media and Political Engagement Worldwide: A Comparative Study* (Cambridge: Cambridge University Press).

Barber, B. (2004) *Strong Democracy: Participatory Politics for a New Age* (Berkeley: University of California Press).

Barnes, S.H., Kaase, M. et al. (eds.) (1979) *Political Action: Mass Participation in Five Western Democracies* (Beverly Hills, CA: Sage).

Bennett, W.L. and Segerberg, A. (2012) 'The Logic of Collective Action', *Information, Communication & Society,* 15 (5), 739–768.

Bennett, W.L. and Segerberg, A. (2011) 'Digital Media and the Personalization of Collective Action: Social Technology and the Organization of Protests Against the Global Economic Crisis', *Information Communication & Society,* 14 (6), 770–799.

Bimber, B., Flanagin, A.J. and Stohl, C. (2009) 'Technological Change and the Shifting Nature of Political Organisation', in A. Chadwick and P. Howard (eds.), *Routledge Handbook of Internet Politics* (London: Routledge), pp. 72–85.

Boyd, D.M. and Ellison, N.B. (2007) 'Social Network Sites: Definition, History, and Scholarship', *Journal of Computer-Mediated Communication,* 13 (1), 1–22.

Boyd, D. and Crawford, K. (2012) 'Critical Questions for Big Data. Provocations for a Cultural, Technological, and Scholarly Phenomenon', *Information Communication & Society,* 15 (5), 662–679.

Calvo, K., Gómez-Pastrana, T., Jiménez, M.S. and Mena, L. (2011) 'Movimiento 15M: Quiénes son y qué Reivindican?' [15M Movement: who are they and their demands?] *Zoom Político,* Fundación Alternativas, no. 2011/04.

Castells, M. (2001) *The Internet Galaxy: Reflections in the Internet, Business and Society* (Oxford: Oxford University Press).

Castells, M. (2012) *Networks of Outrage and Hope: Social Movements in the Internet Age* (London: Polity Press).

Centro de Investigaciones Sociológicas (2011) 'Barómetro junio 2011', [Barometer June 2011], available at: http://www.cis.es, date accessed 1 July 2011.

Chadwick, A. (2012) 'Recent Shifts in the Relationship Between the Internet and Democratic Engagement in Britain and the United States: Granularity, Informational Exuberance and Political Learning', in E. Anduiza, M.J. Jensen and L. Jorba (eds.), *Digital Media and Political Engagement Worldwide: A Comparative Study* (Cambridge: Cambridge University Press), pp. 39–55.

Chew, C. and Eysenbach, G. (2010) 'Pandemics in the Age of Twitter: Content Analysis of Tweets During the 2009 H1N1 outbreak', *PLoS ONE,* 5 (11), e14118.

Coleman, S. and Shane, P. (eds.) (2012) *Connecting Democracy: Online Consultation and the Flow of Political Communication* (Cambridge: MIT Press).

Dalton, R. (2008) *The Good Citizen: How a Younger Generation is Reshaping America* (Washington: CQ Press).

Dimitrova, D.V., Shehata, A., Strömbäck, J. and Nord, L. (2011) 'The Effects of Digital Media on Political Knowledge and Participation in Election

Campaigns: Evidence from Panel Data', *Communication Research,* available at: http://crx.sagepub.com/content/early/2011/11/02/0093650211426004.abstract
D'Orazio, D. (2012) 'Twitter Breaks 400 million Tweet-per-day Barrier, sees Increasing Mobile Revenue', *The Verge,* available at: http://www.theverge.com/2012/6/6/3069424/twitter-400-million-total-daily-tweets, date accessed 6 June 2012.
Dugan, L. (2012) 'Twitter to Surpass 500 million Registered Users on Wednesday', *Mediabistro,* available at: http://www.mediabistro.com/alltwitter/500-million-registered-users_b18842, date accessed 21 February 2012.
Earl, J. and Kimport, K. (2011) *Digitally Enabled Social Change: Activism in the Internet Age* (Cambridge: MIT Press).
Esfandiari, G. (2010) *The Twitter Devolution, Foreign Policy,* available at: http://www.foreignpolicy.com/articles/2010/06/07/the_twitter_revolution_that_wasnt, date accessed 7 June 2010.
Farrell, H. (2012) 'The Consequences of the Internet for Politics', *Annual Review of Political Science,* 15, 35–52.
Finkel, S.E., Muller, E.N. and Opp, K-D. (1989) 'Personal Influence, Collective Rationality and Mass Political Action', *American Political Science Review,* 83 (3), 885–903.
Gladwell, M. (2010) 'Why the revolution will not be tweeted', *New Yorker,* 4 October, available at: http://www.newyorker.com/reporting/2010/10/04/101004fa_fact_gladwell.
González-Bailón, S., Borge-Holthoefer, J., Rivero, A. and Moreno, Y. (2011) 'The Dynamics of Protest Recruitment Through an Online Network', *Scientific Reports,* 1 (197), available at: http://www.nature.com/srep/2011/111215/srep00197/full/srep00197.html
Groves, R.M., Fowler, F.J., Couper, M.P., Lepknowski, J.M., Singer, E. and Tourangeau, R. (2004) *Survey Methodology* (New Jersey: John Wiley and Sons).
Gruzd, A., Wellman, B. and Takhteyev, Y. (2011) 'Imagining Twitter as an Imagined Community', *American Behavioral Scientist,* 55 (10), 1294–1318.
Howard, P.N. (2010) *The Digital Origins of Dictatorship and Democracy: Information Technology and Political Islam* (New York: Oxford University Press).
Inglehart, R.F. (1990) *Culture Shift in Advanced Industrial Society* (Princeton, NJ: Princeton University Press).
Java, A., Song, X., Finin, T. and Tseng, B. (2007) 'Why We Twitter: Understanding Microblogging Usage and Communities', Paper Presented at the Joint 9th WEBKDD and 1st SNA-KDD Workshop '07, San Jose, California, USA.
Jennings, M.K. and van Deth, J.W. (eds.) (1990) *Continuities in Political Action. A Longitudinal Study of Political Participation in Three Western Democracies* (Berlin and New York: de Gruyter).
Kriesi, H. (1995) 'The Political Opportunity Structure of New Social Movements: Its Impact on their Mobilization', in C. Jenkins and B. Klandermans (eds.), *The Politics of Social Protest* (Minneapolis: University of Minnesota Press), 167–198.
Kwak, H., Lee, C., Park, H. and Moon, S. (2010) 'What is Twitter, a Social Network or a News Media?' Proceedings of the 19th International Conference on World Wide Web, Raleigh, North Carolina, USA.
Leyne, J. (2010) 'How Iran's political battle is fought in cyberspace', *BBC Online,* available at: http://news.bbc.co.uk/2/hi/middle_east/8505645.stm, date accessed 11 February 2010.

Lotan, G., Graeff, E., Ananny, M., Gaffney, D., Pearce, I. and Boyd, D. (2011) 'The Revolutions were Tweeted: Information Flows During the 2011 Tunisian and Egyptian Revolutions', *International Journal of Communication,* 5, 1375–1405.

Madianou, M. and Miller, D. (2013) 'Polymedia: Towards a New Theory of Digital Media in Interpersonal Communication', *International Journal of Cultural Studies,* 16 (2), 169–187.

Mandiberg, M. (2012) *The Social Media Reader* (New York: New York University Press).

Margetts, H., Hale, S., Dunleavy, P. and Tinkler, J. (2012) 'Designing the State for Essentially Digital Governance and the Era of Big Data', Paper Presented at the International Political Science Association XXII World Congress of Political Science, July 2012, Madrid, Spain.

Mattes, R. and Bratton, M. (2007) 'Learning about Democracy in Africa: Awareness, Performance and Experience', *American Journal of Political Science,* 51 (1), 192–217.

McAdam, D. (1996) 'The Framing Function of Movement Tactics: Strategic Dramaturgy in the American Civil Rights Movement', in D. McAdam, J.D. McCarthy and M.N. Zald (eds.), *Comparative Perspectives on Social Movements: Opportunities, Mobilizing Structures, and Framing* (Cambridge: Cambridge University Press), pp. 338–355.

McCaughey, M. and Ayers, M. (2003) *Cyberactivism: Online Activism in Theory and Practice* (New York: Routledge).

Micheletti, M. and McFarland, A. (eds.) (2010) *Creative Participation. Responsibility-taking in the Political World* (Boulder and London: Paradigm Publishers).

Morozov, E. (2011) *The Net Delusion: How not to Liberate the World* (London: Allen Lane).

Muller, E.N. and Opp, K-D. (1986) 'Rational Choice and Rebellious Collective Action', *The American Political Science Review,* 80 (2), 471–488.

Norris, P. (2002) *Democratic Phoenix. Reinventing Political Activism* (Cambridge: Cambridge University Press).

Oates, S., Owen, D. and Gibson, R. (eds.) (2006) *The Internet and Politics: Citizens, Voters and Activists* (London: Routledge).

Opp, K.-D. and Hartmann, P. (1989) *The Rationality of Political Protest: A Comparative Analysis of Rational Choice Theory* (Boulder: Westview Press).

Papacharissi, Z. and Oliveira, M.d.F. (2012) 'Affective News and Networked Publics: The Rhythms of News Storytelling on #Egypt', *Journal of Communication,* 62 (2), 266–282.

Public Issue (2011) 'Flash Βαρόμετρο 159: Το κίνημα των Αγανακτισμένων Πολιτών' [Flash barometer 159: The movement of indignant citizens], available at: http://www.publicissue.gr/wp-content/uploads/2011/06/plateies-6-20111.pdf

Rainie, L., and Smith, A. (2012). Social Networking Sites and Politics. *Pew Internet Project,* available at: http://blogs.searchenginewiki.pewinternet.com/~/media/Files/Reports/2012/PIP_SNS_and_politics.pdf

Rainie, L. and Wellman, B. (2012) *The New Social Operating System* (Cambridge, MA: MIT Press).

Rainie, L., Smith, A., Schlozman, K.L., Brady, H.E. and Verba, S. (2012). *Social Media and Political Engagement,* available at: http://pewinternet.org/Reports/2012/Political-engagement.aspx

Richards, J. and Lewis, P. (2011) How Twitter was used to Spread – and Knock Down – Rumours During the Riots, *The Guardian*, 7 December, available at: http://www.guardian.co.uk/uk/2011/dec/07/how-twitter-spread-rumours-riots date accessed 7 December 2011.

Shirky, C. (2011) 'The Political Power of Social Media', *Foreign Affairs,* 90 (1), 28–41.

Smith, A. and Brenner, J. (2012) 'Twitter use 2012', *Pew Internet and American Life Project,* Pew Research Center, available at: http://pewinternet.org/Reports/2012/Twitter-Use-2012.aspx, date accessed 31 May 2011.

Smith, A. and Rainie, L. (2008) 'The internet and the 2008 election', *Pew Internet and American Life Project,* Pew Research Center, available at: http://www.pewinternet.org/Reports/2008/The-Internet-and-the-2008-Election.aspx, date accessed 15 June 2008.

Social-Media Observatory (2012) *Just by Chance? Sentimeter Correctly Predicts #USA2012's final results,* Università degli Studi di Milano, available at: http://voicesfromtheblogs.com/2012/11/07/just-by-chance-sentimeter-correctly-predicts-usa2012s-final-results, /date accessed 7 November 2012.

Sunstein, C. (2008) *Republic.com 2.0* (Princeton: Princeton University Press).

Takhteyev, Y., Gruzd, A. and Wellman, B. (2012) 'Geography of Twitter Networks', *Social Networks,* 34 (1), 73–81.

Tarrow, S. (1996) 'States and Opportunities: The Political Structuring of Social Movements', in D. McAdam, J.D. McCarthy and M.N. Zald (eds.), *Comparative Perspectives on Social Movements: Opportunities, Mobilizing Structures, and Framing* (Cambridge: Cambridge University Press), pp. 41–61.

Theocharis, Y. (2013) 'The Wealth of (Occupation) Networks? Communication Patterns and Information Distribution in a Twitter Protest Network', *Journal of Information Technology & Politics,* 10 (1), 35–56.

Tsaliki, L. (2010) 'Technologies of Political Mobilization and Civil Society in Greece: The Wildfires of Summer 2007', *Convergence,* 16 (2), 151–161.

Tufekci, Z. and Wilson, C. (2012) 'Social Media and the Decision to Participate in Political Protest: Observations from Tahrir Square', *Journal of Communication,* 62 (2), 363–379.

Tumasjan, A., Sprenger, T.O., Sandner, P.G. and Welpe, I.M. (2010) 'Predicting Elections with Twitter: What 140 Characters Reveal about Political Sentiment', *Proceedings of the Fourth International AAAI Conference on Weblogs and Social Media,* pp. 178–185, available at: http://www.Aaai.org/ocs/index.php/ICWSM/ICWSM10/paper/viewFile/1441/1852

Valenzuela, S., Park, N. and Kee, K.F. (2009) 'Is there Social Capital in a Social Network Site? Facebook use and College Students' Life Satisfaction, Trust, and Participation', *Journal of Computer-Mediated Communication,* 14 (4), 875–901.

van de Donk, W., Loader, B.D., Nixon, P.G. and Rucht, D. (eds.) (2004) *Cyberprotest: New Media, Citizens, and Social Movements* (London: Routledge).

Van Laer, J. and Van Aelst, P. (2010) 'Internet and Social Movement Action Repertoires: Opportunities and Limitations', *Information' Communication & Society,* 13 (8), 1146–1171.

Walgrave, S. and Rucht, D. (2010) *The World Says no to War: Demonstrations Against the War on Iraq,* (Minneapolis: University of Minnesota Press).

Waters, R.D. and Williams, J.M. (2011) 'Squawking, Tweeting, Cooing, and Hooting: Analyzing the Communication Patterns of Government Agencies on Twitter', *Journal of Public Affairs,* 11 (4), 353–363.
Yardi, S. and Boyd, D. (2010) 'Dynamic Debates: An Analysis of Group Polarization Over Time on Twitter', *Bulletin of Science, Technology & Society,* 30 (5), 316–327.

# 6

# Stuttgart's Black Thursday on Twitter: Mapping Political Protests with Social Media Data

*Andreas Jungherr and Pascal Jürgens*

Event detection based on textual data is an approach often used in the social sciences. The method has been used predominantly in the fields of international politics (Schrodt 2010) and public opinion research (Landmann and Zuell 2008). Event detection presupposes that major events leave traces in textual documents. By automatically identifying events in publicly available documents, researchers can establish timelines of events relevant to their research. For example, in international politics, researchers work on how to reliably identify political actors, time and topics from official documents, hoping to establish comprehensive and detailed maps of international treaties and conflicts. Based on these maps, they aim to develop models of the dynamics of conflict (Brandt et al. 2011). In public opinion research, one goal is to automatically deduce major events from newspaper coverage. This might be a first step in calculating the impact of these events on changes in public opinion (Landmann and Zuell 2008).

Most research in this area has focused on event detection based on textual data that filter events through structured reports, be it official documents or newspaper articles (Allan 2002; Kleinberg 2003). This has the benefit that researchers are able to analyse a textual corpus focusing on relevant aspects of an event. The authors of these documents (that is, officials and journalists), edited these texts consciously so that they contain relevant information. Thus researchers focusing on these documents potentially find a high signal to noise ratio (that is, relevant information to irrelevant information) in these documents. But exactly the process of filtering relevant information by authors removes these documents one step from the actual events themselves. Official documents or newspaper articles often offer a summary of relevant actors, events or outcomes of a topic under investigation. They are after-the-fact accounts, not observations of unfolding events. Thus potentially relevant steps of the event might be missing in these accounts and remain hidden in analyses based on them. For a researcher interested in regular dynamics of conflicts and treaties, this might seem a reasonable trade-off, but for those interested in the dynamics of protest, the chain of micro-events that constitute a protest event might hold important meaning. Clearly, the analysis of textual data closer to the events of interest holds potential for social scientists. The ever-growing adoption of social media services provides researchers with data of that kind.

Increasingly, people use social media services to document their lives, comment on events or communicate with each other. Although this activity can come in many forms (for example, a user might take a photo of a protester being carried away by the police and directly post it on a photo-sharing service, or instead she might use her mobile phone to film the incident and post it on a video-sharing site), most of it will come in the form of time-coded textual status updates that lend themselves to computer-assisted analysis (for example, a user writes a short update on her Twitter feed that the police is carrying protesters away). Analysing these data offers researchers a closer look at the steps that constitute an event, for example a protest. Unfortunately, this benefit is offset by the noise of unrelated information that surrounds the information of interest. Most social media users do not attempt to document events impartially as they unfold. Most users post updates on mundane details of their lives. They are not necessarily journalists but might be passers-by or participants in social events. Still they might document parts of these events on social media channels. Thus unintentionally each user becomes a sensor of her surroundings. The challenge for researchers attempting to use social media data to document socially relevant events is to cut through the noise of unrelated information and identify those pieces of text that hold meaning.

In this chapter, we show that the analysis of messages published on the microblogging service Twitter can be used to establish a timeline for political events. We analyse Twitter messages by the 80,000 most prominent Twitter users in Germany. In our analysis we focus only on messages commenting on the highly contentious protest against the controversial project 'Stuttgart 21' in the night of 30 September going on 1 October 2010. 'Stuttgart 21' provides us with a case study that shows the potential of event detection with data collected from social media services. We identified relevant tweets by their use of the hashtag #s21.

On 30 September and 1 October 2010 46,789 Twitter messages containing the hashtag #s21 were posted by 7793 of the Twitter users in our sample. In our analysis the protests of that night reacting to the project 'Stuttgart 21' become the event. We are trying to identify the steps contributing to this event by the analysis of the 46,789 Twitter messages containing the hashtag #s21.

For our analysis we use four different approaches to event detection and compare their results. These approaches look for local maxima in the total volume of messages, the first occurrences of messages that were highly retweeted, the first occurrences of URLs on the Internet that were highly linked to and finally by the examination of words that were only prominent during specific time intervals of the protest (Shamma et al. 2011). We show that the microblogging service Twitter is a valuable tool for the mapping of political events.

## Twitter as data source for event detection

The growing use of online tools and social media services has provided companies and researchers with an ever-increasing amount of rich data on human behaviour. Specifically data collected on the microblogging service Twitter (http://twitter.com) has become the focus of various research projects.

Twitter enables users to post short text messages (up to 140 characters in length) on personalised profiles. These Twitter feeds and the messages posted on them have URLs and are publicly accessible. The exceptions are cases in which users explicitly state that their feed is private and thus only accessible to users previously approved by them. Twitter users are able to subscribe to other Twitter-feeds to regularly receive updates. Thus each Twitter account is connected to accounts of users whose owner subscribed to (in Twitter terms 'following') and the accounts of users who decided to subscribe to it ('followers'). The limit of 140 characters per message led to the widespread adoption of usage conventions in which regularly used abbreviations help to discern meaning. If users want to post a Twitter message on a given topic they use a keyword or commonly agreed upon abbreviation and precede it with a '#' (hashtag, for example, tweets commenting on the project 'Stuttgart 21' were marked by the hashtag #s21). This convention helps researchers to automatically identify tweets reacting to specific events, commenting on topics, or adding to a meme. If a user chooses to write a public message directed to another user she can do so by preceding the message with an '@' followed by the username of the addressed person. If a user reads a tweet which she thinks important or witty and wants to bring it to the attention of her followers, she can do so by retweeting it. She can do this by copying the original message preceded by the abbreviation 'RT' – for retweet – followed by '@' and the username of the original author. These two conventions – @message and retweet – enable researchers to extract social networks formed by communication activities by users. This is a powerful addition to the examination of follower/following networks of Twitter users.

Researchers are able to access Twitter's data with various approaches. This chapter cannot offer a systematic overview on different approaches to collect data from Twitter, but two approaches seem to dominate the relevant literature. One approach is to use Twitter's API (application programming interface). An API provides outsiders with standardised access to a service's databases. The API provides researchers with the message, the username of its author, a unique time stamp, the name of the third-party service the message was posted with, and the location where the tweet was sent from (provided a user enabled the geolocation option). Twitter started out with a relatively open data access policy that allowed users to run up to 2000 queries per hour on Twitter's search API. This type of access is no longer provided; instead there are stricter (but unspecified) numbers of queries one can run on Twitter's search API. In addition to this, Twitter offers access to random samples of the total stream of Twitter messages that provide users with a fixed percentage of the total amount of messages posted. It is difficult to determine the data quality provided by the Twitter API. There are indicators that the Twitter API provides researchers with systematically divergent data, dependent on whether researchers used search queries or accessed the sample stream. If unacknowledged, these differences can lead to biased results (González-Bailón et al. 2012). Without access to Twitter's infrastructure, the precise nature of the sampling algorithm cannot be verified. Our dataset is based on a now defunct sampling mechanism which Twitter describes as merely selecting the first N of 100 tweets (White et al. 2012). The ID values of tweets used to increase linearly. Twitter's sampling algorithm then selected messages by calculating the modulus and returning tweets with certain remainder values, depending on the user's access level. All in all we are fairly confident that there is no significant impact of the sampling methodology on our dataset, especially since we only used it in order to bootstrap our own sample of German users. The messages of these users were collected independently of Twitter's random messages sample (see below).

Another approach is the use of third party applications that collect data on Twitter (for example, by using the Twitter API, by scraping Twitter's openly accessible websites, etc.). These applications offer researchers ease of use but potentially introduce a new black box in the data acquisition process. Still, tools like DiscoverText (http://discovertext.com) or yourTwapperKeeper (https://github.com/jobrieniii/yourTwapperKeeper) (Bruns and Liang 2012) are becoming increasingly popular among researchers. A systematic comparison of data provided by these services and the Twitter API remains to be done to assess the potentials and problems associated with each approach. We collected the data here by using Twitter's streaming API.

Research focusing on Twitter could be grouped in three approaches: research interested in specific usage practices and the adoption of Twitter in various communities (Crawford 2009; Marwick and Boyd 2011); research interested in network structures on Twitter and information flows through these networks (Cha et al. 2010; Jürgens et al. 2011); and research interested in using Twitter data to analyse or predict human behaviour and events offline (Asur and Huberman 2010; Chew and Eysenbach 2010; Gayo-Avello et al. 2011; Jungherr and Jürgens 2013). This research clearly falls in the third group.

The idea behind research using Twitter data to detect major events is that each Twitter user is a sensor that documents their observations of reality in their messages. While most of these messages might document mundane details of their daily activities, others might address a social event the user might participate in or an event they accidentally witnessed. For events with high popular appeal, such as TV-shows, or the death of a celebrity, or social relevance e.g. political protests, or natural disasters, it is reasonable to assume that many Twitter users tweet their reactions or observations. In the process of formulating their individual observations of the unfolding events they necessarily code their subjective impressions in a common vocabulary. This makes them automatically identifiable as signals referring to the same object. The sudden increase in messages on a certain event or topic produces automatically discernible patterns since these messages typically share attributes in semantic structure, their vocabulary, the use of hashtags, time stamps or linked content. Thus social events leave an imprint in Twitter data through clearly identifiable clusters of similar messages, which in turn might be automatically detected.

Various research communities have approached event detection with Twitter data with different aims. Some researchers try to detect potentially catastrophic events as they are unfolding and thus use Twitter as an early warning system (Sakaki et al. 2010) or to increase situational awareness in emergencies or humanitarian missions (Verma et al. 2011). Researchers also tried to use Twitter messages to determine the structure of big broadcast events based on the dynamic and persistence of spikes in the use of event specific terms (Shamma et al. 2009; Shamma et al. 2011). Other researchers work on event detection algorithms in the hope of improving real-time search results with Twitter data (Petrovic et al. 2010; Becker et al. 2011; Chakrabarti and Punera 2011; Weng and Lee 2011).

The obvious potential of Twitter as a data source on human behaviour and interests should not blind us to the fact that Twitter's user base is still comparatively small and far from representative (Smith and Brenner 2012). Attempting to draw conclusions on behaviours or interests of the population of a given country based merely on data produced by Twitter users of that country seems highly optimistic (Jungherr et al. 2012). So far, only a few studies have looked at the specific socio demographic composition of Twitter users. Their results suggest that Twitter users in a given country are – at least at this point in the adoption process – far from representative of other Internet users and the population as a whole (Busemann and Gscheidle 2012; Smith and Brenner 2012). This does not invalidate research based on Twitter data, but it means that researchers have to pay special attention to the interpretation of their results.

For the purposes of this chapter we are interested in whether Twitter data allow the automated mapping of events during the unfolding of a political protest. This seems a sensible proposition since Twitter has become a very popular tool for users to comment on politicians, campaigns or political events in a range of countries (Bruns and Burgess 2011; González-Bailón et al. 2011; Jürgens and Jungherr 2011; Jackson and Lilleker 2011; Segerberg and Bennett 2011; Smith 2011; Vergeer et al. 2011; Jürgens and Jungherr 2014). For our research here, the non-representativeness of Twitter users is not an issue. We use Twitter data to examine if patterns in messages addressing the protests against 'Stuttgart 21' (#s21) correspond to offline events. To answer our question we do not need representativeness, we need a high volume of messages. Our analysis becomes possible since 'Stuttgart 21' – as we will show – generated interest among German Twitter users. They commented on the events as they were unfolding. This is positive but does not have to be true for other political events.

## Four approaches to event detection with twitter

In this chapter we look at data documenting all Twitter messages containing the hashtag #s21 on 30 September and 1 October 2010 when major protests took place against 'Stuttgart 21'. We then examine whether different analytical approaches show patterns that correspond to the occurrence of discrete developments in the actual protests. Our main objective is to analyse the potential benefits and limits of different approaches to event detection using Twitter data. It is important to note that we use data on an event that happened in the past. Our analytical approaches can rely on the fact that data patterns at any given point of our analysis can be compared to data patterns at all other points during the time span of interest. This facilitates the analysis. There are other attempts by researchers that use different approaches to event detection in real time (Chakrabarti and Punera 2011; Nikolov 2012). To us this seems motivated less by the attempt to determine the structure of offline events through patterns in online data but more by using online data to determine the most important topics of online buzz at any given moment. The question we are addressing is not 'how can we accurately measure or predict levels of online buzz?' but 'is it possible to detect meaningful events based on the analysis of online data, specifically Twitter?' For our goals, the use of data sets documenting discrete events in the past seems unproblematic.

We compare the results of four approaches to event detection with Twitter data: local maxima in the total volume of messages; the first occurrences of messages that were highly retweeted; the first occurrences of URLs that were highly linked to; and, finally, by the examination of words that were only prominent during specific time intervals of the protest.

- Volume: this approach is solely concerned with the volume of messages and local maxima. This follows a simple assumption: the more users talk about a topic (measured by hashtags), the more important that topic is. By extension, the more they talk about it at a certain point in time, the more important or salient the topic is at this particular moment. While this approach is rather simplistic, there are still valid inferences to be drawn from it. For example, the mere fact that messages using a given hashtag follow a distinct pattern can often be directly interpreted. A sudden rise in tweets will signify rising interest and potentially point to a cause that at first glance might remain invisible to the analyst.
- RTs: this approach focuses only on the occurrence of those tweets that were reposted (retweeted) the most. The premise is that users

will select and redistribute tweets with especially high informative value or of high novelty value. These tweets might potentially refer to key events during the protest.

- URLs: another approach using the same logic focuses on the most popular URLs that were linked to in messages containing the hashtag #s21. This approach offers further information as it might be that digital traces found on Twitter only echo existing reports by established mass media. Thus event detection with social media data would be redundant to event detection based on news reports. If this were true, we expect two observations in the results provided by URLs: (1) time stamps indicated by the first occurrences of popular URLs should be delayed in comparison to the actual protests and possibly also in comparison to the time stamps as provided by local maxima in volume; and (2) most of the salient URLs should link to web pages of established media.
- Peakiness: this term describes an approach introduced by Shamma, Kennedy and Churchill (2011) that offers a less simplistic approach to event detection than the former. Shamma, Kennedy and Churchill introduce the 'peakiness' value as the number of word occurrences within a time window divided by the number of occurrences within the entire reference time span. The value (ranging from zero to one) denotes how densely the use of a word is 'lumped together' in time. A peakiness of .5 means that half of the total uses of a word appear within one time window. Thus it is possible to identify the appearance of new and rare words during a short time span. In our case we can expect that words are very peaky if a clearly named object or action is only referred to during a discrete time span in the complete run of the protests. At the same time, terms which are mentioned more or less constantly are spread out during the whole time span and hence not peaky. The substantial benefit for the detection of discrete steps in an event is that even keywords with a clear relation to the protests are filtered out if they are used ubiquitously. As we will show, there are several of these steps that can be successfully identified through the peaky characteristics of words referring to them.

While the concept of peakiness has advantages, its general applicability remains to be shown. The use of this approach forces researchers to make choices in order to get promising results with their respective data sets. Most notably, researchers will want to set a minimum peakiness threshold for word stems indicating discrete steps of an event in question. Second, the time window for which the peakiness value of a word is calculated has to be chosen carefully: if too small, there may not be any term whose mentions are packed enough to fit into one window, so peakiness will be low overall. If the time window is too long, not much insight into an event can be gained. Additionally, the value obviously depends on the total length and volume of a sample. This means that different datasets can only be compared if some sort of normalisation is used.

We calculated the peakiness of word stems (for example, 'Baum' and its plural, 'Bäume' were counted as multiple occurrences of the same word), hashtags and URLs. We systematically varied the time window for our analysis between one to four hours and compared peakiness results. We found that for our time span of two days and the nature of the events documented by our data, the most relevant results were obtained for time windows of one hour.

## Stuttgart 21

One of Germany's most contentiously discussed topics in 2010 was an infrastructure project in Stuttgart called 'Stuttgart 21'. Stuttgart is a town in the southwest of Germany and the state capital of Baden-Württemberg. 'Stuttgart 21' (#s21) is an infrastructure project with the plan to move Stuttgart's central train station underground to increase its transit capacity. Since its inception in the early 1990s the project has met with strong resistance that reached its zenith in the second half of 2010 with regular demonstrations attended by participants in the tens of thousands. The protests attracted massive attention on various social media channels by both protesters and supporters. This makes 'Stuttgart 21' a promising object to test the mapping of campaigns based on social media data (for a comprehensive discussion of the protests see Gabriel et al. 2013).

From the night of 30 September to 1 October 2010 the protests escalated. Under police protection construction workers started cutting down trees. This led to heavy clashes between police and protesters during which up to 400 people were injured (sueddeutsche.de 2010). The following day, in reaction to the clashes of the night before, between 50,000 and 100,000 (the sources vary) protesters took to the streets (Ternieden 2010). Shortly after the night, that day became known as Black Thursday (Bilger and Raidt 2011). Messages posted on Twitter during this night serve as the basis of our analysis.

Both protesters and supporters of 'Stuttgart 21' relied heavily on social media tools for organisation and visibility during the protests (Jakat 2010; Mader 2010). To mark content relevant to 'Stuttgart 21' both protesters and supporters used the hashtag #s21. In their use of Twitter the protests against 'Stuttgart 21' followed other political campaigns in Germany and Austria; beginning in the summer of 2009 with the #zensursula campaign against a law enabling the blocking of access to websites hosting child pornography (Bieber 2010, 54–60), the #yeaahh flashmobs during the 2009 campaign for the federal election in Germany (Jungherr 2012), the #unibrennt protests for better university education (Maireder and Schwarzenegger 2011) and the supporter campaign of Jochaim Gauck (#mygauck) during the run up to the election of Germany's Bundespräsident (President) in 2010 (Hoffmann 2010). Thus when the protesters against 'Stuttgart 21' started using social media the use of online tools for political movements was well established in Germany and applicable to the protests in Stuttgart (Schimmelpfennig 2010; Stegers 2010).

Social media activity reached its high point in reaction to the events during the night of September 30. Long before TV stations started to cover the protests, protesters themselves streamed video footage via mobile phones (Kuhn 2010). An aggregation site started to collect relevant videos (http://www.cams21.de) to provide a 'mosaic' of the events (Wienand 2010). Together with Twitter messages from the ground these videos documented the events as they unfolded and were quickly linked by German Twitter users. This led to the high visibility of the events well beyond the immediate vicinity of Stuttgart (Reißmann 2010). The intensive coverage on blogs, Twitter, and Facebook quickly led social media users in Germany to take notice of the events in Stuttgart. An impressive amount of ad hoc analyses and link lists followed, which documented and collected the reactions online (Bunse 2010; Pfeiffer 2010a, 2010b).

Both, the nature of the event – a political protest that during the run of two days went through several discrete stages – and the intensive coverage of the events by social media users make the protests of the night of 30 September to 1 October an ideal topic to test the potential of event detection with Twitter data.

## Data acquisition and preparation

As described above, we used the Twitter streaming API to collect the data for this chapter. We focus on messages sent by Twitter users in

Germany. Twitter does not require its users to state their nationality or current location reliably. The service merely encourages its users to provide some information relating to their location on their user profiles along with their local time zone. We used this information and Twitter's random sample stream to construct our sample of German Twitter users. We approached this task in three stages:

- Collecting random tweets from the Twitter streaming API;
- Checking for hints regarding the nationality of the users posting these random tweets. In our case, we performed three checks. We assumed users to be German if they matched any of the following criteria: (1) they had their location set to one of Germany's 10,000 most populous cities (2) their time zone contained 'Germany', 'Deutschland' or 'Berlin' or (3) they used the letter 'ß' (a letter only used in Germany and Austria).
- Once we identified a user as German we collected their followers and those users they themselves followed. With these users we then ran the checks of step 2. This first-degree snowball sample significantly sped up the bootstrapping process and served to identify users who posted less often (and hence whose messages might not appear in Twitter's random sample).

We stopped this sampling process only after three consecutive days yielded less than a 0.1 per cent increase in the number of users identified as German. Once the size of the identified German Twitter population had stabilised, we ranked the users by the number of their followers. The top 80,000 Twitter users, identified by this procedure, constitute our sample of Germany's most prominent Twitters users. For this group, we analysed all published messages on 30 September 2010 and 1 October 2010 (for a more detailed description of the sample as well as empirical tests, see Jürgens 2010).

On these two days the 80,000 German Twitter users in our sample posted 803,201 tweets. 7793 Twitter users of our initial sample of 80,000 posted at least one message containing the hashtag #s21. In total 46,789 Twitter messages included #s21 (see Figure 6.1). When looking at the data we see a strong cyclical pattern of Twitter messages corresponding with day and night rhythms, while most Twitter messages were posted during working hours (this corresponds with findings of Golder and Macy 2011).

In this timeframe, #s21 was by far the most popular #hashtag (46,789 mentions), followed by the longstanding Twitter usage convention 'follow friday' #ff (12,637 mentions), and hashtags identifying tweets

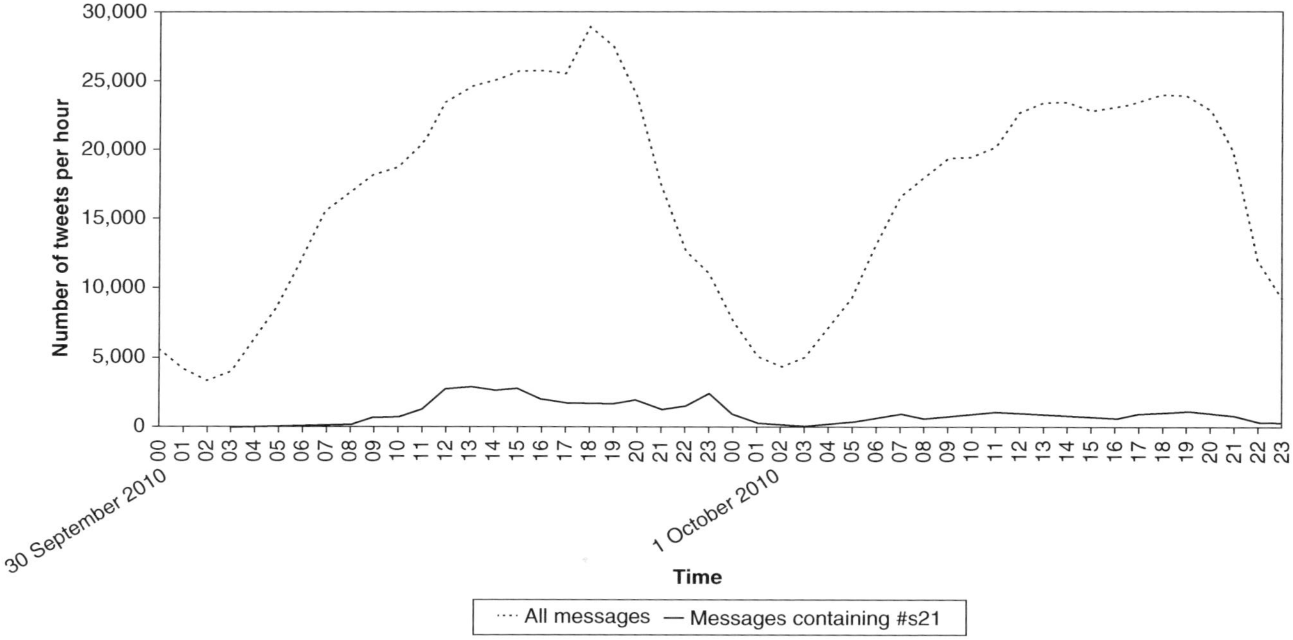


*Figure 6.1* Messages on 30 September and 1 October 2010

commenting on astrology such as #176 (9639 mentions), #ascendant (4481 mentions) or #mediumcoeli (4068 mentions). So while only roughly 10 per cent of the Twitter users in our sample used Twitter to comment on the events in Stuttgart, #s21 was the single most talked about topic on Twitter (see Figure 6.2).

When examining messages containing #s21, we find that a large proportion of these tweets are @messages or retweets. Of the total number of #s21 tweets (46,789) 3389 messages were @messages while 29,138 were retweets. It is interesting to note that the number of @messages per hour remained relatively stable while the number of retweets was highly fluctuating often in connection with spikes in the overall volume of tweets containing #s21 (see Figure 6.3).

## Stuttgart's Black Thursday on twitter: Four attempts at event detection

As described above, we will use four approaches for event detection with Twitter data and compare their results:

- local maxima in the volume of messages containing #s21;
- the first occurrences of tweets that were retweeted very often during the time span of our analysis;
- the first occurrences of URLs that were highly linked to during in our analysis;
- word stems with peaky characteristics.

To compare the quality of the results of these approaches we divided the two days that our analysis focused on in one-hour bins. For each of these 48 bins, we calculated the word stems that were used 50 times or more in Twitter messages containing #s21. Word stems are the 'root' of a word that omits any inflections. For example, the stem of 'driving' would be 'driv'. Collapsing words to their common root serves as a clustering methodology that maps related words to the same category. This drastically shrinks the number of possible items and enhances the power of analyses based on these data. To identify word stems, we use a de facto standard algorithm, the snowball stemmer for German that is provided by the python NLTK software package (see Bird et al. 2009). In identifying word stems we are able to identify words describing the same context but in slightly different forms (for example, 'tree' and 'trees', 'child' and 'children'). The word stems used 50 times or more during each respective hour can serve as a rough indicator as to which words dominated

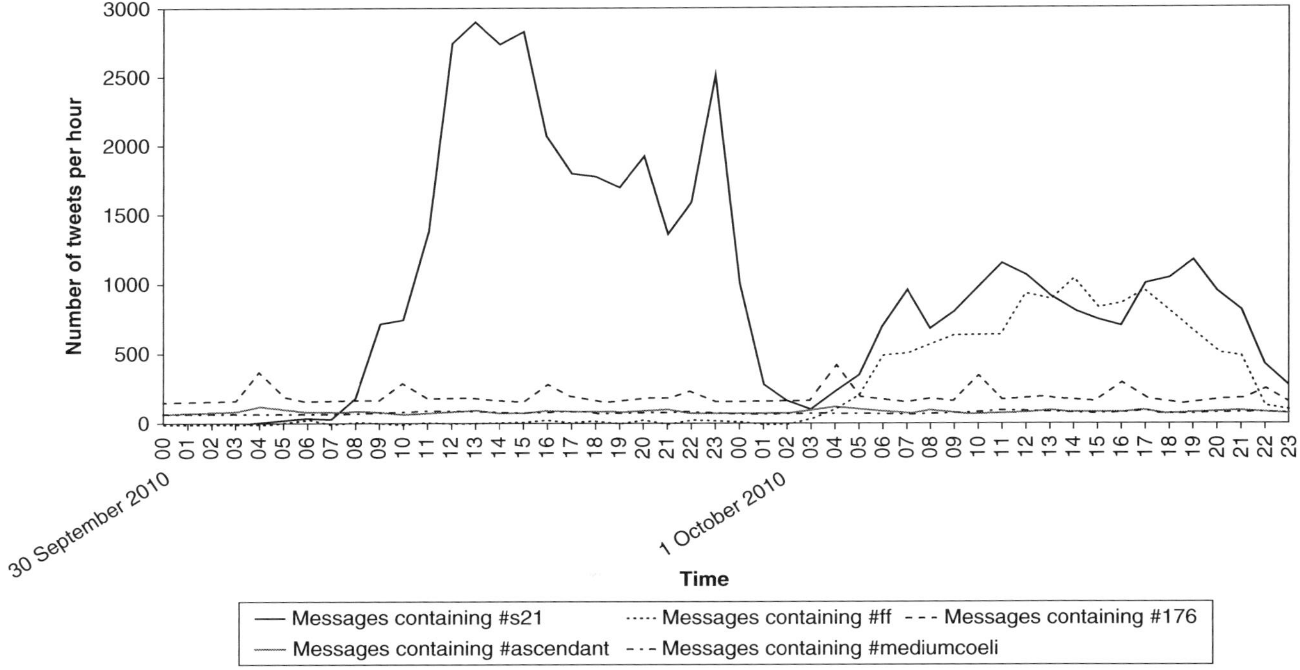


*Figure 6.2* The five most popular hashtags in message sample on 30 September and 1 October 2010

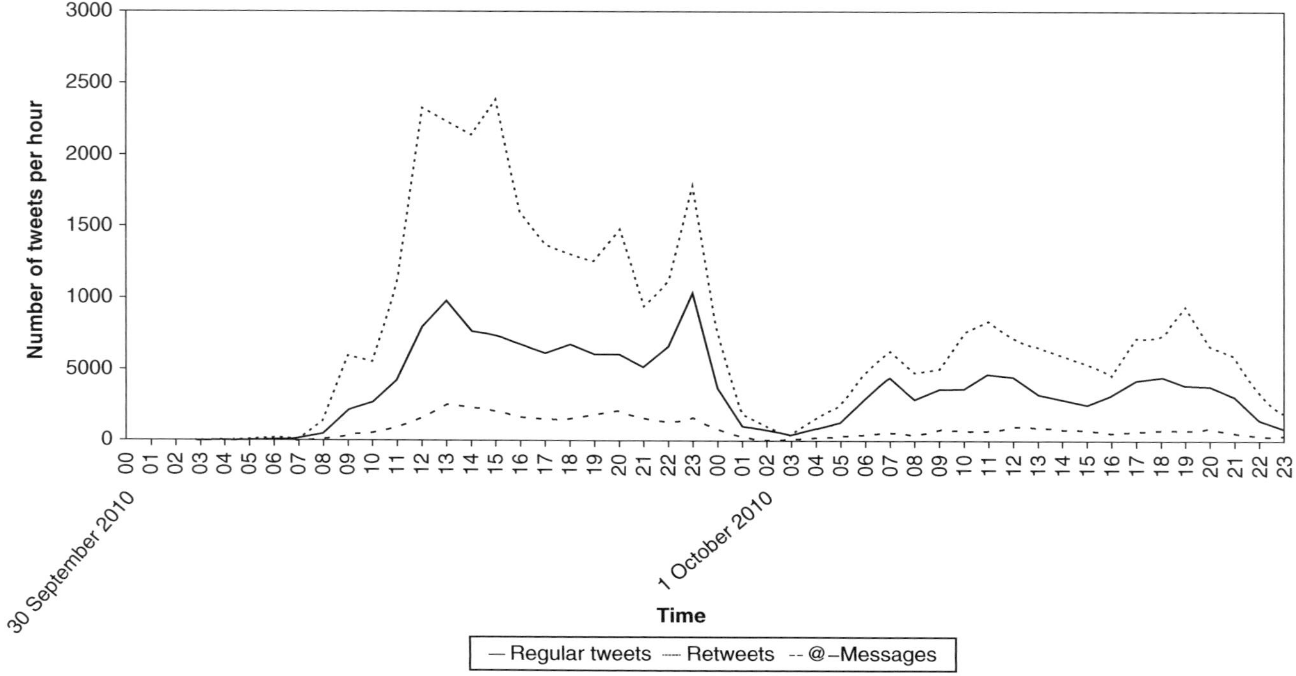


*Figure 6.3* Comparison of normal messages, retweets and @messages containing #s21 on 30 September and 1 October 2010

each hour. We then used the approaches listed above to determine the time intervals of interest

Table 6.1 shows the word stems with at least 50 mentions or more during each hour of 30 September and 1 October 2010. Already a first glance at these words suggests the nature of the events that took place during these hours. We find the German words for 'police', 'park', 'tree', 'tear gas' and 'water cannon'. While it is difficult to discern discrete steps of the protests against 'Stuttgart 21' from these words alone, we are able to discern the general nature of the events. These words represent the focused attention of German Twitter users interested in the events of 'Stuttgart 21' on the days in question. The symbol 'x' in the columns 'Volume', 'RTs', and 'Links' indicate those hours that were identified as significant by the respective event detection approach used. The following section develops each of these approaches and the results of their application in our data.

## Message volume

One simple approach is to examine the fluctuations in the volume of messages containing #s21. In Figure 6.4 we show the total volume of messages containing #s21 in any given hour of the two days in question. The lines mark local maxima were the volume reached relative peaks.

Figure 6.4 indicates that the volume of Twitter messages containing the hashtag #s21 follows a clear day and night rhythm. Still, especially on 30 September the overall volume is much higher than the following day and it shows distinctive patterns between 12:00 and 3:00 p.m. and again at 11:00 p.m. These peaks are clearly detected by an analysis based on local maxima. In Table 6.1, we showed the one-hour bins in which the local maxima fall by the value 'x' in the column 'Volume'. When looking at the corresponding word stems that were used 50 times or more in these bins we find that local maxima correspond with distinct events during the protest. For example, the peak around 1:00 p.m. corresponds with heavy clashes between police and protesters, among them school children. Messages dealing with this event dominate the Twitter discourse over the following hours. The sudden peak at 11:00 p.m. the same day corresponds with a new development in the protest. At that time construction workers started to cut down trees under police protection. This was accompanied by heavy protests and clashes between police and protesters. Thus it can be said that the analysis of local maxima in the volume of Twitter messages commenting on a given topic can provide a first understanding of the development of the event in

*Table 6.1* Word stems used at least 50 times in any given hour

| Bin Number | Date | Time | Volume | RTs | Links | Word stems (50 mentions or more) |
|---|---|---|---|---|---|---|
| 1 | 30 September 2010 | 0:00–1:00 a.m. | | | | |
| 2 | 30 September 2010 | 1:00–2:00 a.m. | | | | |
| 3 | 30 September 2010 | 2:00–3:00 a.m. | | | | |
| 4 | 30 September 2010 | 3:00–4:00 a.m. | | | | |
| 5 | 30 September 2010 | 4:00–5:00 a.m. | | | | |
| 6 | 30 September 2010 | 5:00–6:00 a.m. | | | | |
| 7 | 30 September 2010 | 6:00–7:00 a.m. | x | | | |
| 8 | 30 September 2010 | 7:00–8:00 a.m. | | | | |
| 9 | 30 September 2010 | 8:00–9:00 a.m. | | | | park, polizei |
| 10 | 30 September 2010 | 9:00–10:00 a.m. | | x | x | polizei, park, wasserwerf, baum, nil, schlagstock, demokrati, bestatigt |
| 11 | 30 September 2010 | 10:00–11:00 a.m. | | | | polizei, wasserwerf, schul, http://www.cams21.de/ |
| 12 | 30 September 2010 | 11:00–12:00 a.m. | | | x | wasserwerf, polizei, kind, fur, reizgas, traenengas, schul, #polizeigewalt, 15, friedlich |
| 13 | 30 September 2010 | 12:00–1:00 p.m. | | x | x | polizei, wasserwerf, kind, http://twitpic.com/2tbto, mal, fur, heut, wurd, reizgas, bericht |
| 14 | 30 September 2010 | 1:00–2:00 p.m. | x | | x | polizei, wasserwerf, http://twitpic.com/2tbto, bild, bitt, heut, #dpa, geh, fur, mehr |
| 15 | 30 September 2010 | 2:00–3:00 p.m. | | x | x | polizei, bitt, mehr, prot, heut, wasserwerf, stuttgart, reizgas, beim, uhr |
| 16 | 30 September 2010 | 3:00–4:00 p.m. | x | x | | heut, mensch, uhr, 1000, krankenhaus, uberlastet, prot, augenverletz, erlitt, eil |
| 17 | 30 September 2010 | 4:00–5:00 p.m. | | | | heut, uhr, mahnwach, polizeigewalt, wurd, polizei, prot, viel, polizeieinsatz, 20 |

| | | | | | | |
|---|---|---|---|---|---|---|
| 18 | 30 September 2010 | 5:00–6:00 p.m. | | x | | park, heut, kind, verletzt, uhr, 100, schadelbasisbruch, mahnwach, polizei, sanis |
| 19 | 30 September 2010 | 6:00–7:00 p.m. | | x | x | #swr, kind, demokrati, polizei, heut, geht, fur, #piraten, demo, mahnwach |
| 20 | 30 September 2010 | 7:00–8:00 p.m. | | x | | heut, mehr, eigent, wurd, burg, verletzt, egal, dass, pro, #piraten |
| 21 | 30 September 2010 | 8:00–9:00 p.m. | x | x | | polizist, rech, fur, demokrat, eigent, heut, steh, gegenub, hundert, merk |
| 22 | 30 September 2010 | 9:00–10:00 p.m. | | x | x | polizei, fur, rech, heut, mal, kind, burg, eigent |
| 23 | 30 September 2010 | 10:00–11:00 p.m. | | | x | polizei, polizeifunk, park, geht, fallarbeit, beginn, fur, mal, demonstrant, #cdu |
| 24 | 30 September 2010 | 11:00–12:00 p.m. | x | x | x | baum, polizei, gasmask, kommt, polizist, erst, gefallt, rech, innenminist, baumfallfirma |
| 25 | 1 October 2010 | 0:00–1:00 a.m. | | | | tot, heut, mal, #cdu, fur |
| 26 | 1 October 2010 | 1:00–2:00 a.m. | | | | |
| 27 | 1 October 2010 | 2:00–3:00 a.m. | | | | |
| 28 | 1 October 2010 | 3:00–4:00 a.m. | | | | |
| 29 | 1 October 2010 | 4:00–5:00 a.m. | | | | |
| 30 | 1 October 2010 | 5:00–6:00 a.m. | | | | |
| 31 | 1 October 2010 | 6:00–7:00 a.m. | | | | heut |
| 32 | 1 October 2010 | 7:00–8:00 a.m. | x | | | bundestag, debatt, #bundestag, heut, grun, fur, ab, antrag, schwarzgelb, uber |
| 33 | 1 October 2010 | 8:00–9:00 a.m. | | | | ab, heut, polit |
| 34 | 1 October 2010 | 9:00–10:00 a.m. | | | x | heut, uhr, fur |
| 35 | 1 October 2010 | 10:00–11:00 a.m. | | x | x | rucktritt, fur, ford, heut, innenminist, #rech, rech, bahnhof, polizeieinsatz, brutal |

*Table 6.1* (Continued)

| Bin Number | Date | Time | Volume | RTs | Links | Word stems (50 mentions or more) |
|---|---|---|---|---|---|---|
| 36 | 1 October 2010 | 11:00–12:00 a.m. | x | x | x | fur, bitt, http://youtu.be/W1UYd5LDQXA, uhr, uber, video, weiterverbreit, geht, gewalt, phoenix, video |
| 37 | 1 October 2010 | 12:00–1:00 p.m. | | | | fur, heut, bitt, uhr, geht, http://youtu.be/W1UYd5LDQXA, video |
| 38 | 1 October 2010 | 1:00–2:00 p.m. | | | | fur, heut, geht, bos, schlagzeil, printmedi, preis, #ftd |
| 39 | 1 October 2010 | 2:00–3:00 p.m. | | | | fur, heut, geht, bitt, polizei, schlagzeil, preis |
| 40 | 1 October 2010 | 3:00–4:00 p.m. | | | | heut, fur, bitt, uber, abstimm |
| 41 | 1 October 2010 | 4:00–5:00 p.m. | | x | | demo, heut, fur, 1900, schlossgart, livestream, ab, www.polizei.co, www.krieg.co, http://bit.ly/a0aFpA |
| 42 | 1 October 2010 | 5:00–6:00 p.m. | | | | heut, polizei, gest, schon, #rech, #mappus, fur, wurd, baum |
| 43 | 1 October 2010 | 6:00–7:00 p.m. | | | x | eisenbahnbundesamt, demo, frau, seit, fur, heut, 100000, gest, fall, db |
| 44 | 1 October 2010 | 7:00–8:00 p.m. | x | | x | mappus, polizei, 100000, demonstrant, ja, uhr, uber, rucktritt, konnt, gesprach |
| 45 | 1 October 2010 | 8:00–9:00 p.m. | | | | mappus, slomka, #zdf, #mappus, wurd, frau, heutejournal, fur, mal, gesprach |
| 46 | 1 October 2010 | 9:00–10:00 p.m. | | | | mappus, fur, neu, lug, polizei, masseein, abstand, #mappus, schon |
| 47 | 1 October 2010 | 10:00–11:00 p.m. | | | | fur |
| 48 | 1 October 2010 | 11:00–12:00 p.m. | | | | |

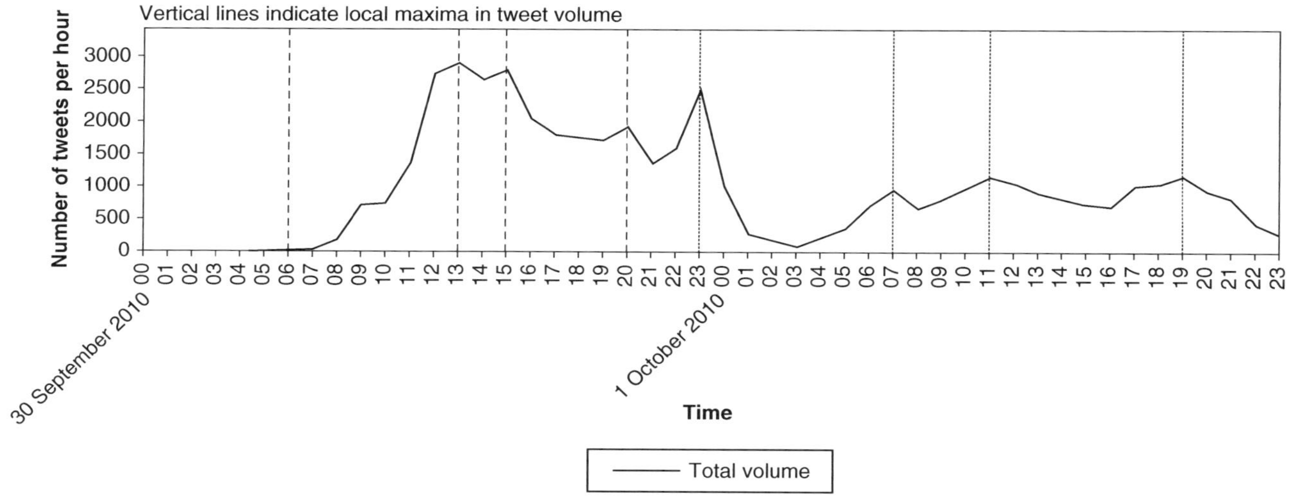


*Figure 6.4* Tweet volume per hour (local maxima)

*Note*: The vertical lines identify significant hours as detected by local maxima. Local maxima are detected if tweet volume is lower both before and after a local point.

question. They indicate important time spans during the event while the words used most often during these time spans allow a view on the elements of the event that held public attention.

## Retweets

Another approach to the detection of events is the identification of messages that were retweeted often. We identified the 20 tweets in our data set that were retweeted most often during the two days in question (see Table 6.2). The number we chose, 20, is rather arbitrary. Still, we find that in our case the number of retweets a message received stabilised after the twentieth rank. For other analyses or other time spans, a different number of retweets might be better suited. The frequency of retweets ranged from 271 at the top to 75 at the bottom of our 20 most often retweeted messages. We then identified the time these tweets were originally posted and checked what kind of information these tweets held on the protests (see Figure 6.5).

As shown in the columns 'Volume' and 'RTs' of Table 6.1 the 20 most popular retweets identified more time bins than the previous approach through local maxima. Still, there is no large difference in the time bins identified by both methods. Messages that were highly retweeted were posted mostly during the active hours of the protest in Stuttgart. When looking at the word stems that were used in the hours indicated by popular tweets we roughly get the same picture of the protest as when looking at the word stems in hours indicated by local maxima. Also when looking at the content of the most often retweeted tweets themselves we do not get a more detailed look at the events in Stuttgart. This is largely due to the fact that only a small minority of those tweets contained actual information on the event itself. Most messages that were retweeted intensively contained either generic commentary on the events (for example, 'Pro or against #s21 does not really matter. You don't beat up your citizens. Full stop' (ID=0)) or satirical content (for example, 'How do I remember the 11880 [the number of Germany's telephone information]? Hundred 11-year-old democrats stand against 88 policemen and have 0 chance. #s21' (ID=4)). While this content is highly popular among retweeters, maybe because it crystallises their thinking or reaction to the events, these tweets do not help researchers interested in the development of the unfolding protest. However, when looking at tweets that were less often retweeted we increasingly find tweets of activists that contain actual information on different stages of the protest. For example, 'The police does not let journalists through,

*Table 6.2* Top 20 RTs in Twitter messages on 30 September and 1 October, 2010 containing the #keyword #s21

| ID | Count | Date | Time | Tweet | Type |
|---|---|---|---|---|---|
| 0 | 271 | 30 September 2010 | 7:46:09 p.m. | RT @dingler_g4: Pro oder contra #s21 ist eigentlich egal. Man prügelt seine Bürger nicht. Punkt. | Commentary |
| 1 | 248 | 30 September 2010 | 3:08:30 p.m. | RT @tazgezwitscher: EIL (dapd) + + + 1.000 Menschen haben Augenverletzungen erlitten, Krankenhäuser in Stuttgart überlastet #s21 | Misinformation |
| 2 | 150 | 30 September 2010 | 5:50:30 p.m. | RT @triffy: Stuttgart 21: Kirche zeigt sich empört, das Verprügeln kleiner Jungs sei ihre Aufgabe! #s21, 150 | Satire |
| 3 | 148 | 30 September 2010 | 9:08:20 a.m. | RT @fasel: Schlagstöcke und Wasserwerfer, die Grundpfeiler einer gesunden Demokratie #S21 | Commentary |
| 4 | 139 | 30 September 2010 | 8:10:46 p.m. | RT @ChrMll: Wie ich mir 11880 merke? Hundert 11-jährige Demokraten stehen 88 Polizisten gegenüber und haben 0 Chance. #s21 | Satire |
| 5 | 127 | 30 September 2010 | 2:53:45 p.m. | RT @zebramaedchen: Wenn Iraner jetzt aus Solidarität unter Location 'Stuttgart' eintragen, wird es ernst. #s21 | Satire |
| 6 | 124 | 30 September 2010 | 9:23:38 p.m. | RT @Schmidtlepp: Bahnhof des himmlischen Friedens = 天安火车站 #S21 | Satire |
| 7 | 123 | 30 September 2010 | 2:26:35 p.m. | RT @C_Holler: BREAKING+ + + Demokratiefeindliche Ökostalinisten behindern Stuttgarts Polizei beim Blumengießen. #S21 | Satire |
| 8 | 121 | 30 September 2010 | 6:24:17 p.m. | RT @eldersign: In einer Demokratie kann man bedenkenlos Kinder mit auf eine Demo nehmen, in einem #Polizeistaat nicht. #S21 | Commentary |
| 9 | 121 | 30 September 2010 | 12:55:46 p.m. | RT @forschungstorte: dieses bild soll um die welt gehen: #s21 http://twitpic.com/2tbtod #dpa – sowas passiert in #deutschland | Media |

*Table 6.2* (Continued)

| ID | Count | Date | Time | Tweet | Type |
|---|---|---|---|---|---|
| 10 | 113 | 1 October 2010 | 10:52:18 a.m. | RT @saschalobo: Das Gegenteil von höflich heisst seit gestern bahnhöflich. #S21 | Satire |
| 11 | 103 | 30 September 2010 | 12:24:11 p.m. | RT @phlox81: Und vergesst nicht, wenn es nach der #CDU ginge, würde da jetzt auch die #Bundeswehr mitmischen! #s21 | Satire |
| 12 | 98 | 1 October 2010 | 11:03:59 a.m. | RT @NineBerry: Bitte dieses Video weiterverbreiten: http://youtu.be/W1UYd5LDQXA #s21 | Protest media |
| 13 | 94 | 1 October 2010 | 11:19:46 a.m. | RT @pillenknick: Der Preis für die böseste Schlagzeile zu #S21 in Printmedien geht an die #FTD: http://twitpic.com/2tlg9t | Media |
| 14 | 94 | 30 September 2010 | 8:19:11 p.m. | RT @ChrMll: Wie praktisch: Wenn die Revolution am Sonntag kommt, bleibt sogar der Nationalfeiertag der gleiche. #s21 | Satire |
| 15 | 91 | 30 September 2010 | 12:46:44 p.m. | RT @ZDFonline: Der Konflikt um Stuttgart 21 eskaliert – laut Augenzeugen mit Pfefferspray und Wasserwerfern http://bit.ly/czGpM7 #s21 #p... | Media |
| 16 | 90 | 30 September 2010 | 11:27:12 p.m. | RT @tauss: Die #s21 Baumfällfirma kommt übrigens aus dem Wahlkreis von Innenminister Heribert Rech (Karlsdorf b. Bruchsal) | Information |
| 17 | 87 | 30 September 2010 | 4:59:14 p.m. | RT @tazgezwitscher: 100 verletzte Kinder, 1 Schädelbasisbruch – und die Sanis dürfen nicht in den Park. (Quelle: Parkschützer) #s21 http... | Misinformation |
| 18 | 82 | 30 September 2010 | 2:13:06 p.m. | RT @abrissaufstand: bitte! wir brauchen mehr Sanitäter & Ärzte #S21 sie sprühen Reizgas willkürlich und massiv in die Menge #S21 | Information |
| 19 | 75 | 1 October 2010 | 4:52:52 p.m. | RT @KnirpsStore: Schirm durch einen Wasserwerfer kaputt gegangen? Wir unterstützen gerne friedliche Demos. Mail an s21@knirps-store.de<mailto:s21@knirps-store.de> #s21 | Satire |

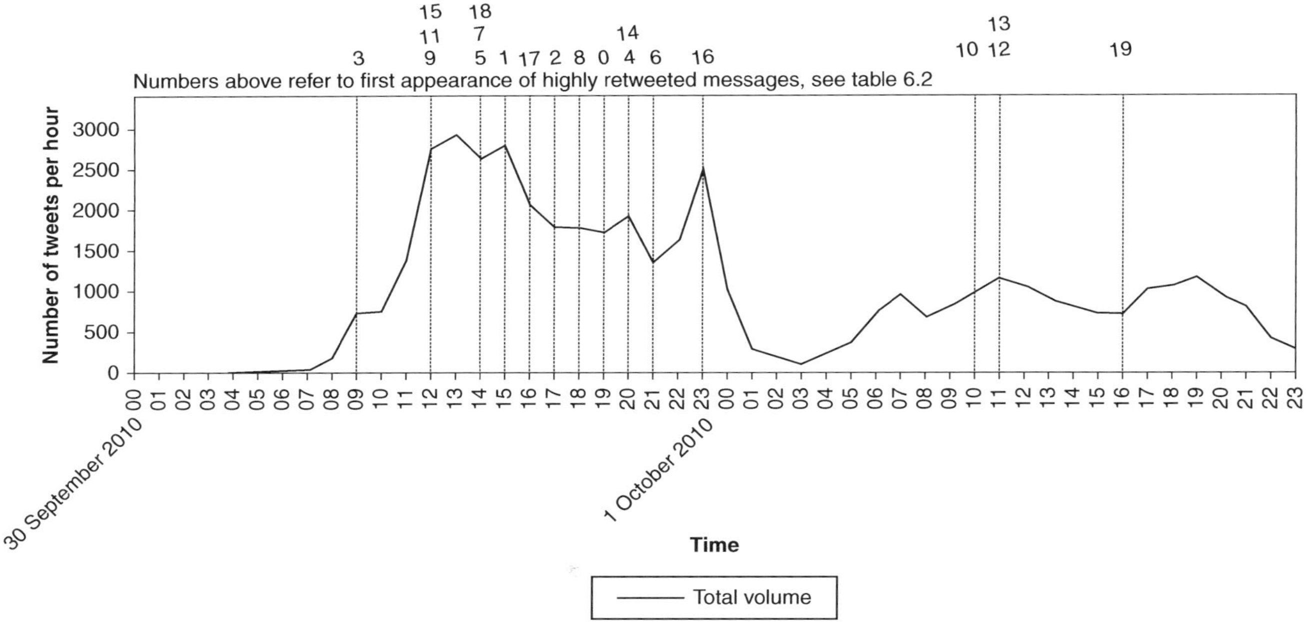


*Figure 6.5* Tweet volume (Retweets)

*Note*: The vertical lines identify significant hours as detected by the first appearance of the 20 most retweeted messages.

even those with official credentials', or 'They said via microphone that one man has lost his eyesight through a water cannon'. So activists used Twitter consciously to distribute information about the protests and to organise it, as has also been shown in other cases (Jungherr 2009), but these tweets did not receive as much retweet attention as tweets containing generic or satirical commentary.

Another indicator shows potential problems with expecting tweets containing actual information on the protests to be highly retweeted when examining which applications people used when tweeting about the protests, we found that applications for mobile phones, which can be used to post messages on Twitter on the go, were used to publish only about a quarter of the total tweets containing the hashtag #s21. This means that most of the volume of tweets commenting on the events actually comes from users sitting in front of desktop computers or notebooks who followed the protests from afar. For those users, satirical or witty tweets are of course more attractive to retweet than messages containing procedural information.

So while the time of the initial posting of popular retweets often corresponds with time bins identified by peaks in total volume of messages the actual content of the most popular retweets does not provide a better understanding of the unfolding events. While local maxima helped us understand which words were used by most users in their attempt to comment on #21, popular retweets help us understand which messages these users considered to be most representative for their own reactions to the events.

## URLs

As a third approach to the identification of relevant time bins, we can use domains that were popularly linked to in tweets containing #21. After identifying the domains linked to most often in #s21 tweets, we measured the time when they were first posted and marked the corresponding time bin (see Figure 6.6).

Again we find that most time bins identified by this method correspond with those identified by local maxima or retweets (see column 'URLs' in Table 6.1). Again we find that the word stems used most often in those time bins do not provide us with very specific information about the development of the protest. So, do the linked domains tell us something about the protests that we did not know before?

In Table 6.3 we documented the 20 most popular domains linked to in #s21 tweets. As before, 20 is an arbitrary number that is useful

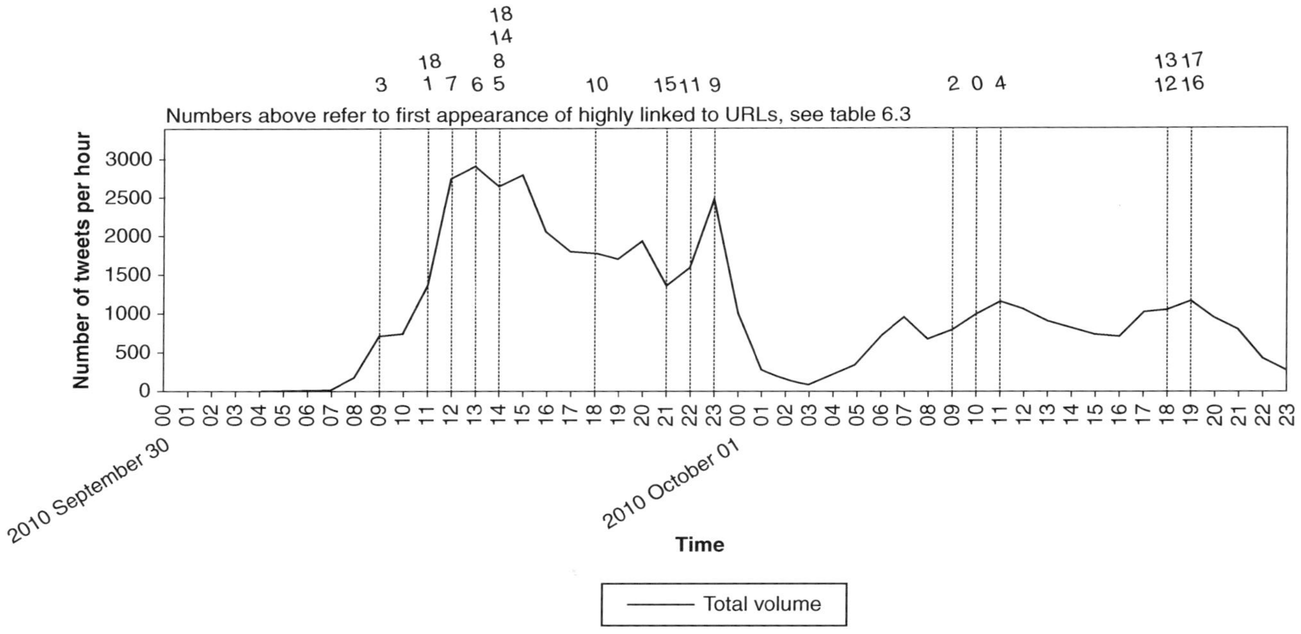


*Figure 6.6* Tweet volume (URLs)
*Note*: The vertical lines identify significant hours as detected by the first appearance of the 20 most linked to URLs.

*Table 6.3* Top 20 websites linked with Twitter messages on 30 September and 1 October 2010 containing the #keyword #s21

| ID | Website | Description | Type | Link Count |
|---|---|---|---|---|
| 0 | http://www.youtube.com/verify_age?next_url=/watch%3Fv%3DW1UYd5LDQXA%26feature%3Dyoutu.be | Videoclip of protest | Protest media | 311 |
| 1 | http://fluegel.tv/ | Videostream of protest | Protest media | 308 |
| 2 | http://www.campact.de/bahn/ml4/mailer | Campact mail campaign in reaction to protests | Campaign | 246 |
| 3 | http://www.cams21.de/ | Videostream of protest | Protest media | 204 |
| 4 | http://twitpic.com/2tlg9t | Picture of newspaper article on protest | News | 203 |
| 5 | http://piratenpad.de/s21 | Public pad of Germany's Pirate party, used to coordinate protests | Party content | 175 |
| 6 | http://bambuser.com/channel/terminal.21/broadcast/105357 | Videostream of protest | Protest media | 160 |
| 7 | http://www.heute.de/ZDFheute/inhalt/30/0,3672,8116958,00.html | News coverage of protest | News | 149 |
| 8 | http://www.amnestypolizei.de/ | Campaign by Amnesty International for transparency of police actions | Campaign | 120 |
| 9 | http://fxneumann.de/2010/10/01/ohnmacht-wut-und-repraesentative-demokratie/ | Blog post in reaction to protest | Blog | 103 |

| | | | | |
|---|---|---|---|---|
| 10 | http://images.zeit.de/politik/deutschland/2010-09/bg-stuttgart21-bilder/20754237-540x304.jpg | News photo of protest | News | 101 |
| 11 | http://www.ustream.tv/channel/kaputtgart-21 | Videostream of protest | Protest media | 96 |
| 12 | http://twitpic.com/2tp8ui | Twitpic of official document concerning the protests | Protest media | 95 |
| 13 | http://www.piratenpartei.de/Pressemitteilung-100930-PIRATEN-entsetzt-ueber-Traenengaseinsatz-gegen-Schueler-bei-S21-Demo | Official press statement of Germany's Pirate party in reaction to the police action | Party content | 85 |
| 14 | http://twibbon.com/join/Oben-bleiben-s21 | Support Twibon for protesters against #s21 | Protest media | 83 |
| 15 | http://twitpic.com/2tpka5 | Twitpic of protest | Protest media | 81 |
| 16 | http://twitpic.com/2tpk9o | Twitpic of protest | Protest media | 80 |
| 17 | http://twitpic.com/2tb48b | Twitpic of protest | Protest media | 72 |
| 18 | http://taz.de/!59135/ | Newscoverage of protest | News | 70 |
| 19 | http://wiki.piratenpartei.de/Landesverband_Baden-W%C3%BCrttemberg/Arbeitsgruppen/Presse/S21 | Wiki of Germany's Pirate party collecting press reactions to Stutgart21 | Party content | 68 |

in this specific analysis but that could be expanded. It is interesting to note that most linked domains do provide access to media provided by the protesters themselves. Links to video or audio live streams that document the unfolding protests are particularly popular. In this, the 'Stuttgart 21' protests mirror other recent practices among political activists (Pickard 2006; David 2010). It is also interesting to note that although many of the links go to video streams, nearly no digital photographs taken by protesters themselves are detected among the most popular links. There are some links to pictures, but these tend to be snapshots of newspaper articles or links to photographs taken by professionals. In documenting the #s21 protests on 30 September and 1 October 2010, digital photography by activists themselves had only a marginal role. Although the linked domains offered other Twitter users on that evening a more detailed look at the unfolding events, they do not provide much information for researchers looking for the development of the process. Still, popularly linked domains provide us with an impression of what Twitter users were paying attention to while publicly commenting on the events.

With regard to the questions stated above, we find that popular URLs provide us with similar time bins as other event detection approaches and that content of established media are not overrepresented. Social media data thus seems to offer a view of unfolding events independent of media accounts.

## Peakiness

In our final approach, we identify relevant time bins by the relative frequency of word stems. We identified those word stems that were used at least 100 times during the two days and received at least 50 per cent of their mentions during one single hour (see Table 6.4). Shamma et al. (2011) call this pattern 'peaky'.

We used the hours indicated by the appearance of word stems with peaky characteristics and compared them to the hours indicated by the three previous approaches (see Table 6.1). Again we find that most hours identified by this approach correspond quite well with those identified by the other approaches (see Figure 6.7). Since the calculation of peakiness occurs in slices of one hour each, the indicated moments of relevant activity have a maximum precision of one hour.

Following the pattern of peaky word stems, four major phases of the protests can be identified. After a first onset around 9 a.m. which is connected to a first sighting of water cannons, the main phase of

*Table 6.4* Peaky word strems, hashtags and links

| ID | Word stem | Date | Time | Example | Type |
|---|---|---|---|---|---|
| 0 | krankenhaus | 30 September 2010 | 3:00–4:00 p.m. | RT @Tschuly82: Ungesicherte Infos ca. 1000 Verletzte #s21 in den Krankenhäusern in #Stuttgart | Misinformation |
| 1 | uberlastet | 30 September 2010 | 3:00–4:00 p.m. | bitte NICHT mit Reizgasverletzungen in die Stuttgarter Krankenhäuser; diese sind komplett überlastet #S21 bitte RT | Misinformation |
| 2 | 1000 | 30 September 2010 | 3:00–4:00 p.m. | meinen 1000ten tweet widme ich dem widerstand in stuttgart: nicht aufgeben, weitermachen! #S21 | Non-specific |
| 3 | augenverletz | 30 September 2010 | 3:00–4:00 p.m. | Augenverletzungen dokumentieren: Augenarztpraxis am Olgaeck, Charlottenstraße 23 #S21 | Information |
| 4 | eil | 30 September 2010 | 3:00–4:00 p.m. | RT @Roland_Veile: #S21: Bitte sofort alle in den #Park | Non-specific |
| 5 | erlitt | 30 September 2010 | 3:00–4:00 p.m. | EIL (dapd) + + + 1.000 Menschen haben Augenverletzungen erlitten, Krankenhäuser in Stuttgart überlastet #s21 | Misinformation |
| 6 | dapd | 30 September 2010 | 3:00–4:00 p.m. | EIL (dapd) + + + 1.000 Menschen haben Augenverletzungen erlitten, Krankenhäuser in Stuttgart überlastet #s21 | Misinformation |
| 7 | http://youtu.be/W1UYd5LDQXA | 1 October 2010 | 11:00–12:00 a.m. | Bitte dieses Video weiterverbreiten: http://youtu.be/W1UYd5LDQXA #s21 | Protest media |
| 8 | chanc | 30 September 2010 | 8:00–9:00 p.m. | RT @stoddnet: Keine Chance, wenn selbst Kinder geschlagen werden #s21 | Non-specific |
| 9 | 88 | 30 September 2010 | 8:00–9:00 p.m. | @Debe1887 Und wieder wirst du bestätigt in einigen deiner Aussagen. #S21 | Non-specific |

*Table 6.4* (Continued)

| ID | Word stem | Date | Time | Example | Type |
|---|---|---|---|---|---|
| 10 | polizeifunk | 30 September 2010 | 10:00–11:00 p.m. | Darf man eigentlich einen Livestream des Stuttgarter Polizeifunks vertwittern? http://www.ustream.tv/recorded/9913851 #s21 | Protest media |
| 11 | 11jahrig | 30 September 2010 | 8:00–9:00 p.m. | 'Tagesspiegel' berichtet von Gewalt gegen 11jährige Schüler und 60 jährige Frauen. http://bit.ly/a9d97W #s21 | Media |
| 12 | 11880 | 30 September 2010 | 8:00–9:00 p.m. | Wie ich mir 11880 merke? Hundert 11-jährige Demokraten stehen 88 Polizisten gegenüber und haben 0 Chance. #s21 | Non-specific |
| 13 | http://twitpic.com/2tcutw | 30 September 2010 | 3:00–4:00 p.m. | Hehe: Wer nicht hört bekommt auf die Fresse! RT @scheelm: http://twitpic.com/2tcutw #s21 | Media |
| 14 | hinlang | 30 September 2010 | 12:00–1:00 p.m. | #s21 proteste in #stuttgart: ein beamtensprecher erklärt auf #taz online, die polizei kann ruhig mal hinlangen: http://tinyurl.com/38rzazd | Media |
| 15 | baumfallfirma | 30 September 2010 | 11:00–12:00 p.m. | Baumfällfirma aus Ba-Wü: Gredler & Söhne, Waldstrasse 17, 76689 Karlsdorf-Neuthard, Tel: 07251–9443–0 Fax: -9443–22, #S21 | Information |
| 16 | wahlkreis | 30 September 2010 | 11:00–12:00 p.m. | RT @lutz__h: Wahlkreisbüro von Stefan #Mappus, #CDU, Pforzheim: 07231/1458–0 #S21 | Information |
| 17 | gasmask | 30 September 2010 | 11:00–12:00 p.m. | gasmasken – Polizei hat Gasmasken #s21 | Information |
| 18 | behind | 30 September 2010 | 2:00–3:00 p.m. | schlagzeile morgen in der BILD: 'wildgewordene schüler und rentner behindern friedliche baumfällarbeiten' #s21 | Satire |

| | | | | | |
|---|---|---|---|---|---|
| 19 | weiterverbreit | 1 October 2010 | 11:00–12:00 a.m. | RT @JulianMuetsch: Mahnwache zu #S21 um 19Uhr vor dem Mannheimer HBF! Bitte Weiterverbreiten! | Information |
| 20 | breaking | 30 September 2010 | 2:00–3:00 p.m. | Breakingnews: In #Stuttgart gehen derzeit #Polizisten brutal gegen friedliche Demonstranten – darunter viele #Schüler – vor. #S21 | Non-specific |
| 21 | demokratiefeind | 30 September 2010 | 2:00–3:00 p.m. | RT @C_Holler: BREAKING+ + + Demokratiefeindliche Ökostalinisten behindern Stuttgarts Polizei beim Blumengießen. #S21 | Non-specific |
| 22 | blumengiess | 30 September 2010 | 2:00–3:00 p.m. | RT @C_Holler: BREAKING+ + + Demokratiefeindliche Ökostalinisten behindern Stuttgarts Polizei beim Blumengießen. #S21 | Satire |
| 23 | okostalinist | 30 September 2010 | 2:00–3:00 p.m. | RT @C_Holler: BREAKING+ + + Demokratiefeindliche Ökostalinisten behindern Stuttgarts Polizei beim Blumengießen. #S21 | Satire |
| 24 | beginn | 30 September 2010 | 10:00–11:00 p.m. | die parkräumung und baumfällung beginnt. #S21 | Information |
| 25 | schadelbasisbruch | 30 September 2010 | 5:00–6:00 p.m. | RT @hellertaler: fluegel.tv: Über 100 verletzte Kinder, ein Schädelbasisbruch, diverse sonstige . . . . heute ist was zerbrochen. Vertr. #s21 | Misinformation |
| 26 | arzt | 30 September 2010 | 2:00–3:00 p.m. | @Kyra2001: #S21 Augenärzte und Ärzte werden noch gebraucht. Vor allem #Augenärzte Vor Ort! Augenverletzungen S21 | Information |

*Table 6.4* (Continued)

| ID | Word stem | Date | Time | Example | Type |
|---|---|---|---|---|---|
| 27 | parkschutz | 30 September 2010 | 5:00–6:00 p.m. | RT @Cymaphore: Kranwagen im Schlosspark in #Stuttgart wird blockiert #S21 #K21 #Parkschützer | Information |
| 28 | sanis | 30 September 2010 | 5:00–6:00 p.m. | Verletzte: Demosanis: Biergarten, Rotes Kreuz: Cannstatter Ende des mitt. Schlossgartens, Rettungswagen am Südausgang #S21 bitte RT | Information |
| 29 | #bundestag | 1 October 2010 | 7:00–8:00 a.m. | #S21: Bitte alle #Berliner und #Berlinnerinnen. Demonstriert bitte vor dem #Bundestag gegen Stuttgart21. | Information |
| 30 | willkur | 30 September 2010 | 2:00–3:00 p.m. | bitte! wir brauchen mehr Sanitäter & Ärzte #S21 sie sprühen Reizgas willkürlich und massiv in die Menge #S21 | Information |
| 31 | sanitat | 30 September 2010 | 2:00–3:00 p.m. | Das Zelt der Sanitäter ist auf der Wiese zwischen Biergarten und Cafe Nil #S21 | Information |
| 32 | spruh | 30 September 2010 | 2:00–3:00 p.m. | jetzt prügeln und sprühen sie auch noch aufs Deeskalationsteam ein #s21 #WTF | Information |
| 33 | #bundeswehr | 30 September 2010 | 12:00–1:00 p.m. | Und vergesst nicht, wenn es nach der #CDU ginge, würde da jetzt auch die #Bundeswehr mitmischen! #s21 | Commentary |
| 34 | mitmisch | 30 September 2010 | 12:00–1:00 p.m. | RT @phlox81: Und vergesst nicht, wenn es nach der #CDU ginge, würde da jetzt auch die #Bundeswehr mitmischen! #s21 | Commentary |
| 35 | fallarbeit | 30 September 2010 | 10:00–11:00 p.m. | fällarbeiten – An alle Stuttgarter Parkschützer: AUF IN DEN PARK!!! Baumfällarbeiten beginnen nun! http://www.parkschuetzer.de/webcam #s21 #k21 | Information |

| | | | | | |
|---|---|---|---|---|---|
| 36 | sonntag | 30 September 2010 | 8:00–9:00 p.m. | Heute die Demokratie mit Füßen treten und am Sonntag Geschwollene Reden über Einheit in Frieden und Freiheit halten . . . #s21 | Non-specific |
| 37 | mind | 1 October 2010 | 7:00–8:00 p.m. | RT @Sugg__: Mindestens 2 Wasserwerfer sind schon im Park!!! #S21 #Aufstand #WehrtEuch | Non-specific |
| 38 | karlsdorf | 30 September 2010 | 11:00–12:00 p.m. | Baumfällfirma aus Ba-Wü: Gredler & Söhne, Waldstrasse 17, 76689 Karlsdorf-Neuthard, Tel: 07251–9443–0 Fax: -9443–22, #S21 | Information |
| 39 | antrag | 1 October 2010 | 7:00–8:00 a.m. | Begründung war übrigens, das sei eine Spontandemo, die müsste schriftlich beantragt werden. #dortmund #s21 | Information |
| 40 | nil | 30 September 2010 | 9:00–10:00 a.m. | RT @robin_wood: #Wasserwerfer am Café Nil im Park. #S21 | Information |
| 41 | seltsam | 30 September 2010 | 1:00–2:00 p.m. | Gute Nacht, seltsame Welt! Denk' ich an Deutschland in der Nacht, so bin ich um den Schlaf gebracht . . . #Polizeistaat #S21 | Non-specific |
| 42 | praktisch | 30 September 2010 | 8:00–9:00 p.m. | @JoGoebel naja, in einer repräsentativen demokratie äußern sich praktisch alle parteien stellvertretend für gewisse gruppen, oder? #s21 | Non-specific |
| 43 | phoenix | 1 October 2010 | 11:00–12:00 a.m. | Stuttgart #s21 live im Bundestag! #phoenix | Information |

*Table 6.4* (Continued)

| ID | Word stem | Date | Time | Example | Type |
|---|---|---|---|---|---|
| 44 | bruchsal | 30 September 2010 | 11:00–12:00 p.m. | bruchsaler – Schichtwechsel hinterm Zaun. Rheinland-Pfalz wurde durch aggresive Bruchsaler abgelöst. #S21 | Information |
| 45 | nationalfeiertag | 30 September 2010 | 8:00–9:00 p.m. | Wie praktisch: Wenn die Revolution am Sonntag kommt, bleibt sogar der Nationalfeiertag der gleiche. #s21 | Non-specific |
| 46 | sekundentakt | 30 September 2010 | 7:00–8:00 p.m. | Im sekundentakt kommen Tweets. Ab in die Trending Topic, zeigt der Welt was hier passiert! #s21 | Non-specific |
| 47 | sek | 30 September 2010 | 3:00–4:00 p.m. | RT @HMSzymek: Die "Wichtigen" in Zivil sind eher SEKs bei der Menge. #s21 | Information |
| 48 | http://bit.ly/czGpM7 | 30 September 2010 | 12:00–1:00 p.m. | Der Konflikt um Stuttgart 21 eskaliert – laut Augenzeugen mit Pfefferspray und Wasserwerfern http://bit.ly/czGpM7 #s21 #parkschützer | Media |

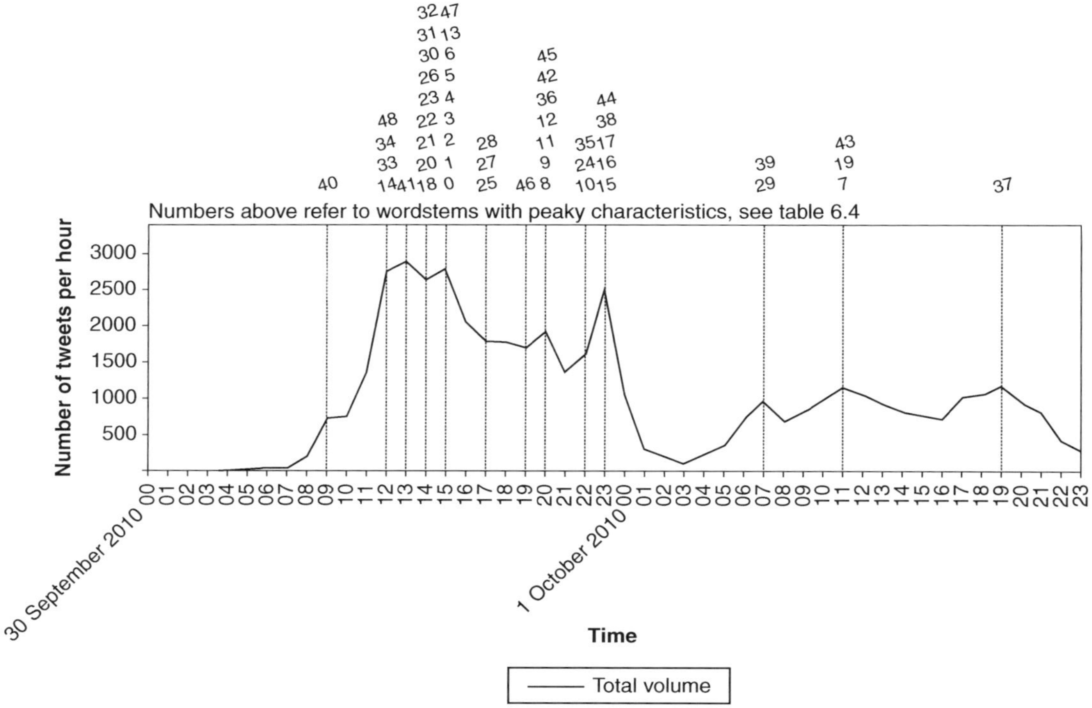


*Figure 6.7* Tweet volume (peakiness)

*Note*: The vertical lines identify significant hours as detected by word stems with peaky characteristics. Peakiness is assumed at 0.5 (50 per cent of occurrences within this hour) for all word stems that appeared at least 100 times on 30 September and 1 October 2010.

the demonstration starts around 12 a.m. It is characterised by content that comments rather than reports (for example, 'breaking', entry 20 in Table 6.4). The main theme, apart from the general mentioning of protests, are reported injuries through tear gas and water cannons ('sanitat' = medic, entry 31 in Table 6.4). From 3 p.m. onwards, links to live streams start to appear (items 0–6 in Figure 6.7). The intermediary period (5–7 p.m.) is dominated by humorous meta-coverage. The second major sub-event happens during the night, when trees are first being chopped down ('fallarbeit' = logging work, item 35 in Table 6.4). The following day is characterised by meta-coverage and links to media stories (for example, 'phoenix', a German TV station, item 43 in Table 6.4).

Overall, isolating peaky word stems provides researchers with a general yet relevant summary of the event in question. In most cases, however, the context from entire tweets is still needed in order to interpret the meaning of word stems.

## Conclusion: Event detection with social media data

We presented four distinct approaches for the detection of events in social media data. All four approaches – based on volume alone, salient retweets, salient URLs and a metric called 'peakiness' (Shamma et al. 2011) – were applied to the same two-day dataset documenting protests reacting to the construction of a new train station in Stuttgart, Germany.

Even at first glance, it is apparent that tweets addressing the protests (containing the #s21 hashtag) seem to develop parallel to the actual events. During crucial phases of the protest, the volume of messages commenting on #s21 rises. This extends a basic observation: at its most simple level, the volume of Twitter messages over time mirrors basic human activity patterns – high volume during waking hours and on weekends, low volume during the night. What do the four approaches chosen by us add to that basic observation?

- Volume: the analysis of local maxima in the volume of tweets succeeds in finding significant time bins. Times indicated by this approach coincide with the most active phases of the protests. It should be noted that while in this case activity online corresponds with activity offline, this might not always be the case. That is, in general, protests might occur but might go unnoticed on Twitter. Also, Twitter users might discuss protests without any corresponding offline event.

- Retweets: examining the tweets that, during the run of our analysis, were retweeted the most we also find a temporal structure of the protests. We find that the time bins marked by the date of the original publication of these tweets largely match the time bins indicated by local maxima in message volume. Beyond the identification of key points in the timeline, retweets also supply a first glance at what is happening at these moments. Still, a cursory analysis of the 20 most retweeted messages (cf. Table 6.2) shows that most of the time their content does not address the various stages of the protest, but instead mostly offers humorous commentary. Thus the content of the most salient tweets does not offer a map of the protests, but instead provides an overview of the social media objects (for example, pictures, links, jokes) connected to the protests in Stuttgart that were amplified by commentators of the event and not the view of activists present at the protests.
- URLs: examining the times when the most salient URLs were initially linked to offers another temporal structure of the events. The results for the Stuttgart dataset show that Twitter messages did not trail accounts of traditional media. The time bins indicated by popular URLs often overlap with the time bin indicated by local maxima in message volume. Many of the referenced websites provide live coverage of the protests through video streams (cf. Table 6.3, column 'type' and there all entries that were labelled 'protest media'). So we can clearly state that at least some users used Twitter in combination with other social media channels to cover the events as they were unfolding. While we still cannot claim that the URL analysis yields an appropriate overall picture of the event itself, it has become clear that (at least, in this case) Twitter messages tracked the protest dynamics with little to no delay.
- Peakiness: so far it has become clear that the approaches described above merely offer coarse maps of the actual event. The peakiness approach offers a somewhat more detailed account of the events. The approach clearly identified time bins that corresponded with important stages in the development of the protest. In addition, it identifies and locates many peaky word stems that are descriptive of important changes in the situation. Good examples for this are the mentioning of gas masks, the moment when trees were first chopped down ('Fällarbeiten') as well as reported eye injuries ('Augenverletzung') (cf. Table 6.4). In contrast to the approaches focusing on salient tweets and URLs – that rely on the prominent visibility of a small subset of all messages (by an even smaller subset of users) – peakiness

is able to detect meaningful trends based on messages posted by a widely distributed group of users. Therein lays its biggest advantage: it is not constrained to the recognition of the few most prominent phenomena. Even if thousands of people decided to independently tweet about a certain moment without referencing each other, the peak would still be detected as long as they use roughly the same vocabulary. A caveat remains in that many of the peaky word stems fail to provide meaningful information on their own. As such, the method is not suited for fully automated analyses. As one tool among many for exploratory analysis, however, it offers a different and valuable new approach to the data.

In this chapter, we investigated the analytical potential of four approaches to event detection with data collected on a social media channel, namely Twitter. We have argued that although these approaches provide a somewhat successful overview over the events, their scientific value remains limited by the lack of representativeness of the original data set. Thorough inferences about real-world protests still require direct, unbiased observations that are unavailable in social media and other media channels (Lang and Lang 1953). We see the potential of analyses based on social media data mainly in their capacity to structure large quantities of unknown data and aid researchers in exploratory sighting. Depending on the respective research question, such data potentially then need corroboration by studies that are based on representative samples of the population under study.

## References

Allan, J. (ed.) (2002) *Topic Detection and Tracking: Event-based Information Organization* (Boston: Kluwer Academic Publishers).

Asur, S. and Huberman, B.A. (2010) *Predicting the Future with Social Media*, available at: http://arxiv.org/abs/1003.5699.

Becker, H., Naaman, M. and Gravano, L. (2011) 'Beyond Trending Topics: Real-World Event Identification on Twitter', in *Proceedings of the Fifth International AAAI Conference on Weblogs and Social Media* (Menlo Park, CA: The AAAI Press), pp. 438–441.

Bieber, C. (2010) *Politik Digital: Online zum Wähler* (Salzhemmendorf: Blumenkamp Verlag).

Bilger, C. and Raidt, E. (2011) 'Schwarzer Donnerstag: Ein lauter Tag hallt nach, Stuttgarter Zeitung', available at: http://www.stuttgarter-zeitung.de/inhalt.schwarzer-donnerstag-ein-lauter-tag-hallt-nach.94770415-a4dd-4957-8422-a689eaa2909e.html.

Bird, S., Loper, E. and Klein, E. (2009) *Natural Language Processing with Python* (Sebastopol, CA: O'Reilly Media).

Brandt, P.T., Freeman, J.R. and Schrodt, P.A. (2011) 'Real Time, Time Series Forecasting of Inter- and Intra-State Political Conflict', *Conflict Management and Peace Science,* 28, 41–64.

Bruns, A. and Burgess, J. (2011) '#Ausvotes: How Twitter Covered the 2010 Australian Federal Election', *Communication, Politics & Culture,* 44 (2), 37–56.

Bruns, A. and Liang, Y.E. (2012) 'Tools and Methods for Capturing Twitter Data During Natural Disasters', *First Monday* 17 (4), available at: http://firstmonday.org/htbin/cgiwrap/bin/ojs/index.php/fm/article/viewArticle/3937/3193.

Bunse. V. (2010) '#S21: Man prügelt seine Bürger nicht... *Kaffee bei mir?*', available at: http://opalkatze.wordpress.com/2010/09/30/s21-man-prugelt-keine-burger/.

Busemann, K. and Gscheidle, C. (2012) 'Web 2.0: Habitualisierung der Social Communitys', *Media Perspektiven,* 7–8, 380–390.

Cha, M., Haddadi, H., Benevenuto, F. and Gummadi, K.P. (2010) 'Measuring User Influence in Twitter: The Million Follower Fallacy', in *Proceedings of the Fourth International AAAI Conference on Weblogs and Social Media* (Menlo Park, CA: The AAAI Press), pp. 10–17.

Chakrabarti, D. and Punera, K. (2011) 'Event Summarization Using Tweets', in *Proceedings of the Fifth International AAAI Conference on Weblogs and Social Media* (Menlo Park, CA: The AAAI Press), pp. 66–73.

Chew C. and Eysenbach G. (2010) 'Pandemics in the Age of Twitter: Content Analysis of Tweets During the 2009 H1N1 Outbreak', *PLoS ONE* 5/11, e14118.

Crawford, K. (2009) 'Following You: Disciplines of Listening in Social Media', *Continuum: Journal of Media & Cultural Studies,* 23 (4), 525–535.

David, G. (2010) 'Camera Phone Images, Videos and Live Streaming: A Contemporary Visual Trend', *Visual Studies,* 25 (1), 89–98.

Gabriel, O.W., Schoen, H. and Faden-Kuhne, K. (2013) *Die Volksabstimmung über 'Stuttgart 21'* (Leverkusen: Opladen Budrich).

Gayo-Avello, D., Metaxas, P.T. and Mustafaraj, E. (2011) 'Limits of Electoral Predictions Using Twitter', in *Proceedings of the Fifth International AAAI Conference on Weblogs and Social Media* (Menlo Park, CA: The AAAI Press), pp. 490–493.

Golder, S.A. and Macy, M.W. (2011) 'Diurnal and Seasonal Mood Vary with Work, Sleep, and Daylength Across Diverse Cultures', *Science,* 333 (6051), 1878–1881.

González-Bailón, S., Borge-Holthoefer, J., Rivero, A. and Moreno, Y. (2011) 'The Dynamics of Protest Recruitment Through an Online Network', *Scientific Reports* 1, Article number 197.

González-Bailón, S., Wang, N., Rivero, A., Borge-Holthoefer, J. and Moreno, Y. (2012) 'Assessing the Bias in Communication Networks Sampled from Twitter', available at: http://ssrn.com/abstract=2185134.

Hoffmann, T. (2010) 'Netzgemeinde Mobilisiert für Gauck', *taz.de,* available at: http://www.taz.de/!53629/.

Jackson, N. and Lilleker, D. (2011) 'Microblogging, Constituency Service and Impression Management: UK MPs and the use of Twitter', *The Journal of Legislative Studies,* 17 (1), 86–105.

Jakat, L. (2010) '"Astroturfing" – Geheimkampf um Botschaften im Netz', *sueddeutsche.de,* available at: http://www.sueddeutsche.de/politik/streit-um-stuttgart-astroturfing-geheimkampf-um-botschaften-im-netz-1.1008550.

Jungherr, A. (2009) *The DigiActive guide to Twitter for Activism,* available at: http://andreasjungherr.net/wp-content/uploads/2011/10/Jungherr-2009-Digiactive-Guide-to-Twitter-for-Activism.pdf.

Jungherr, A. (2012) 'The German Federal Election of 2009: The Challenge of Participatory Cultures in Political Campaigns', *Transformative Works and Fan Activism,* 10, available at: http://journal.transformativeworks.org/index.php/twc/article/view/310/288.

Jungherr, A. and Jürgens, P. (2013) 'Forecasting the Pulse: How Deviations from Regular Patterns in Online Data Can Identify Offline Phenomena', *Internet Research* 23(5), 589–607.

Jungherr, A., Jürgens, P. and Schoen, H. (2012) 'Why the Pirate Party Won the German Election of 2009 or the Trouble with Predictions: A Response to Tumasjan, A., Sprenger, T. O., Sander, P. G., & Welpe, I. M. "Predicting Elections with Twitter: What 140 Characters Reveal About Political Sentiment" ', *Social Science Computer Review* 30 (2), 229–234.

Jürgens, P. (2010) *Stell' Dir vor du twitterst und keiner hört zu. Themen und Öffentlichkeit auf Twitter,* Unpublished Master's Thesis at the Institut für Publizistik, Universität Mainz, Germany.

Jürgens, P. and Jungherr, A. (2011) 'Wahlkampf vom Sofa aus: Twitter im Bundestagswahlkampf 2009', in E.J. Schweitzer and S. Albrecht (eds.), *Das Internet im Wahlkampf: Analysen zur Bundestagswahl 2009* (Wiesbaden: VS Verlag für Sozialwissenschaften), pp. 201–225.

Jürgens, P. and Jungherr, A. (2014) 'The Use of Twitter During the 2009 German National Election', *German Politics*. In Publication.

Jürgens, P., Jungherr, A. and Schoen, H. (2011) 'Small Worlds with a Difference: New Gatekeepers and the Filtering of Political Information on Twitter', in *Proceedings of the ACM WebSci'11*, New York, NY, ACM, available at: http://www.websci11.org/fileadmin/websci/Papers/147_paper.pdf.

Kleinberg, J. (2003) 'Bursty and Hierachical Structure in Streams', *Data Mining and Knowledge Discovery*, 7 (4), 373–397.

Kuhn, J. (2010) 'Live aus der Baumkrone', *sueddeutsche.de,* available at: http://www.sueddeutsche.de/digital/stuttgart-protestvideos-im-netz-live-aus-der-baumkrone-1.1007082.

Landmann, J. and Zuell, C. (2008) 'Identifying Events Using Computer-Assisted Text Analysis', *Social Science Computer Review,* 26, 483–497.

Lang, K. and Lang, G.E. (1953) 'The Unique Perspective of Television and Its Effect: A Pilot Study', *American Sociological Review,* 18 (1), 3–12.

Mader, F. (2010) 'Schwabenstreich im Netz', *sueddeutsche.de,* available at: http://www.sueddeutsche.de/politik/protest-gegen-stuttgart-schwabenstreich-im-netz-1.998202.

Maireder A. and Schwarzenegger, C. (2011) 'A Movement of Connected Individuals: Social Media in the Austrian Student Protests 2009', *Information, Communication & Society* 15 (2), 171–195.

Marwick, A.E. and Boyd, D. (2011) 'I Tweet Honestly, I Tweet Passionately: Twitter Users, Context Collapse, and the Imagined Audience', *New Media & Society,* 13 (1), 114–133.

Nikolov, S. (2012) *Trend or No Trend: A Novel Nonparametric Method for Classifying Time Series,* Unpublished Master's Thesis, Cambridge, MA: Massachusetts Institute of Technology.

Petrovic, S., Osborne, M. and Lavrenko, V. (2010) 'Streaming First Story Detection with Application to Twitter', in *NAACL '10: Proceedings of the 11th Annual Conference of the North American Chapter of the Association for Computational Linguistics* (Stroudsburg, PA: ACL), pp. 181–189.

Pfeiffer, T. (2010a) 'Stuttgart21 im Spiegel von Twitter', *web evangelisten*, available at: http://webevangelisten.de/stuttgart21-im-spiegel-von-twitter/.

Pfeiffer, T. (2010b) 'Stuttgart 21: Auf Facebook redet man nicht mit "den Anderen"', *web evangelisten*, available at: http://webevangelisten.de/stuttgart21-auf-facebook/.

Pickard, V.W. (2006) 'United yet Autonomous: Indymedia and the Struggle to Sustain a Radical Democratic Network', 28 (3), 315–336.

Reißmann, O. (2010) 'Riesenwut auf #S21-Polizeieinsatz', *Spiegel Online*, available at: http://www.spiegel.de/netzwelt/web/0,1518,720701,00.html.

Sakaki, T., Okazaki, M. and Matsuo, Y. (2010) 'Earthquake Shakes Twitter Users: Real-time Event Detection by Social Sensors', in *Proceedings of the 19th International World Wide Web Conference, WWW '10* (New York, NY: ACM), pp. 851–860.

Schimmelpfennig, M. (2010) 'Auf Twitter mehr Bewegen: Ideen, den Widerstand zu stärken', *Copywriting*, available at: http://copywriting.de/archives/1103.

Schrodt, P.A. (2010) 'Automated Production of High-Volume, Near-Real-Time Political Event Data', paper presented at the Annual Meeting of the American Political Science Association, Washington, 2–5 September 2010.

Segerberg, A. and Bennett, L. (2011) 'Social Media and the Organization of Collective Action: Using Twitter to Explore the Ecologies of Two Climate Change Protests', *The Communication Review*, 14 (3), 197–215.

Shamma, D.A., Kennedy, L. and Churchill, E. F. (2009) 'Tweet the Debates: Understanding Community Annotation of Uncollected Sources', in *Proceedings of the First SIGMM Workshop on Social Media, WSM '09* (New York, NY: ACM), pp. 3–10.

Shamma, D.A., Kennedy, L. and Churchill, E.F. (2011) 'Peaks and Persistence: Modeling the Shape of Microblog Conversations', in *Proceedings of the ACM 2011 Conference on Computer Supported Cooperative Work* (New York, NY: ACM), pp. 355–358.

Smith, A. (2011) *Twitter and Social Networking in the 2010 Midterm Elections*, Pew Internet & American Life Project, available at: http://pewinternet.org/~/media//Files/Reports/2011/PIP-Social-Media-and-2010-Election.pdf.

Smith, A. and Brenner, J. (2012) *Twitter Use 2012*, Pew Internet & American Life Project, available at: http://pewinternet.org/Reports/2012/Twitter-Use-2012.aspx.

Stegers, F. (2010) 'The Revolution Will Be Televised Streamed via Mobile', *onlinejournalismus.de*, available at: http://www.onlinejournalismus.de/2010/09/30/stuttgart-21-demo-the-revolution-will-be-televised-streamed-via-mobile/.

Sueddeutsche.de (2010) 'Die ersten Bäume sind gefallen', available at: http://www.sueddeutsche.de/politik/protest-gegen-stuttgart-die-ersten-baeume-sind-gefallen-1.1006862.

Ternieden, H. (2010) 'Machtdemonstration gegen Mappus', *Spiegel Online*, available at: http://www.spiegel.de/politik/deutschland/0,1518,720840,00.html.

Vergeer, M., Hermans, L. and Sams, S. (2011) 'Is the Voter only a Tweet Away? Micro-Blogging During the 2009 European Parliament Election Campaign in the Netherlands', *First Monday*, 16 (8), available at: http://www.uic.edu/htbin/cgiwrap/bin/ojs/index.php/fm/article/viewArticle/3540/30.

Verma, S., Vieweg, S., Corvey, W.J., Palen, L, Martin, J.H., Palmer, M., Schram, A. and Anderson, K.M. (2011) 'Natural Language Processing to the Rescue? Extracting "Situational Awareness" Tweets During Mass Emergency', in *Proceedings of the Fifth International AAAI Conference on Weblogs and Social Media* (Menlo Park, CA: The AAAI Press), pp. 386–392.

Weng, J. and Lee, B. (2011) 'Event Detection in Twitter', in *Proceedings of the Fifth International AAAI Conference on Weblogs and Social Media* (Menlo Park, CA: The AAAI Press), pp. 401–408.

White, J.S., Matthews, J.M. and Stacy, J.L. (2012) 'Coalmine: An Experience in Building a System for Social Media Analytics', *Proc. SPIE 8408, Cyber Sensing 2012*, 84080A.

Wienand, L. (2010) 'Mobiles Kamera-Einsatzkommando: Die "Volksreporter" von Stuttgart 21', *Rhein-Zeitung*, available at: http://www.rhein-zeitung.de/nachrichten/computerundmedia_artikel,-Mobiles-Kamera-Einsatzkommando-Die-Volksreporter-von-S21-_arid,151852.html.

# 7
# Analysing 'Super-Participation' in Online Third Spaces

*Todd Graham and Scott Wright*

Over the past two decades, there has been much debate concerning the Internet's ability to facilitate and support public deliberation and extend the public sphere (cf. Gimmler 2001; Papacharissi 2002; Dahlgren 2005; Coleman and Blumler 2009). The belief that the Internet may play a significant role in reducing some of the deliberative deficit of Western democracies has sparked much interest in the potential benefits and drawbacks of online communication. Following the initial euphoria over the possibility of a 'new' Internet-based public sphere, along with its critical response, a growing body of innovative empirical research into online deliberation has emerged in its wake. Scholars have been interested in how citizens use the Internet to express themselves, not only during election time, but also how it is used for political purposes in citizens' everyday lives. In particular, there is growing research focusing on online, everyday political talk.

Building on the work of Habermas and other deliberative democratic theorists (cf. Barber 1984; Mansbridge 1999; Dryzek 2000), scholars, including the authors of this chapter, have argued that at the heart of civic culture should be a talkative electorate and that the Internet affords citizens the communicative space necessary to rehearse, debate and elaborate the important political and societal issues of the day. Under this account, political conversation becomes one of the essential ways to democratically organise society. It is through ongoing participation in informal political talk whereby citizens become aware of other opinions, discover the pressing issues of the day and develop and transform their preferences. Such talk prepares members of society for participation in the political system. Thus, understanding political talk that occurs in these spaces is important because of its links with other expressions of political engagement from voting in an election to protesting in the streets.

Given its emphasis on user participation and interaction, the Internet is a potentially fruitful place to look if one is interested in political talk. Indeed, the Internet is positively awash in all types, forms and styles of communication and interaction. Net-based public-sphere researchers have studied the nature of online political talk and tried to understand the emerging practices by examining them through the lens of deliberative ideals. Though scholars have analysed online discussions in a variety of ways and in a diverse range of online spaces and contexts, one of the most common findings is that online environments, from discussion forums to Twitter, typically feature highly active minorities of content creators (Dahlberg 2001; Jensen 2003; Coleman 2004; Jankowski and van Os 2004; Davis 2005; Winkler 2005; Albrecht 2006; Dunne 2009; Graham 2010; Anstead and O'Loughlin 2011; Halpern and Gibbs 2013). Given their link to theories of deliberative democracy, such active minorities are typically framed negatively: it is thought that they dominate interactions and crowd out other voices. However, while the existence of the active minority is not in dispute, their actual impact remains unclear: research is scant, focuses primarily on political discussion forums and typically does not move beyond quantitatively observing their existence. This is problematic because we cannot assume that their impact is negative. Regular participants can be an important part of a community (Oldenburg 1999).

The lack of research may, in part, be because analysing highly active participants raises a series of methodological challenges. By definition, such users create an awful lot of content. The spaces in which their participation grows also tend to be very large. Given that the largest forum has over two billion posts, there is potentially an awful lot of data that must be considered. Moreover, such data is typically not presented in ways that make it easy for the researcher to access it, in part to stop scraping 'bots' from getting access to the data. The small number of studies that have focused in more detail on the active minority have confounded expectations: their impact is largely positive because they help to keep debates going, act as 'old hands' and provide continuity that would otherwise not exist in the more ephemeral online world (Albrecht 2006; Kies 2010).

This chapter focuses on our attempts to overcome these methodological challenges and analyse the participatory patterns and discursive activity of what we call super-participants. Our principal contribution in this area (Graham and Wright 2014) focuses on the www.moneysavingexpert.com (MSE) discussion forum. It is one of the largest forums in the United Kingdom and has received nearly 30 million posts. Until recently, the forum (and broader website and email list) was owned by the finance guru and campaigner Martin Lewis. We used a large-scale quantitative content analysis that covered all of the users, alongside a detailed qualitative, hand-coded content analysis. While smaller in scale, this still required a large number of posts to be analysed, and this raises its own challenges.

First, we will discuss why active minorities (that is, super-participants) are typically framed negatively by reviewing the normative frameworks commonly used to analyse online political talk. Second, we present a typology for identifying and categorising super-participants, a framework that can be used to conceptualise super-participation in online forums. Third, we explain and describe the methods that we developed for analysing super-participants. As relative novices to the scraping of data, we explain some of the challenges that we faced, as well as how we eventually overcame them. We then outline our qualitative approach and provide some methodological insight for future research on super-participation. Finally, we discuss the methodological implications of our work.

## Analysing online political talk

Research into online deliberation has developed in various directions over the past two decades. There are studies on the use of online consultations (Beierle 2004; Coleman 2004; Fishkin 2009; Kies 2010; Astrom and Gronlund 2012); moderation and the design of forums (Coleman and Gotze 2001; Edwards 2002; Wright 2006, 2009; Wright and Street 2007); the extent to which such spaces facilitate contact between opposing perspectives (Sunstein 2002; Stromer-Galley 2003; Wojcieszak and Mutz, 2009; Brundidge 2010); and comparisons between face-to-face and online deliberation (Wojcieszak et al. 2009; Baek et al. 2012). However, one of the most popular strands of research has focused on the deliberativeness of online forums; that is, research that has utilised public sphere ideals as a means of evaluating online communicative practices (Schneider 1997; Wilhelm 1999; Dahlberg 2001; Tsaliki 2002; Graham and Witschge 2003; Jensen 2003; Jankowski and van Os 2004; Papacharissi 2004; Davis 2005; Winkler 2005; Albrecht 2006; Stromer-Galley 2007; Strandberg 2008; Dunne 2009; Graham 2008, 2010, 2012; Halpern and Gibbs 2013).

Measuring the deliberativeness of online political talk requires a normative framework of the process of deliberation of the public sphere: researchers construct a set of criteria that embody the ideal, which are then operationalised into measurable concepts and employed in an empirical analysis. Habermas's work (for example, 1984, 1987, 1989, 1990, 1996) – particularly his theory of communicative rationality and discourse ethics – has been highly influential in this process because, as Dahlberg (2004a) has rightly argued, it provides one of the most systematically developed critical theories of the public sphere. However, there is a lack of consistency among researchers as to what criteria should be included, which is mainly due to different interpretations of Habermas's work.[1] For example, Schneider's (1997) pioneering analysis of Usenet newsgroups employed four criteria of the idealised public sphere: equality, diversity, reciprocity and quality. In another prominent study, Wilhelm (1999) identified four criteria: exchange of opinions, rationality, opinion homogeneity and degree of listening.[2] Although there have been a variety of normative frameworks developed, one of the most common conditions employed by past studies has been *discursive equality*.

Discursive equality, not to be mistaken for inclusion (that is, access to the debate), refers to the normative claim that all participants are equal. As Barber (1984, 183) maintains, 'So it is with democratic talk, where no voice is privileged, no position advantaged, no authority other than the process itself acknowledged.' Under the deliberative democratic account, discursive equality requires: that the rules and guidelines that coordinate and maintain the process of deliberation do not privilege one individual or group of individuals over another; that participants have an equal opportunity to express their views and question the position of others; and that participants respect and recognise each other as having an equal voice and standing within this process.[3] Thus, it has been typically employed by researchers at two levels: analysing the formal and informal rules and management of those rules for acts of exclusion and inequality; and identifying communicative exclusions and inequalities that occur in communicative practices. The latter is of particular interest when it comes to understanding why active minorities have been typically framed in a negative light.

In the past, discursive equality has been examined from two angles: equal distribution of voice and substantial equality. The most common measurement of discursive equality has been the equal distribution of voice indicator (Dahlberg 2001; Jensen 2003; Coleman 2004; Jankowski and van Os 2004; Davis 2005; Winkler 2005; Albrecht 2006;

Dunne 2009; Graham 2010; Halpern and Gibbs 2013; Schneider 1997; Strandberg 2008). Researchers measure the number of participants along with their share of the postings, thereby determining the concentration of participation. Forums that maintain a distribution of voice skewed towards a small group of frequent posters are considered discursively unequal because they threaten the participatory opportunities of other participants. Thus, under this account, super-participants are viewed as impeding deliberation because the sheer number of their postings alone drowns out the voices of others. Furthermore, there is often an (implicit) assumption made in the literature that, because of their volume of participation, super-participants dictate the agenda and style of debate.

Substantial equality requires that participants respect and recognise each other as having an equal voice and standing in the deliberative process. One common approach to assessing the level of substantial equality has been to code discussion threads for acts of exclusion and inequality primarily through identifying instances of aggressive and abusive posting behaviour. For example, Hill and Hughes (1998, 52) coded discussion forums for flaming: 'personal, ad hominem attacks that focus on the individual poster not the ideas of the message'. Similarly, Graham (2008, 26) coded discussion threads for degrading: 'A message that degraded – to lower in character, quality, esteem, or rank – another participant and/or participant's argument or opinion'. Coming from a slightly different angle, Papacharissi (2004) coded online discussions for acts of 'incivility and impoliteness'. Under these accounts, high levels of aggressive and abusive communicative practices jeopardise deliberation, because they foster an environment of disrespect and inequality.

The problem with many of these studies is that they tend to make assumptions about the behaviour of super-participants, yet, do not examine in any great detail (if at all), their communicative practices. Regarding the equal distribution of voice indicator, it may be true that the volume of heavy posters alone may make it difficult for other voices to be heard, and there is some participant survey evidence to support this claim (Schultz 2000; Beierle 2004). However, the volume of participation says little about how super-participants are actually behaving in those online forums. Nevertheless, the assumption that super-participants tend to dominate the agenda and style of debate is often made. Those studies that do focus on participants' communicative practices and the style of debate tend to neglect the volume of participation. Moreover, they typically focus on acts of exclusion and inequality while ignoring posting behaviours that might facilitate a more egalitarian communicative environment. On those rare occasions when researchers have analysed the communicative practices of active minorities, they have found their impact to be largely positive (Albrecht 2006; Kies 2010). For example, Albrecht's (2006, 72) analysis revealed that active users did not dominate the agenda or style of debate, but rather, they 'behaved as "old hands", giving advice and providing other participants with an overview of the debate'. As we can see, there is a need for research that not only focuses on active participants but moves beyond simply identifying acts of inequality and exclusion. However, before we turn to our research design, we need to provide some conceptual clarity regarding *super-participation*: what is a super-participant exactly?

## A typology of super-participation

In response to the lack of research, we have developed a typology of what we call super-participants, which has three categories of super-participation. The hope is that the typology will encourage future research into the impact of super-participants and provide a useful theoretical framework to structure empirical analysis. While there are numerous typologies of online participants/actors, few give any weight to the volume of participation. Even where length of membership is an element, they do not give any detail on levels of posting that they consider approximate to their categories (Kim 2000). Our typology provides quantitative definitions while not falling into the trap of thinking that these are the only form of super-participation.

The three categories of super-participation are super-posters (SP1s), agenda-setters (SP2s) and moderators and facilitators (SP3s).

### Super-posters

SP1s are the people who post very regularly to a discussion forum. Our definition has been informed by existing research. Moreover, as there are thousands, if not millions of forums, many of which are very well established and often with similar designs, rules and organisational structures – it is possible to set generalisable parameters: an SP1 is defined as any user that has created more than 2 per cent of all messages on a forum with between 20,000 and 99,999 posts and any user who has made more than 2000 posts on a forum with over 100,000 thousand messages.

### Agenda-setters

SP2s are people who repeatedly start new discussion threads in online forums. As the name suggests, they help to set the parameters of debate and participation. The crucial importance of agenda-setting is finally receiving the attention it deserves (Bua 2012), though less work has been conducted online (see Himelboim et al. 2009 for an exception). Informed by existing research, an SP2 is defined as any person who has created more than 200 threads.

### Moderators and facilitators

SP3s are people who set the tone of a forum and can normally moderate, manage or otherwise advise broader participants. This can be a formal or informal role, and they can be paid professionals or recruited from within forum participants on a voluntary basis. The precise role of facilitators is determined by the forum managers. SP3s often shape the activities of SP1s and SP2s.

Interestingly, the categories hold across different online contexts, suggesting that super-participation is a broader phenomenon. The methodologies and research discussed here largely focus on SP1s.

## Methodology

We opted for a multi-method research design, using quantitative and qualitative content analysis. Thus, in order to analyse how SP1s communicate, we have undertaken both a broad quantitative content analysis and a detailed qualitative content analysis. Our selection of the case and coding frame is informed by our earlier work that has argued that there is a need for more analysis of informal political talk in non-political online forums – third spaces – using inclusive definitions of both politics and what counts as deliberation (Graham 2008, 2010, 2012; Graham and Harju 2011; Wright 2012a, 2012b). Thus, we propose to analyse the www.moneysavingexpert.com (MSE) discussion forum.

### Quantitative method: The scrape

While electronic forms of online content make it more readily accessible to researchers, there are still many significant methodological challenges that must be met. First, significant parts of the content are either held privately – in the back-end of the website – or made public in a partial manner. One particular issue that we faced was that some of the user statistics that we hoped to capture were actually capped at the 300 most recent examples (such as posts thanked) and thus we had to work within this limitation. Where the data is made public, it may be subject to legal restrictions such as copyright that must be considered. There are also increasingly sophisticated techniques that attempt to stop screen scrapers and the like from parsing the data. These restrictions have occurred for several reasons. First, there are concerns over privacy. Second, people's online data is often commercially valuable – either for legal or illegal ends – and limiting access can make sense (it can be sold, for example). Third, some screen scrapers and crawlers can create financial costs for the websites that they 'attack', and lead to reliability issues.[4] In attempting to stop malicious attempts, researchers can get caught in the crossfire.

Handling what is now described as the 'big data' produced online is a relatively new concern for social scientists. The typical approach is for social scientists to work alongside computer scientists – drawing together a wide range of complimentary skill sets (for example, the FITNA Project).[5] Indeed, several of the projects reported on in this volume rely on such collaborations. Nevertheless, there are limitations. Speaking from our personal experience, it can be hard to identify and recruit computer scientists. In part, this is because the kinds of task that we need help with are just too basic; they have limited value to computer scientists, and thus this relies on good will if they are not linked to a research bid.

We considered several approaches to getting the data off the forum and into an analysable format. It is worthwhile discussing the trials and tribulations we experienced, because it highlights the challenges social scientists with limited direct experience of scraping can meet when trying to tap into 'big data'. While we had both used scraping tools in the past (Wright 2006; Graham 2009), we had either relied on people with a computer programming background or used off-the-shelf packages. Initially, we asked on prominent discussion lists for help with scraping, but drew a blank. Fortuitously, we noticed that our target forum included a list of all the users on the forum along with various metadata, including posting frequency. Moreover, the forum software allows the researcher to sort the data according to these criteria. This made accessing the data significantly easier. It should be noted that, in the absence of a list, applying the techniques discussed below would be either unlikely to work or prohibitively time-consuming and thus the ability to write script would be necessary.

Without an obvious tool or script to remove the data, we initially tried cutting and pasting the user list into a spreadsheet. Unfortunately, this proved problematic because it was not possible to extract the bits of data we wanted directly into a spreadsheet. Instead, we had to copy and paste most of the page into a Word document first and then sort and extract the columns. This process was slowed down because most users have an avatar (image) attached to their profile. While undertaking this laborious process, a colleague with knowledge of writing screen scraping scripts offered to help us. Unfortunately, the first two attempts at scraping the data did not work correctly. At the third attempt, the scrape worked. The data was verified by checking that the number of users matched what was presented. A random sample of participants was also checked to make sure that the data (number of signatures and so on) matched. In the interim, fearing that the script would not work, we redoubled our efforts to find scraping tools that did not require programming skills. We managed to identify several that could be applied to the list (though not to the secondary level data contained on individual user profiles) and conducted our own scrape using Google Docs. We will now present some of the tools that we have found helpful. Before we present this, however, it would be helpful to discuss the kind(s) of data that are necessary to analyse super-participation.

To analyse SP1s, the key information that is required is frequency and volume of posting; length of membership; the text of messages; the username of a participant; and the thread structure. Forums often feature further, interesting pieces of information such as the number of likes a post receives, the number of likes a participant makes and personal information such as occupation. The basic raw data can then be subjected to quantitative and qualitative analysis. For example, the usernames can be coded for gender or use of anonymity, and this information can be used to further break down the analysis for comparative research.

Initially a site-map generator can be used, if the URL range either is not known or is not presented sequentially. Rather than clicking on each page and copying and pasting the URL, these tools scrape off all of the URLs from a root (for example, epetitions.direct.gov.uk). Of course, it is still necessary to verify and remove unwanted URLs. There are several potential tools such as http://www.xml-sitemaps.com – with Google providing a helpful list.[6] The Google Docs extraction function works across several formats, including tables. The researcher inserts a formula (for example, =IMPORTHTML("URL"; "table"; X) that commands it to scrape off a table on the given web page. Outwit Hub offers both free and a paid-for 'pro' scraper. Other interesting tools include Yahoo's Dapper, Google Chrome's XPath extension scraper, NodeXL and Webharvy. These enable the researcher to identify and scrape discrete aspects of a web page that is not necessarily in a table format. You click on the text that you are interested in (for example, the username of a person), and then you mark this as a username and they can scrape off each username on the page. You can mark up multiple areas of the same page. Where there are a series of pages with a similar structure, you apply the scrape across the different pages and link them together.

Once the data is extracted, a useful data-cleaning and sorting tool is Google/Open Refine. This allows the researcher to correct blemishes in data that can affect your ability to manipulate it. For example, if you wanted to sort names, if there is a space or number in front of the name, they will be presented out of order and this can be amended. Similarly, if the same code is accidentally stored under different names (for example, R&D or Research and Development), the tool makes it easy to standardise these.

One final point to bear in mind is that some online environments give access to at least some of their data much more readily. In particular, websites such as Facebook and Twitter provide an Application Programming Interface (API) that allows script developers to gain access to some of their data (400 track keywords, 5000 follow user IDs and twenty-five 0.1–360 degree locations in the case of Twitter) and will also offer data streams such as the Twitter 'fire hose' for a price. There are now many tools available that allow the user to tap into such feeds and code data (for example, Discovertext). Unfortunately, there typically aren't APIs for discussion forums. This is because they can be underpinned by a different architecture, so the script has to be tweaked for each case. One concern is that the difficulties of getting access to the data from online environments that do not have an API will lead researchers to focus on websites that do. There are also some concerns about the limitations of the data gained from APIs as elsewhere in this volume.

## Qualitative content analysis

The aim of the qualitative content analysis was to investigate SP1's posting behaviour by moving beyond the manifest coding of volume and frequency: how are SP1s actually behaving in these online spaces? In this section, we start by discussing some of the challenges we faced regarding the selection of the population and sample. This was not as straight forward as it might seem, namely due to the sheer amount of data produced by SP1s. We then discuss the method and coding scheme adopted. The aim here is not only to highlight some of the key issues one has to deal with when analysing SP1s' posts, but also to provide some insight into developing a coding scheme for investigating SP1s' impact on public debate.

We identified a total 2052 SP1s who had contributed 11.8 million posts. Given the vast amount of data, the first challenge we encountered was selecting the population and sample for analysis. We avoided selecting a random sample of SP1s from the list of 2052 participants because the posting rates within the group differed considerably from 2001 posts to 116,074 posts for the most active user. Rather, we wanted to select a sample that accounted for this diversity. Another issue we had to contend with was dormant SP1s (or closed accounts): participants that had not posted in five or more years. Given the limitations of the search function of the website, accessing their data was not possible. Taking all this into account, we selected 25 SP1s: beginning with the most frequent poster, every 80th SP1 active during 2008–2012 was selected for analysis.

We limited the analysis to 25 SP1s. This was done for two reasons. First, practically speaking, the coding scheme adopted for analysis was time-consuming. Second, and more importantly, we felt that to understand SP1s posting behaviour, it was essential to analyse a substantial number of postings for each SP1 rather than taking more SP1s with fewer postings. Many of our SP1s posted comments over a diverse range of sub-forums and/or types of threads. Consequently, by taking a larger sample for each SP1, we were able to provide a more comprehensive account. Naturally, selecting the population and sample depends largely on the depth of the coding scheme along with the time and resources available to the research team. However, if one is interested in analysing posting behaviours of SP1s, we would recommend taking fewer SP1s with more postings than vice versa. As we will see, collecting the actual sample presents a whole new set of challenges and difficulties.

There are two important factors to consider when it comes to collecting the sample for analysis: the context unit of analysis and thread size. The context unit of analysis plays an essential role when coding posting behaviour. There are arguably various contexts that a researcher may want to consider (for example, the forum, sub-forum, a particular event), depending on the research aim and focus. That being said, one of the most significant contexts is the discussion thread. In order to code posting behaviour (the function of a post), you need to read the postings in the context of the entire discussion thread; in other words, you need to read the whole thread. Thus, when compiling the sample for analysis, our unit of selection was the discussion thread, as opposed to the individual post.

One of the advantages of human coding is that trained coders do a much better job of taking the context unit of analysis into account while coding in comparison to the automated coding software available today. However, one drawback is the amount of data one is left with for analysis. For example, although the unit of analysis is a single post, you may have to read through thousands of postings in order to code just 100 comments from a single SP1. When collecting the sample, one of the difficulties we faced was that many SP1s posted one to three comments per thread. Consequently, collecting the data became a balancing act between identifying enough threads (with enough posts) for analysis along with the practical consideration of the time needed to read through the threads and code SP1s' posts.

One way to help deal with possible data overload and help organise systematically the collection of the sample is to take thread size into account. In our case, thread size ranged from a single post to 27,000 (plus) postings. We decided to take different-sized threads into account, not only for practical reasons, but also because behaviour might vary between small and large threads (something we noticed in our previous research). Upon investigation, we discovered that most threads did not exceed 600 postings, and those that did were usually set over several years. Thus, we distinguished between three sizes: small threads ($<$ 100 postings), medium threads ($\geq$100 and $<$ 300 postings) and large threads ($\geq$300 and $\leq$600 postings).

Given that the unit of selection was the thread and not the post, several rounds of sampling were carried out in order to gather 100 posts for each of the 25 SP1s. In the first round, two small, two medium and two large threads for each SP1 were randomly selected. For those SP1s where 100 postings were not collected, a second round of sampling was conducted by randomly selecting another set of small, medium and large threads. Any SP1 where 100 or more postings were still not obtained, we then proceed to select randomly small, medium and large threads until this was achieved in a final round of sampling. A 100 post requirement was set because, in our case, it provided us with enough data for investigating posting behaviour while avoiding data overload when it came to reading and coding the threads.

When it came to developing a coding scheme, there were various challenges we encountered. First, there were few studies that analysed the posting behaviour of SP1s, which made adopting coding categories difficult. The coding schemes that were available focused primarily on specific communicative forms such as argumentation and other deliberative norms. Since our aim was to move beyond these normative frameworks and beyond coding for acts of inequality and exclusion, we decided to employ a qualitative content analysis (Mayring 2000), which utilised both deductive and inductive coding techniques. More specifically, we initially adopted Graham's (2008) coding scheme, which was developed to analyse the deliberativeness of online political talk while employing an inductive coding method via the use of feedback loops. During several rounds of coding, some of the initial codes were modified, merged and deleted while, via inductive coding, new codes were created until a final set of coding categories was deduced. The final product (in addition to our findings of course) was a tested content analysis codebook, which can be used for future research.

Second, another issue that we had to sort out was whether to make the codes for behaviour mutually exclusive. The aim of the analysis was to identify the *primary* behaviour (function of the post). However, a post can potentially serve multiple functions; a user can address multiple participants, issues and/or subjects. For example, in a single post, a participant can give advice on applying for child benefits to one person while, later in the same post, debate the recent austerity policies being implemented by the government. In order to compensate for this, a single post could be coded as having multiple behaviours when it was clear that a participant was addressing multiple issues or participants (using different behaviours), as the example above illustrates. However, this can become quite complicated, particularly for long posts. Thus, clear coding rules and procedures for dealing with such cases are required.

Finally, we were interested not only in how SP1s were behaving, but also whether their behaviour served any positive function. Our analysis, along with (our) previous research, indicates that there are several types of behaviour that seem to enhance the quality of debate and/or foster an egalitarian communicative environment. The goal here is not to provide a complete breakdown of these various posting behaviours (see Graham and Wright 2014), but rather, to provide some insight into the types of SP1 behaviour that researchers could use to help develop future coding schemes.

There were three groups of behaviour that SP1s exhibited that seemed to serve a positive function and, we would argue, should be taken into account when investigating the impact of SP1s on public debate: consultative and supportive, pedagogical and social bonding-based communicative forms. Consultative and supportive communicative forms were quite common among SP1s. This refers to behaviours such as advice giving, helping and various other support-based behaviours.

Pedagogical communicative forms such as informing, clarifying and interpreting were also common among SP1s, particularly during extended (political) debates. SP1s here helped foster a more productive debate by, for example, clarifying and summarising the position for others. Social bonding-based communicative forms were the most common among SP1s. This included behaviours such as banter, chatter and storytelling. At first, they might not seem like the behaviours one should be looking for when analysing the quality of debate. However, this type of behaviour among SP1s fostered a friendly communicative environment; it kept the debate going; and it seemed to create a sense of community among forum participants.

## Conclusion

Highly complex online environments such as discussion forums raise numerous potential research questions, often necessitating a multi-method and interdisciplinary approach. One basic problem that we have faced is that there simply is not enough space in a standard research article to cover all of the ground that we would like. This means that compromises have to be made – be it to the literature cited, or to the methodological detail. In this example, we could only analyse SP1s. Such compromises are often picked up at the review stage, and thus a very careful balance has to be struck.

As has been noted, undertaking screen scraping can be difficult. While there are a number of excellent tools available, they have limitations and need refinement to fit specific cases, and this requires the ability to write script. How might we open up scraping to a broader audience? While we did end up managing to do this – even trying to write our own scraping script – it is not particularly efficient: what takes us days to get right would probably take a programmer two minutes! But how might we overcome this?

One idea is that a team of computer scientists (perhaps research students) could be gathered together under the auspice of the e-Social Science Centre or its successors and social scientists could effectively bid for their support in tool development through research proposals. A similar idea has been used in the United States in relation to surveys. As surveys can (1) be expensive to run; (2) people may not have the relevant expertise to run a survey; and (3) they may only be interested in one or two questions – an ongoing panel survey was set up and scholars could bid to have their questions included. Another idea is that computer science departments could ask scholars in other departments to submit research projects for which they need programming support, and these can then be offered to dissertation students as research projects. This might be to develop a screen scraper, for example. In the meantime, we encourage researchers to explore the wide range of 'off the shelf' tools that now exist: when combined together they can be very powerful. Of course, getting the data is but a necessary first step, and how to analyse and interpret 'big data' is an ongoing area of debate. While machine learning continues to improve, for the reasons discussed above, we believe that there will always be an important place for studies that combine large-scale quantitative and qualitative hand-coded content analyses such as that deployed here.

## Notes

1. See Dahlberg (2004a) for critical account of past normative frameworks based on Habermas's work.
2. See Dahlberg (2004b), Graham (2009) and Kies (2010) for comprehensive normative frameworks.
3. For a more elaborate theoretical account of discursive equality, see, for example, Cohen (1997, 74) and Benhabib (1996, 68).
4. Screen scraping, also known as web scraping, is a computer software technique of extracting information/data from websites.
5. http://www.lboro.ac.uk/departments/socialsciences/research/projects/fitna project/
6. http://code.google.com/p/sitemap-generators/wiki/SitemapGenerators

## References

Albrecht, S. (2006) 'Whose Voice Is Heard in Online Deliberation? A Study of Participation and Representation in Political Debates on the Internet', *Information, Communication & Society*, 9 (1), 62–82.

Anstead, N. and O'Loughlin, B. (2011) 'The Emerging Viewertariat and BBC Question Time: Television Debate and Real Time Commenting Online', *International Journal of Press/Politics*, 16 (4), 440–462.

Astrom, J. and Gronlund, A. (2012) 'Online Consultations in Local Government: What Works, When and How', in S. Coleman and P. Shane (eds.), *Connecting Democracy: Online Consultation and the Flow of Political Communication* (Cambridge, MA: MIT Press), pp. 75–96.

Baek, Y.M., Wojcieszak, M. and Delli Carpini, M.X. (2012) 'Online Versus Face-to-Face Deliberation: Who? Why? What? With What Effects?', *New Media & Society*, 14 (3), 363–383.

Barber, B.R. (1984) *Strong Democracy: Participatory Politics for a New Age* (Berkeley, CA: University of California Press).

Beierle, T.C. (2004) 'Engaging the Public Through Online Policy Dialogues', in P. Shane (ed.), *Democracy Online: The Prospects for Democratic Renewal Through the Internet* (New York: Taylor & Francis), pp. 155–66.
Benhabib, S. (1996) 'Toward a Deliberative Model of Democratic Legitimacy', in S. Benhabib (ed.), *Democracy and Difference: Contesting the Boundaries of the Political* (Princeton, NJ: Princeton University Press), pp. 67–94.
Brundidge, J. (2010) 'Encountering "Difference" in the Contemporary Public Sphere: The Contribution of the Internet to the Heterogeneity of Political Discussion Networks', *Journal of Communication,* 60 (4), 680–700.
Bua, A. (2012) 'Agenda Setting and Democratic Innovation: The Case of the Sustainable Communities Act 2007', *Politics,* 32 (1), 10–20.
Cohen, J. (1997) 'Deliberation and Democratic Legitimacy', in J. Bohman and W. Rehg (eds.), *Deliberative Democracy: Essays on Reason and Politics* (Cambridge, MA: MIT Press), pp. 67–92.
Coleman, S. (2004) 'Connecting Parliament to the Public via the Internet', *Information, Communication & Society,* 7 (1), 1–22.
Coleman, S. and Blumler, J.G. (2009) *The Internet and Democratic Citizenship* (Cambridge: Cambridge University Press).
Coleman, S. and Gotze, J. (2001) *Bowling Together: Online Public Engagement in Policy Deliberation* (London: Hansard Society).
Dahlberg, L. (2001) 'Extending the Public Sphere Through Cyberspace: The Case of Minnesota E-Democracy', *First Monday: Peer-Reviewed Journal on the Internet* 6 (3), available at http://firstmonday.org/htbin/cgiwrap/bin/ojs/index.php/fm/article/view/838/747, date accessed 9 July 2013.
Dahlberg, L. (2004a) 'Net-Public Sphere Research: Beyond the "First Phase"' *Javnost – The Public,* 11 (1), 5–22.
Dahlberg, L. (2004b) 'The Habermasian Public Sphere: A Specification of the Idealized Conditions of Democratic Communication', *Studies in Social and Political Thought,* 10, 2–18.
Dahlgren, P. (2005) 'The Internet, Public Spheres, and Political Communication: Dispersion and Deliberation', *Political Communication,* 22 (2), 147–162.
Davis, R. (2005) *Politics Online: Blogs, Chatrooms and Discussion Groups in American Democracy* (London: Routledge).
Dryzek, J.S. (2000) *Deliberative Democracy and Beyond: Liberals, Critics, Contestations* (Oxford: Oxford University Press).
Dunne, K. (2009) 'Cross Cutting Discussion: A Form of Online Discussion Discovered within Local Political Online Forums', *Information Polity,* 14 (3), 219–232.
Edwards, A.R. (2002) 'The Moderator as an Emerging Democratic Intermediary: The Role of the Moderator in Internet Discussions About Public Issues', *Information Polity,* 7 (1), 3–20.
Fishkin, J. (2009) *When the People Speak: Deliberative Democracy and Public Consultation* (Oxford: Oxford University Press).
Gimmler, A. (2001) 'Deliberative Democracy, the Public Sphere and the Internet', *Philosophy & Social Criticism,* 27 (4), 21–39.
Graham, T. (2008) 'Needles in a Haystack: A New Approach for Identifying and Assessing Political Talk in Nonpolitical Discussion Forums', *Javnost – The Public,* 15 (2), 17–36.

Graham, T. (2009) 'What's Wife Swap Got to Do with It? Talking Politics in the Net-Based Public Sphere'. PhD Dissertation (University of Amsterdam: Amsterdam), available at http://dare.uva.nl/record/314852, date accessed 9 July 2013.

Graham, T. (2010) 'Talking Politics Online Within Spaces of Popular Culture: The Case of the Big Brother Forum', *Javnost – The Public,* 17 (4), 25–42.

Graham, T. (2012) 'Beyond "Political" Communicative Spaces: Talking Politics on the Wife Swap Discussion Forum', *Journal of Information Technology and Politics,* 9 (1), 31–45.

Graham, T. and Harju, A. (2011) 'Reality TV as a Trigger of Everyday Political Talk in the Net-Based Public Sphere', *European Journal of Communication,* 26 (1), 18–32.

Graham, T. and Witschge, T. (2003) 'In Search of Online Deliberation: Towards a New Method for Examining the Quality of Online Discussions', *Communications: The European Journal of Communication Research,* 28 (2), 173–204.

Graham, T. and Wright, S. (2014) 'Discursive Equality and Everyday Talk Online: The Impact of "Super-Participants" ', *Journal of Computer-Mediated Communication,* 19 (3), 625–642.

Habermas, J. (1984) *The Theory of Communicative Action. Vol. 1, Reason and the Rationalization of Society* (Boston, MA: Beacon Press).

Habermas, J. (1987) *The Theory of Communicative Action. Vol. 2, Lifeworld and System: A Critique of Functionalist Reason* (Boston, MA: Beacon Press).

Habermas, J. (1989) *The Structural Transformation of the Public Sphere: An Inquiry into a Category of Bourgeois Society* (Cambridge, MA: Polity Press).

Habermas, J. (1990) *Moral Consciousness and Communicative Action* (Cambridge, MA: MIT Press).

Habermas, J. (1996) *Between Facts and Norms: Contributions to a Discourse Theory of Law and Democracy* (Cambridge, MA: MIT Press).

Halpern, D. and Gibbs, J. (2013) 'Social Media as a Catalyst for Online Deliberation? Exploring the Affordances of Facebook and YouTube for Political Expression', *Computers in Human Behavior,* 29 (3), 1159–1168.

Hill, K.A. and Hughes, J.E. (1998) *Cyberpolitics: Citizen Activism in the Age of Internet* (New York: Rowman & Littlefield).

Himelboim, I., Gleave, E. and Smith, M. (2009) 'Discussion Catalysts in Online Political Discussions: Content Importers and Conversation Starters', *Journal of Computer-Mediated Communication,* 14 (4), 771–789.

Jankowski, N.W. and van Os, R. (2004) 'Internet-Based Political Discourse', in P. Shane (ed.), *Democracy Online: The Prospects for Political Renewal Through the Internet* (New York: Taylor & Francis), pp. 181–194.

Jensen, J.L. (2003) 'Public Spheres on the Internet: Anarchic or Government Sponsored – A Comparison', *Scandinavian Political Studies,* 26 (4), 349–374.

Kies R. (2010) *Promises and Limits of Web-Deliberation* (Basingstoke: Palgrave Macmillan).

Kim, A.J. (2000) *Community Building on the Web* (Berkeley, CA: Peachpit Press).

Mansbridge, J. (1999) 'Everyday Talk in the Deliberative System', in S. Macedo (ed.), *Deliberative Politics: Essays on Democracy and Disagreement* (Oxford: Oxford University Press), pp. 211–239.

Mayring, P. (2000) 'Qualitative Content Analysis', *Forum: Qualitative Social Research,* 1, available at: http://www.qualitative-research.net/index.php/fqs/article/view/1089, date accessed 9 July 2013.
Oldenburg, R. (1999) *Great Good Place: Cafés, Coffee Shops, Bookstores, Bars, Hair Salons and Other Hangouts at the Heart of a Community* (New York: Marlow & Company).
Papacharissi, Z. (2002) 'The Virtual Sphere: The Internet as a Public Sphere', *New Media & Society,* 4 (1), 9–27.
Papacharissi, Z. (2004) 'Democracy Online: Civility, Politeness, and the Democratic Potential of Online Political Discussion Groups', *New Media & Society,* 6 (2), 259–283.
Schneider, S.M. (1997) 'Expanding the Public Sphere Through Computer Mediated Communication: Political Discussion about Abortion in a Usenet Newsgroup'. PhD Dissertation (Massachusetts Institute of Technology, Cambridge, Massachusetts).
Schultz, T. (2000) 'Mass Media and the Concept of Interactivity: An Exploratory Study of Online Forums and Reader Email', *Media, Culture & Society,* 22 (2), 205–221.
Strandberg, K. (2008) 'Public Deliberation Goes On-Line? An Analysis of Citizens' Political Discussions on the Internet Prior to the Finnish Parliamentary Elections in 2007', *Javnost – The Public,* 15 (1), 71–90.
Stromer-Galley, J. (2003) 'Diversity of Political Conversation on the Internet: Users' Perspectives', *Journal of Computer-Mediated Communication,* 8 (3), available at: http://jcmc.indiana.edu/vol8/issue3/stromergalley.html, date accessed 9 July 2013.
Stromer-Galley, J. (2007) 'Assessing Deliberative Quality: A Coding Scheme', *Journal of Public Deliberation,* 3 (1), 1–35.
Sunstein, C.R. (2002) *Republic.com* (Princeton, NJ: Princeton University Press).
Tsaliki, L. (2002) 'Online Forums and the Enlargement of Public Space: Research Findings from a European Project', *Javnost – The Public,* 9 (2), 95–112.
Wilhelm, A.G. (1999) 'Virtual Sounding Boards: How Deliberative Is Online Political Discussion?', in B.N. Hague and B.D. Loader (eds.), *Digital Democracy: Discourse and Decision Making in the Information Age* (London: Routledge), pp. 154–178.
Winkler, R. (2005) *Europeans Have a Say: Online Debates and Consultations in the EU* (Vienna: The Austrian Federal Ministry for Education).
Wojcieszak, M.E, Baek, Y.M. and Delli Carpini, M.X. (2009) 'What Is Really Going On? Structure Underlying Face-to-Face and Online Deliberation', *Information, Communication & Society,* 12 (7), 1080–1102.
Wojcieszak, M.E. and Mutz, D.C. (2009) 'Online Groups and Political Discourse: Do Online Discussion Spaces Facilitate Exposure to Political Disagreement?', *Journal of Communication,* 59, 40–59.
Wright, S. (2006) 'Government-Run Online Discussion Forums: Moderation, Censorship and the Shadow of Control', *British Journal of Politics and International Relations,* 8 (4), 550–568.
Wright, S. and Street, J. (2007) 'Democracy, Deliberation and Design: the case of online discussion forums, *New Media & Society,* 9 (5), 849–869.
Wright, S. (2009) 'The Role of the Moderator: Problems and Possibilities for Government-Run Online Discussion Forums', in T. Davies and S.P.

Gangadharan (eds.), *Online Deliberation: Design, Research, and Practice* (Stanford, CA: CSLI Publications), pp. 233–242.
Wright, S. (2012a) 'Politics as Usual? Revolution, Normalization and a New Agenda for Online Deliberation', *New Media & Society,* 14 (2), 244–261.
Wright, S. (2012b) 'From "Third Place" to "Third Space": Everyday Political Talk in Non-Political Online Spaces', *Javnost – The Public,* 19 (3), 5–20.

# Part III

# Mixed Methods and Approaches for the Analysis of Web Campaign

# 8

# A Mixed-Methods Approach to Capturing Online Local Level Campaigns Data at the 2010 UK General Election

*Rosalynd Southern*

The emergence of the Web as a political campaigning tool has challenged social researchers to develop innovative methods of data capture that can account for unique aspects of web campaigning including personal websites, social media and campaign emails. This chapter sets out a mixed-methods methodology for measuring candidates' online web campaigns by form and interactivity at the 2010 UK general election. The methodology uses a quantitative content analysis of both Web 1.0 and Web 2.0 campaigning materials and combines this with a qualitative analysis of email responses sent by the candidates themselves during the campaign. These three datasets can be used to provide different perspectives on supply-side online campaigning and can be used to compare whether drivers of engagement are the same or different for Web 1.0 and Web 2.0 types of campaigning. The purpose of this chapter is not to present any results from the study, but to highlight a proposed methodology for capturing data which is applicable to an area of study which is often overlooked – that is, candidate-level online campaigning. This methodology aims to improve upon past studies into these areas with an updated approach that is more appropriate for the development and expansion in online technology in political campaigning recent years.

Since the last UK general election in 2005, communications on the Web have changed dramatically, mainly driven by the rapid mainstreaming of social media tools such as Facebook, Twitter and YouTube. One of the main advantages of campaigning with these new Web tools is their potential for interactivity. In the past, candidate campaign sites have often been criticised for there lack of interactivity or even overall activity (Gibson and Ward 2003; Coleman and Ward 2005). UK websites in the 2001 general election were lacklustre in utilising technology to its full potential, often just reproducing offline campaigning materials on a web page with little attempt at interaction or dialogue with site visitors. Little appeared to change in the 2005 general election (Ward 2005). Web 2.0, while it can be used as a top-down one-way communication medium, has the potential to facilitate interaction as this is one of its key functions, and so one would expect that candidates may be more likely to exhibit interaction in their campaigns via these new media. No other study to date has attempted to measure candidates' Web 2.0 campaigning activity in the United Kingdom. As this is a new technology, measuring how interactive candidates' Web 2.0 campaigning requires a new methodological approach.

To develop an effective coding scheme of a candidate's Web 2.0 interactivity, it is important to set out how such information would be used. The first research question would be to what extent are candidates using online methods? Furthermore, a second research question would be what factors affect the adoption of online campaigns, with particular reference to party size and resources in line with the current literature on normalisation (Gibson and Römmele 2006; Strandberg 2009; Sudulich and Wall 2009). A final research question taps into the second strand of normalisation often debated in the literature, which is how online methods of campaigning are being used (Norris 2003; Foot and Schneider 2006; Gulati and Williams 2007). This final question would assess the type of communication being exhibited by candidates – that is, do patterns of online use support a broadcast model of communications, or is there genuine evidence for interactivity and engagement.

## Existing methods for researching online election campaigning

There have been few studies to date which examine candidate-level online campaigns data using a systematic and comprehensive approach and no standardised approach across research studies. Certain researchers (Margolis and Resnick 1997; Mann and Stewart 2000) have used a qualitative approach to produce ethnographic or discourse analysis studies of web campaigns. However, by far the most common, method used to study online campaigning has been a semi-quantitative content or 'feature' analysis approach similar to traditional content analysis of texts. This applies a pre-set coding scheme to websites to code and measure their contents, which is more appropriate if one wishes to systematically measure Web use trends over time and control for other variables. Setting up a fixed set of criteria, based on clear concepts, to measure Web use was an approach used by Gibson and Ward (2000) and Foot and Schneider (2002) when assessing party campaign sites and election orientated websites, respectively. Gibson and Ward (2000) set out their criteria based on party function in general and its relation to media communication. From this theoretical starting point, they suggested five functions of party and candidate websites information provision, campaigning, resource generation, networking and promotion of participation. These functions of sites are then measured by taking word counts of different information provisions such as manifestos and policies, candidate biographies and campaign news. Presence of upward information flows such as donation forms were recorded and lateral information flows such as the number of links to other affiliated or supporter sites were also noted. Interactivity was measured by gathering the presence or absence of features such as email contact provision, games and polls and the promotion of participation was measured by noting the presence of a means to become a member, sign up for postal votes and online chats and debates. The coding scheme was then applied to the Australian and UK Labour Party sites as case studies to illustrate how the coding scheme worked in practice.

Foot and Schneider (2002) adopt a similar approach whereby they archived and collected different types of online activity although they captured this not just for party and candidate sites but for all election oriented sites during the 2000 US presidential election season between July and December. This produced a data corpus of nearly one million unique web pages from 5000 different websites, including about 750 candidate websites. They identified three distinct types of online campaign activity: co-production, carnival and mobilisation. Examples of co-production exhibited by sites included urging site visitors to provide feedback on local campaigns and providing them with a questionnaire of their views which would let them know which candidate held views closest to their own. Carnival activities referred to activities which subvert political norms and include insulting political actors, gimmicks, and satire and parody sites claiming to be the official sites of candidates. Mobilisation was defined here as a two-step process and only recorded if the text was 'Tell your friends to vote for Smith' rather than 'Vote for Smith'. Although this method involves manual coding and so can be limited in terms of dataset size, it has the advantage of producing large enough amounts of data to be used in a variety of ways to explain different aspects of Web use.

With the emergence of Web 2.0 more recently, this method has been adapted to incorporate Web 2.0 elements into the content analysis, which has sometimes been termed Web 1.5. (Lilleker and Jackson 2009), due to Web 2.0 elements being included in the coding but using the same coding method used for Web 1.0 elements. The approach suggested in this study uses different coding schemes for Web 1.0 and Web 2.0 to account for the different ways in which they can be, and are, used. Foot and Schneider (2006), produce a typology by which to measure political communication in election and use this to collect features of sites that fall into four categories: information provision; promotion of interaction between supporters and organisations; external connectivity; and mobilisation (of others as described above). Stein (2009) largely replicates this typology in her study of a random sample of 750 various US social movement organisation sites, with the addition of categories for hosting of creative works and resource generation. Gulati and Williams (2007) also use the Web 1.5 approach in their analysis of candidate Web communication in the 2006 congressional elections. They measured the presence of candidate websites and furthermore recorded the presence of informational content, features of engagement and mobilisation tools. Features of engagement included certain Web 2.0 applications such as a having a Facebook profile and having a blog. Only the presence or absence of these features was collected, however, with no attempt to measure how Web 2.0 was being used or whether it was being used interactively.

Building on these studies, the mixed methodology approach proposed in this chapter aims to capture evidence of actual interaction by candidates, rather than simply recording the presence of tools that can be used for interaction or whether candidate were members of certain social networks. Web 2.0 applications are especially prized for their interactive capabilities and their social networking and information sharing capabilities. It is important to not only capture candidates' use of Web 2.0 tools but the extent to which they were using them interactively. This information can help to answer several important questions that surround online campaigning notably how far the Web is promoting or undermining normalisation (that is, whether larger parties are continuing to dominate online as they do in offline campaigning) and about how far the Web may be a driver of campaign change.

There are few studies to date which have analysed the use of emails by candidates at election time. Jackson (2003, 2008) has examined UK MPs' use of e-newsletters and interviewed both candidates who sent them and citizens who received them on their view towards them. MPs who use email newsletters reported feeling that they were an aid to retaining or even converting voters and in the same study interviews with recipients of e-newsletters reported that up to 25 per cent of those questioned said that receiving the newsletter had made them change their prior party affiliation (Jackson 2008). MPs reported that they felt using a more personalised approach (that is, using their name and talking about localised issues) was more effective at building and retaining these links. However, as Jackson (2003) pointed out in an earlier study, this 'relationship marketing' approach benefits an incumbent candidate more than it would a challenger who does not have as much time to forge lasting relationships and simply has to secure a 'sale', that is, vote (O'Malley et al. 1999).

The content of candidate emails has not been analysed before in the UK context and it is of interest here to be able to ascertain whether candidates appear to be using their email correspondence in a more personal way, answering specific questions and offering help, or whether they are using a more direct-marketing approach which is designed to promote the party or the candidate in a rather top down manner in an obvious effort to simply secure a vote and what factors may be driving these different approaches. The coding scheme devised here is designed to be able to capture this information.

## Why mixed methods?

Mixed-methods research designs, such as that proposed here, hold certain general advantages in that they can expand the scope and breadth of information gathered and can help to offset the limitations of using either single method alone (Bryman 1984). Combining different types of data adds explanatory power to findings as this method allows the researcher to look past the headline findings from surveys and ascertain how or why certain patterns are emerging.

For collecting data on candidates' use of personal websites the first approach used was a quantitative content analysis study that developed existing schemes to apply pre-set criteria to ascertain the extent of candidates' use of different types of web presence (see below). This approach was decided upon as it would produce a dataset with fixed, objective categories which would be large enough to allow for a detailed analysis when combined with secondary data as control variables.

A second more in-depth coding scheme was used to capture candidates' Web 2.0 use. Again, a fixed set of criteria was produced based on interactivity and a candidate's Web 2.0 use was coded in line with this, which will be laid out in more detail later in this chapter. This Web 2.0 dataset complements the first as it provides more detail, depth and texture, creating a more rounded picture of Web use for campaigning. This approach therefore produces two datasets which will be suitable for statistical modelling, both having clear and distinct categorisations which can form either the dependent or an independent variable in other models. The third source of data was collected using a quasi-experimental design in which an email was sent to candidates which purported to be from an ordinary voter. This allows for a qualitative text-based analysis to be done which reveals in detail how candidates use the Internet. This evidence can also be used to create another quantitative source of data by coding the emails again against a fixed set of criteria. There are obvious ethical issues with the adoption of this approach which are discussed in more detail later in the chapter. The coding scheme for the content analysis is detailed below.

## Data collection and categorisation

Specifically, three Internet-use datasets were compiled:

- Basic type of Web presence. This dataset can be used to answer the first and second research questions. That is, the extent to which candidates were campaigning online and the factors associated with campaigning online.
- Web 2.0 use. This dataset can also be used to provide more information to answer the first and second research questions, but can also help to answer the final research question – how was the Web being used to campaign? Was Web being used to broadcast a message in a one-way manner or was the use more interactive?
- Email responsiveness. This data source can also be used to answer all three research questions.

Data was collected during the election campaigning period itself, that is, between the time point of dissolution of Parliament and the day of the general election itself. This provided a window of four weeks in which to collect the appropriate level and type of data required. The scope for data collection was wide but the obvious time constraints made it important to focus on collecting data that would provide the most comprehensive answers to the research questions.

## Website content analysis

To answer the first research question, set out above, an objective measure of the extent and type of candidates' Web use at the general election was needed. This could be split intuitively into the more traditional sphere of campaigning – personal campaign websites – and the more cutting-edge Web 2.0 technology.

### Dataset (1) type of website: Basic categorisation

It was decided that only candidates standing in England would be included in the sampling frame. There were numerous reasons for this. Often in Scotland and Wales, nationalist parties such as the Scottish National Party and Plaid Cymru are second, or even first-place, parties in certain constituencies. This would have led to potential inconsistencies in the analysis and collection of data and possibly reduced the number of comparisons possible across constituencies or region. Every candidate in England for the six largest parties (Labour, Conservatives, Liberal Democrats, UK Independence Party, Green Party and the British National Party), 2425 cases in total, had their Web presence checked during the first week of the campaign, and they were categories according to the above criteria. It was decided that only to six largest parties would be included in the analysis as this would still allow for comparisons between larger and smaller parties, but would ensure that the list of parties was not too long. As patterns of adoption may vary even amongst parties of similar size, it would be advantageous to keep parties separate at the analysis stage rather than grouping them by size, and so the six main parties was deemed optimal for these purposed.

The data gathering for this section of the study was conducted in the first week of the campaign. It started the day after Parliament was dissolved, to give time for each candidate to launch their campaign sites and also for any incumbent MPs to redirect traffic from the site that held while in office to their site as a candidate, in line with the rules on migrated campaigning content set out by the Electoral Commission, by which MPs who were re-standing as a candidate must set up a different campaign site. This part of the study took the form of assessing, in relatively simple terms, whether the candidate had a personal web presence or not.

It was decided that rather than a simple binary measure of presence/absence (that is, 1 for there being a personal web presence found, 0 for no presence being found) that the presence would be split up according to the three main types of candidate website found after initial piloting. The categories of websites were as follows: (1) A personal profile on a central party page; (2) A personal site that conformed to a party-driven design (also known as 'Web in a Box'); and (3) An individually designed independent site. The sites were coded 1, 2 and 3 according to their corresponding number above and missing sites were coded 0 and entered onto a spreadsheet.

The advantage of categorising the sites in this way is that this variable can be used to answer more questions than a simple binary measure. As online campaigning has become more ubiquitous and sophisticated, a binary measure is becoming increasing outdated. As adoption of some sort of web-presence approaches near universality a binary measure effectively becomes meaningless and so a new measure is required. This more nuanced coding scheme accounts for this change and will reveal a clearer and more detailed picture of the patterns of campaign website adoption among candidates than has been produced in the United Kingdom so far.

It is likely that the candidates who spent a higher amount of their campaign budget on a personal website attach a greater importance to the Internet's ability to procure votes. This feeds into the central question of e-campaigning research – how important a tool is the Internet and in this case what proportion of candidates deem the Internet significant in the battle for votes and what are their characteristics?

The data gathered for this study allowed for a broad analysis of candidate website adoption. Using the present variable as the dependent variable here provides some answers to the first research question above. Which candidates thought that a high-quality, independent and individual campaigning website was important enough to spend some of their campaign budget on? Did this differ by individual-level independent variables such age, gender, incumbency, ethnicity or party? Furthermore, did this differ by constituency-level variables such as marginality, region or rurality?

The data for the control variables was collected from various independent sources. The information on marginality was sourced from the Rawlings and Thrasher Notional Majorities 2010, which adjusts marginality from the last election based on boundary changes and bi-elections. Information on rurality was obtained from the Office of National Statistics, using percentage or agricultural workers. Socio-demographic information on the candidates was available from the Parties themselves, and information on the incumbency was accessed via the UK Electoral Commission.

**Dataset (2) Web 2.0 use: Interactivity**

The issue of how candidates were using the Web in their campaigns is becoming an increasingly important one. Because of this, the interactivity of the candidates web use is a chief concern. Furthermore, the responsiveness of the candidates – that is, directly replying to their potential voters via email, complements and enhances the question of responsiveness, or interactivity.

*Sampling*

Unlike the data on presence, it was not possible to analyse Web 2.0 use for every candidate for the six main parties in England due to time pressures. Consequently, a sub-sample of the adoption data was used. For the Web 2.0 data, there was an initial concern that there may not be sufficient data for analysis. Web 2.0 applications are still relatively new and there is a history among MPs, candidates and politicians in general for being slow to adopt new means of campaigning (Ward 2005).

For this reason, the decision was taken to select the sample based on marginality alone. In the seats where 'every vote counts' it was always more likely that each candidate would be trying everything possible to mobilise those crucial few floating voter. This meant that overall there was a higher probability that candidates in these seats would be using Web 2.0 to campaign. As such, the findings from this study are representative of these constituencies, rather than the campaign overall.

Marginality in UK elections has no fixed definition and it changes from election to election and can even change during the campaign for an election, usually based on opinion polls at the time. For instance, during the 2010 campaign, it was thought that around 30 seats went from safe to marginal after the first televised Leaders' Debates (*Daily Telegraph* 16 April 2010). Any seats where a Liberal Democrat candidate was in second place by less than a certain amount would have been safe before the debates but marginal after, due to the potential gain in the vote share due to a 14 per cent 'bounce' in the opinion polls for the Liberal Democrats.

Due to this fluidity of marginality as a concept, a 2010 specific sampling frame was formulated, to consist of 2010's 'most marginal' seats in England. To ensure the greatest accuracy and precision possible, the Rallings and Thrasher notional marginality data were used to select the sampling frame. These notional marginalities take into account boundary changes that have occurred since the last election. They show the election results from 2005 as they would have been had the 2010 boundary changes been in place, if voting patterns had been the same. They also take into account and adjust for any local election there have been and the changes in voting behaviour at these elections.

Due to the predicted 4.9 per cent national swing at the time the sample was selected (Forecast Report), any seat with a Labour incumbent and a Conservative candidate in second place, which needed only a 5 per cent swing to unseat said incumbent was removed from the dataset. This was on the basis of that fact that Labour election strategists were likely to pull back their battle lines, so to speak, and be less likely to funnel campaign resources towards fighting for these seats, giving them up as lost to any Conservative candidates in second place.

Once these constituencies had been removed, any other seat which required up to and including a swing of 12 per cent to unseat the incumbent was included in the sample. Seats with potentially atypical results were also left in. For example, Brighton Pavilion, with its predicted Green Party victory and Barking, which was being targeted heavily by the BNP. This provided a 177 constituency case sample and a total of 751 candidates in each of these seats.

## Web 2.0 content analysis

Although categorising the websites does give some texture to the data that will complement any further work on quality, the level of analysis can only be superficial. A further measure was needed to give depth to the data collected as well as the breadth in the 'Adoption' set. These divide into: (1) use of Web 2.0 – five platforms of Facebook, Twitter, YouTube, Flickr and blogging; and (2) inter-operability.

### Web 2.0 use

The most dramatic change in Internet use since 2005 has been the advent of social media-that is, networking sites such as Facebook, microblogging sites such as Twitter and media sharing sites such as YouTube and Flickr (collectively often referred to as Web 2.0). Their interactive nature has been debated at some length with suggestions that they may have the potential to accelerate pluralism and to facilitate political networking and engagement (Castells 2007; Gueorguieva 2008). The ethos of Web 2.0 compliments the collection of data at constituency level. A constituency is a set community, and so the grass roots, 'bottom up' philosophy of Web 2.0 facilitates this culture, in a way that may not be so viable at the national level. At election time, party activists tend rally around their party's chosen candidate and become a tighter community, using networks to support them. It is these networks which are potentially facilitated and strengthened by Web 2.0 and so focussing on the constituency-level activity is an important and yet largely overlooked area for study.

Using Web 2.0 gives candidates the potential to engage with their voters in an interactive way that is not really possible through any other medium. For this reason, it is important to be able to measure how interactively a candidate is using the technology so as to ascertain the level of quality according to a framework which is appropriate in the Web 2.0 context.

The framework needed to include measures for not only the presence of use of certain Web 2.0 application, but also the frequency of use, the level of use and whether the applications were being used in the way they were intended, to fulfil their purpose as a campaigning tool. All these combined give an overall, comprehensive picture of the quality of each candidate's use of Web 2.0 technologies.

The four most popular different types of Web 2.0 were chosen to comprise the quality score: Facebook, Twitter, YouTube and blogging. These were then subject to the following measures:

- Static: This is a basic measure of whether the candidate was using the type of Web 2.0 or not. The candidate uses the technology but has not updated the feed etc. in the past week. This is little better than a leaflet through the door in terms of getting the campaign message across.
- Active: The candidate is using the type of Web 2.0 and has updated the page in the past week. However, the candidate has not left the feed open for comment or questions and so there is only a one-way or 'broadcast' model of communication here. Due to the one-way nature of the communication this is no real improvement on a Web 1.0 activity such as a weekly email newsletter/bulletin.
- Open: In an improvement on 'active' use the candidate is updating content regularly (that is, in the past week) and has left the

feed/wall/post open for comments or questions. Therefore, the candidate is allowing some two-way interaction, but there is no demonstrable evidence that the candidate is taking these comments on board or even reading them.

- Interactive: This was the highest level of effective use in this coding scheme. This is where the candidate was not only opening up their Facebook wall, Twitter feed etc. for comment but there was demonstrable evidence that the candidate had read the contributions from their potential supporters and had responded. This showed a very clear two-way flow of communication between candidate and voter.

**Inter-operability**

In order to assess candidate e-campaigning as a whole, a further measure was needed to address the extent to which candidates had married up Web 1.0 and Web 2.0 technologies. This inter-operability measure was an attempt to capture how well a candidate was 'advertising' their use of Web 2.0 on their central site, and also if they were making potential voters aware of other Web 2.0 applications through their different social media sites.

The importance of capturing this information should not be underestimated as it may be that a candidate is using the individual forms of Web 2.0 well and at a high level of interactivity, but without multichannel connections they will not reach their full potential. Data was therefore gathered noting any embedded links to Web 2.0 applications on a candidate's home page and, furthermore, any embedded links to other forms of Web 2.0 from Facebook or Twitter.

**Email analysis: Dataset (3)**

The third part of the data capture was a quasi-experimental email study. This was done to extend the understanding of candidates' effectiveness in using the Internet during the campaign. As well as looking at how responsive and interactive they were via their Web 2.0 platforms it was also considered that personalised responses to online contact via email was important. This is due to the fact that a poor response to an email from a constituent may potentially harm said constituent's opinion of not only the politician in question but could lead to a broader malaise or disengagement with politics in general. A thoughtful, engaged or helpful response to an email query may help to bridge the gap between elector and elected and could foster greater political engagement. The data collection here involved sending an identical email to each of the candidate in the quality sample only. This was to add another dimension to the quality score in terms of an actual response by the candidates.

Although email is very much considered to be part of Web 1.0, a response from an email is the most quantifiable and consistent way to measure a candidate's responsiveness over the Internet. In terms of an experiment, this was the only type of Internet use that could be assessed in experimental conditions. This is mainly due to the inconsistent nature of responsiveness among candidates who utilise the Web 2.0 technology. Although a candidate may be open for comment on their blog, for instance, they may not actually reply to the comments. So the only reliable and systematic way of gauging the responsiveness is via direct email. If the candidate has a working email address, (this can be known from having an email 'bounce') then the candidate has received an email. A failure to garner a response is a confirmation that the candidate is unresponsive. A reply shows very clearly that the candidate is responsive to the concerns of their potential constituents but also it is important to consider the nature of the reply. Email addresses of all the candidates chosen in the above quality sample were gathered from their personal websites or main party sites.

An email was drafted in a colloquial style (the email is reproduced in Appendix 9.1). It was imperative that none of the candidates deduced that this was not a genuine email and alluding to being a student would help make sure that no candidate was discouraged from replying to me because my email address showed I was studying at Manchester. A university domain address was required in order to send the emails by bulk, as other email platforms such as hotmail, Gmail, etc., have anti-spam devices which would have preventing me sending numerous emails. This would have made this part of the data gathering too time consuming.

Clearly the email study posed ethical issues in that I was not a constituent of the candidate receiving the email. The email was carefully drafted to avoid any such claim being made and was signed by myself. A lack of disclosure of my identity as a researcher was considered important to the experimental nature of the study and the need to create 'real world' conditions, as well as producing a high response rate.

At this stage a concern arose due to the regional structures of some of the Parties, particularly the smaller ones. Due to funding restraints some of the parties only keep around 12 offices-located by region. It was thought that even though the email addresses may all look distinct and individual, they may all be re-routed to one address, all picked up and replied to by a party secretary or other official, thus jeopardising this part of the study. In an attempt to avoid this situation, the step was taken to send the emails out in separate batches, stratified across region, so that no one region would receive a large amount of emails at the same time. The emails were sent out two weeks before the day of the election to allow enough time for responses.

The responses that were received were then coded for a range of characteristics. Firstly the time if took for the respondent to reply was recorded. The email was then matched with secondary data that had already been gathered so that candidate characteristics such as party, gender and incumbency could be identified.

In order to assess the whether candidates were attempting to engage with voters or whether email was being used simply for 'one size fits all' electioneering the content of the emails was also categorised. Firstly, it was recorded whether the email was from the candidate themselves or was sent from another member of staff from the campaign. Of course this is not easy to be certain of as even if the sender was purporting to be the candidate themselves if may not be but some of the senders explicitly stated that they were a secretary or communications assistant. If the sender claimed to be the candidate themselves if was recorded as such, the reasoning being that a voter would likely take this at face-value and feel they had received a personal response rather than one from another staff member. Secondly, the responses were categorised in accordance with whether they dealt directly with the specific question asked by the 'voter' or whether a more templated or general answer was provided. To this end the emails were coded as:

1) Answered the question directly and specifically (that is, made particular reference to youth employment);
2) Provided an answer which referred to a related topic but did not specifically answer the question (for example, wrote about the economy or tuition fees);
3) Sent a general election email which did not even mention the topic asked about in the email.

In addition to this it was recorded whether the candidate used the voter's name and whether they offered further help or clarification on the points made-that is, whether they were offering to enter into dialogue with the voter. To ensure that the coding scheme was clear and reliable some inter-coder reliability checks were carried out. A sample

50 emails was given to two extra coders and then the responses compared with each other and the codes assigned by myself. There was a high level of reliability, with only two discrepancies which were applied to cases which were on the borderline between two categories.

This can then be used to assess the first research question (the extent on online campaigning) but also the second two research questions: what factors were associated with online campaigning via email; and how was email being used to campaign – whether to simply electioneer or attempt to actually engage.

## Interviews

Finally, three interviews were carried out on one candidate from each of the largest parties (Labour, Conservatives and Liberal Democrats). This was so that a little more qualitative texture could be provided to any patterns found in the data. It was decided that these should be carried out even if there were only a limited number of respondents as it may provide some information about website adoption that was not picked up in the quantitative data. To reduce the research costs candidates from the North West region were interviewed. The questions asked are produced in Appendix 9.2.

## Summary

As a result of the way the data has been collected three different types of online campaigning can be assessed. This provides three different perspectives of web campaigning and allows us to compare 'older' types of online campaigning (email and websites) with the more cutting-edge Web 2.0 and see whether there were different factors associated with adoption different types and styles of online campaigns. This data allows us to assess not only who was using online campaigning but also how they were using it and whether this is continuing patterns of normalisation in web campaigning or undermining them. These data can be analysed by controlling for a range of individual level control variables (party size, gender, budget, etc.) as well as constituency level variables (rurality, education level, student presence).

All three datasets can be used to assess the extent to which online campaigning was a feature at the 2010 UK general election (research question one). Considering all three types will allow us to build a detailed and broad picture of overall adoption of web campaigns in the United Kingdom.

In addition to this all three datasets can be used to assess the factors associated with the adoption of online campaigns and enable us to access information about whether there are different associated factors for different types of online campaign. Furthermore, datasets two and three provide information about the nature of online campaigning and whether it is being used as a supplement to other top-down, one-way 'broadcast' modes of political communication or whether online channels are fostering a move towards more interactive and engaged styles of communication.

Finally, a proposed approach for data analysis for investigating each question has been presented.

- Research question one: Frequency tables providing information about the extent of each different type of online campaigning at the 2010 UK general election.
- Research question two: Along with basic descriptive statistics and statistical tests assessing the relationship between different independent variables and the adoption of each type of online campaign, binary regression models can be run on the data to assess the impact of differing independent variables on the overall adoption of each type of web campaign.
- Research question three: To separate out the differing levels of interactivity on display it is necessary to perform ordinal or multinomial logistic regression models to adequately answer this question, as the dependent variable has up to five categories.

## Conclusions

This methodology provides three distinct facets to the data captured. Altogether these elements provide an empirically rich dataset which has breadth as well as depth and texture. With such large datasets, and detailed information, a nuanced analysis of Internet activity and its drivers should be possible. The large N produced by the quantitative methods will allow for a robust analysis of several research questions. Dataset 1 can be used as a dependent variable analysing the adoption of websites by local candidate controlling for several influencing factors, or it can be used as an independent variable with the potential to evaluate the role of candidate website use in winning votes. Datasets 2 and 3 are complementary as, once merged, they can provide what is possibly the most rounded measure of candidates' actual engagement with voters via the Web to date. However each dataset is valuable individually, Dataset

2 is useable as a dependent variable for assessing why certain candidates choose to run interactive web campaigns, while Dataset 3 has the potential to form a textual analysis of how candidates engage via email or to be converted into a quantitative measure to scrutinise the extent of adoption of this type of Web 1.0 and the different factors driving it.

This approach improves on earlier studies of Web use by candidates in the United Kingdom by collecting a much larger sample of use than has been attempted before. Every candidate who stood in England has their website recorded and ranked, providing a more accurate picture of website campaign use, evaluated by a consistent and objective measure. In terms of engagement, actual instances of interaction by candidates are measured directly, rather than simply measuring the presence of interactive features. This approach is systematic and comprehensive and has the advantage that it can be applied almost uniformly across the main types of Web 2.0, allowing for meaningful comparisons. In the email study section of the data the actual correspondence for the candidates and how they communicate with the electorate are documented, providing a valuable and unique resource for this area of study. The mixed-methods approach is important as without the different types of data combined certain aspects of the diverse area of candidate-level Web campaigning could be overlooked. As such it provides one of the most comprehensive insights into this area of study and one that would be of valuable to utilise in future studies.

## Appendix 9.1

Hi there,

I watched the leaders debate on TV the other night, I have to say that as a student I didn't really feel that any of the politicians up there addressed the question that me and most of my friends are really concerned about – employment opportunities for graduates. There are a lot of stories in the media right now about how much debt students are facing to get good qualifications and how they are finding it really hard to find a job.

I would like to know more specifically what you and your party will do to help address these problems. I haven't decided who I am going to vote for yet!

Thanks

Rosalynd

## Appendix 9.2

(1) Around how many emails did you receive from potential voters during the campaign?
(2) Were you aware of a central policy on Internet campaigns during the campaign?
(3) Were candidates encouraged to run an individual web campaign or was it something each individual decided on themselves?
(4) Were they encouraged/compelled to post a profile on the central party page during the campaign?
(5) Were candidates encouraged to use Web 2.0 such as Twitter to connect with potential voters?
(6) What were perceived as the potential benefits of using these?
(7) The public nature of Internet campaigning and the sometimes adversarial nature of a general election campaign could attract criticism/abuse from people with opposing views on a candidates own spaces. Do you think this puts a lot of candidates off from using digital media in their campaigns?
(8) Did you feel more comfortable going 'off message' on Web 2.0 as this is a more bottom-up type of media?
(9) Do you feel there are any downsides to campaigning online?
(10) What do you feel are the advantages of online campaigning?

## References

Bryman, A. (1984) 'The Debate about Quantitative and Qualitative Research: A Question of Method or Epistemology', *The British Journal of Sociology*, 35 (1), 76–92.

Castells, M. (2007) 'Communication, Power, and Counterpower in the Network Society', *International Journal of Communication*, 1, 238–266.

Coleman, S. and Ward, S.J. (2005) *Spinning the Web: Online Campaigning During the 2005 General Election* (London: Hansard Society).

Daily Telegraph. (2010) 'General Election 2010: Liberal Democrats Surge after Nick Clegg's TV Debate Performance', available at: http://www.telegraph.co.uk/news/politics/liberaldemocrats/7597522/General-Election-2010-Liberal-Democrats-surge-after-Nick-Cleggs-TV-debate-performance.html, date accessed 16 April 2010.

Foot, K. and Schneider, S. (2000) 'Online Action in Campaign 2000: An Exploratory Analysis of the U.S. Political Web Sphere', *Journal of Broadcasting and Electronic Media*, 46 (2), 222–244.

Foot, K. and Schneider, S. (2006) *Web Campaigning* (Cambridge, MA: MIT Press).

Gibson, R.K. and Römmele, A. (2006) 'Down Periscope: the Search for High-Tech Campaigning at the Local Level in the 2002 German Federal Election', *Journal of E-Government*, 2 (3), 85–111.

Gibson, R.K. and Ward, S.J. (2000) 'A Proposed Methodology for Studying the Function and Effectiveness of Party and Candidate Web Sites', *Social Science Computer Review,* 18, 301–319.

Gibson, R.K. and Ward, S.J. (2003) 'On-line and On Message? Candidate Websites in the 2001 General Election', *British Journal of Politics and International Relations,* 5 (2), 188–205.

Gueorguieva, V. (2008) 'Voters, MySpace, and YouTube: The Impact of Alternative Communication Channels on the 2006 Election Cycle and Beyond', *Social Science Computer Review,* 26 (3), 288–300.

Gulati, J. and Williams, C. (2007) 'Closing the Gap, Raising the Bar: Candidate Web Site Communication in the 2006 Campaigns for Congress', *Social Science Computer Review,* 25, 443–465.

Jackson, N. (2003) 'Vote Winner or a Nuisance: Email and British MPs' Relationship with their Constituents', paper presented at the UK Political Studies Association Conference, Leicester.

Jackson, N. (2008) 'MPs and their e-Newsletters: Winning Votes by Promoting Constituency Service', *The Journal of Legislative Studies,* 14 (4), 488–499.

Lilleker, D. and Jackson, N. (2009) 'Building an Architecture of Participation? Political Parties and Web 2.0 in Britain', *Journal of Information Technology & Politics,* 6 (3–4), 232–250.

Mann, C. and Stewart, F. (2000) *Internet Communication and Qualitative Research* (Thousand Oaks, CA: Sage).

Margolis, M. and Resnick, D. (1997) 'Campaigning on the Internet: Parties and Candidates on the World Wide Web in the 1996 Primary Season', *The Harvard International Journal of Press/Politics,* 2, 59–78.

Norris, P. (2003) 'Preaching to the Converted: Pluralism, Participation and Party Websites', *Party Politics,* 9 (1), 21–46.

O'Malley, L., Petterson, M. and Evans, M. (1999) *Exploring Direct Marketing International* (London: Thomson Business Press).

Stein, L. (2009) 'Social Movement Web use in Theory and Practice: A Content Analysis of U.S. Movement Websites', *New Media Society,* 11, 749–771.

Strandberg, K. (2009) 'Online Campaigning: An Opening for the Outsiders? An Analysis of Finnish Parliamentary Candidates' Websites in the 2003 Election Campaign', *New Media and Society,* 11, 835–854.

Sudulich, L. and Wall, M. (2009) 'Keeping Up with the Murphys? Candidate Cybercampaigning in the 2007 Irish General Election', *Parliamentary Affairs,* 62 (3), 456–475

Ward, S.J. (2005) 'The Internet and 2005 Election: Virtually Irrelevant?', in A. Geddes and J. Tonge (eds.), *The Nation Decides: The 2005 General Election* (Basingstoke: Palgrave), pp. 188–206.

# 9
# From Websites to Web Presences: Measuring Interactive Features in Candidate-Level Web Campaigns During the 2010 UK General Election

*Benjamin J. Lee*

This chapter focuses on the methodological issues surrounding the study of online constituency campaigning during the 2010 UK general election. More specifically, it considers the use of content analysis schemas for understanding the nature of interactivity in election campaigns. In doing so, it addresses two research questions: first, it seeks to measure the extent to which constituency campaigns could be identified and catalogued online; second, it aims to measure how interactive such presences were. In considering these questions, the chapter also assesses the challenges facing researchers in the Web 2.0 era more generally and the future of content analysis in a multi-platform environment.

2010 represented the first general election in the United Kingdom in which Web 2.0 was widely available as a tool for campaigners. Web 2.0 refers collectively to a group of services that emerged following the dot-com crash of the early twenty-first century (O'Reilly 2005). In particular, tools such as Twitter and Facebook seemingly offered much potential for campaigners looking for new ways to connect to a jaded public. The apparently highly successful use of Web 2.0 in Barack Obama's primary and later presidential campaign was regarded by at least some UK politicians with envious eyes (Crabtree 2010). But aside from simply adopting new campaign tools, if 2010 was to be any different to the Web campaigns that had preceded it, it was necessary to verify that campaigners had actually made use of the features built into Web 2.0 tools or had incorporated interactive elements into their Web 1.0 sites. The question at the core of this study was not so much did campaigns use Web 2.0, but more *how* did campaigns use Web 2.0?

To answer this question, this study uses content analysis to analyse or 'code' constituency level campaign websites. This in itself has been a learning process requiring the researcher to test and adapt established frameworks in order to fit the precise question (i.e. to accurately measure the use of interactive features by campaigns). It has also been a challenge to account for the rapid pace of technological change; content analysis typically addresses a single document at a time, but in the case of constituency campaigns the 2010 election was markedly different as campaigns had begun to outgrow single Web 1.0 presences and to establish numerous Web 2.0 profiles. What had previously been a tried and tested method posed significant challenges in the Web 2.0 era.

Beyond this introduction the chapter goes on to explore some of the theoretical background of this study, focusing in particular on political interpretations of interactivity and previous studies based both in the United Kingdom and globally. It then provides a summary of content analysis as a method for understanding campaign Web presences, and also highlights the challenges of constructing a content analysis schema that remains relevant in the Web 2.0 era. The challenges of content analysis in the Web 2.0 era are further explored through a comparison of the Web campaigns identified through content analysis and those reported by party electoral agents themselves through national survey data. The chapter then briefly explores the findings of the content analysis evaluating campaigns use of interactive features during the campaign. Finally, by way of conclusion, this chapter identifies some of the future issues and possible solutions for the application of content analysis methods more generally in the Web 2.0 era.

## The problems and possibilities of interaction

As long as the Web has existed, it has been seen as having a political dimension and what has particularly excited politicians, journalists, academics and futurists are the expanded possibilities for communication and interactivity. The earliest writers saw digital communications as opening up new possibilities for political discourse (Rheingold 1993; Negroponte 1996). In particular, citizens were no longer required to be the passive recipients of information and could instead break out of the 'broadcast paradigm' by searching out their own information (Rheingold 1993, 308). As discussion moved beyond broad futurist predictions and became more systematic and applied, utopian predictions for the political Web dimmed and in some cases writers even saw the Web more as a tool for the status quo than radical change (Margolis and Resnick 2000). The arrival of highly interactive Web 2.0 services revived interest in the political possibilities of interactive digital technologies with a range of tools and new social networks seemingly bringing candidates and electors closer together than ever before (Lilleker and Jackson 2010).

One key issue in the literature surrounds the issue of what exactly constitutes interactivity. Within the bounds of this chapter, interactivity can be thought of as the exchange of information between the user and the developer of a website, in this case political campaigns. This can take place either in real time, or more likely, asynchronously (such as by email). The key element, however, is that information is being exchanged and the site is not simply about the top down dispersal of information to an audience. Many writers have gone on to distinguish between different types of interactivity. Stromer-Galley (2000) differentiates between what she terms human interactivity, exchanging information with another person, and media interaction, exchanging information with the site itself, effectively with machines. Similarly, Gibson et al. (2003) distinguish between what they term site-based interaction and other, more intense interactivity, in the most extreme cases direct exchanges with party elites. There have also been attempts to develop ever-finer granulated levels of distinction such as Jackson and Lilleker's (2009) use of a 30-point scale of interactivity for political websites. For this study, such a distinction was thought overly complex, especially given the resource requirements inherent in populating such a detailed schema. A central question for researchers working with limited financial resources, labour availability and time scales is the feasibility of applying a schema to the data. Generally, the greater the level of detail in the schema, the more time and resources required to code the available data. Studies seeking to apply content analysis to large datasets are inevitably forced to find a balancing point between the level of detail captured by the schema and the availability of resources. Even so, it is still necessary to elaborate beyond the site-based versus dialogue dichotomy. Much Web campaigning is opaque and off limits to researchers who are unable to negotiate special access. Details such as the content of emails or private messages sent on social networks or through websites, as well as the volume of such traffic, are often inaccessible. This leaves researchers only able to document indicators of the behaviours taking place rather than the behaviour itself. For example, researchers can note whether a campaign includes an email address on its website, but not if it responded to emails sent to that address or the level of detail included in any answer. In contrast, there may though be opportunities to analyse public dialogue such as comment sections, walls or through @replies on Twitter. This creates a distinction between potential dialogue, which cannot be directly measured, and public dialogue, which can be directly observed.

In theory at least, the possibility of these kinds of online interactivity is highly relevant to political campaigns. Many writers have seen the ability to interact online as a great boon to campaigns, opening up new channels of communication between campaigners and the most attentive and connected citizens (Norris 2003; Römmele 2003; Ward and Gibson 2003). In particular, the Web creates the potential for what Foot and Schneider (2006) term a transactional relationship, creating a clear bond between campaigns and their supporters. The ability to interact online offers the potential for campaigns to address the collective action problems that have dogged them as they have grown increasingly professionalised (Green and Smith 2003). In essence, interactivity could give members of political parties, and those interested in their campaigns, a greater sense of involvement and agency through allowing them to engage directly with campaigns and candidates rather than limiting them to a bystander role, bypassed by professional campaign managers.

Of course, not all are so optimistic about the potential for interaction online. In summing up the 2001 election Coleman (2001) dismissed online interactivity as a campaign tool, arguing that it was not surprising that campaigners avoided expending resources to talk to people who were highly unlikely to vote for them in any event. This has become a mainstay for those with a more pessimistic view of campaigns and interactivity, why should campaigns open themselves to the chaos and political risks that accompany allowing users to 'have their say'? The most incisive explanation of this view comes from Stromer-Galley (2000) who argued that campaigns would avoid interactivity: first, because it was burdensome; second, because they had no control over what could be posted in such a space; and finally, because allowing the public to directly question the campaign would challenge the deliberate ambiguity on which campaigns rely. Her argument was that by making campaigns too accountable online interactivity would force them to reveal the often-unpopular details of plans rather than sell a grander but less detailed vision.

Empirically, the pessimistic interpretation of interactivity seems to have won out, with very few researchers reporting large amounts of interactivity taking place. At the UK constituency level, prior to 2010, only one study had been conducted, and it concluded that only a tiny minority of campaigns were using two-way interactive features on their websites, with only 8 per cent of campaigns using less interactive features such as guest books or forums (Ward and Gibson 2003). There have been similar findings looking at the national level UK party sites in both the 2001 and 2005 elections (Coleman 2001; Bartle 2005). Even more recent comparative studies including the United Kingdom have found interactive features to be significantly underdeveloped (Gibson et al. 2008).

2010 was expected to be somewhat different. Since its inception in 1989 as a new kind of information storage system, the Web has been in an unceasing process of evolution (Berners-Lee 1989). The period following the 2005 UK general election was characterised by the emergence of a new series of services referred to collectively as Web 2.0. As a concept, Web 2.0 is problematic to define as it has come, to some extent, to mean all things to all people. The publishers O'Reilly coined the term Web 2.0, defining it as seven specific headings, only some of which are relevant in a political science context (O'Reilly 2005). O'Reilly were unquestionably writing with a commercial aim, attempting to find out why some companies had collapsed in the 'dot com crash' and what made those who had survived different. In the academic sphere, a number of writers have tried to refine the concept (Anderson 2007; Chadwick 2009). Arguably, the most interesting concept to emerge, however, from the definition of Web 2.0 has been the 'architecture of participation'. The idea that where Web 1.0 was constructed mainly of static Web pages designed to impart information, Web 2.0 relies on developing frameworks that encourage users to populate them with their own content. Archetypal Web 2.0 services such as Facebook and Twitter provide no content themselves but instead make it easy for users to post their own. Berners-Lee himself has criticised the idea that Web 2.0 represents anything new, arguing that Web 1.0 was always intended to be interactive presumably through the use of hyperlinks (Anderson 2007). In practice, he is correct, but the difference emerges in the simplicity with which users of Web 2.0 can interact, without the need for their own Web space or knowledge of html.

So what of political campaigns in the Web 2.0 era? Currently, little is known beyond preliminary work conducted on national-level sites. Jackson and Lilleker (2009) have argued that at the national level Web 2.0 is in practice Web 1.5, with campaigns still doing their upmost to maintain control of their Web presences. Beyond this, though, the

2010 Election represented the first opportunity to evaluate Web 2.0 in a 'war time' situation. Certainly, Obama's 2008 US presidential victory loomed large with at least one UK party trying actively to emulate his digital campaign (Crabtree 2010). In truth though, Obama's victory was complex and it is difficult to disentangle the impact of savvy online campaigning from Obama's rock star status and the offline campaign. In particular, the creation of bespoke networks such as MyBO smacked of campaigns trying to create their own social networks that they controlled rather than being forced to rely on 'civilian' spaces. Consequently, when it came to the 2010 UK election, other than the unique US experience, there was little to help predict the use of interactive features in the campaign. As such, therefore, two questions remained to be answered in the UK context: first, how can the use of interactive features in constituency-level campaigns be effectively measured? Second, did the availability of Web 2.0 trump earlier findings and give rise to more authentically interactive campaigns?

## Data and methods

The main tool available for developing this kind of in-depth understanding of political websites has been content analysis. This technique has undergone three main iterations, beginning with qualitative approaches rooted in ethnography (Margolis et al. 1997). These were slowly superseded by more quantitative approaches to content analysis, but these still relied on researcher observation and time-consuming manual coding (Ward and Gibson 2003). Recently, automated approaches have become available which dramatically increase the potential of this kind of content analysis, allowing for a large number of sites to be coded, relatively quickly. In some cases, this development has been linked with hyperlink network analysis (HNA) to give a picture of both the structure of a particular network and the content. Hindman (2009) put this into practice looking at political websites using Support Vector Machine Classifiers (SVM) that were able to automatically classify the crawled websites. For the purposes of this study, however, the technical requirements of an automated approach could not to be met, and so a manual approach (detailed below) was adopted.

## The 2010 content analysis schema

Developing a content analysis schema to operate in a Web 2.0 environment required some alterations to the standard pattern of a single site focussed schema. Three platforms were chosen as the focus: first, Web 1.0 sites were still the mainstay of political campaigning in the United Kingdom in 2010 and were deemed likely to represent a campaign's best efforts. Second, Facebook was by far the most prominent social network in the United Kingdom at the time of the election and so campaigns were thought to favour this network over other contenders such as Bebo and Orkut. Finally, Twitter was also of interest given that its very public facing design seemed likely to make it a hotbed of campaign interactivity. A main goal of this exercise was to allow comparison between platforms, and so every effort was made to identify equivalent behaviours on platforms where they existed. For example, joining a mailing list on a Web 1.0 site was thought equivalent to following a profile on Twitter or 'friending' someone on Facebook. The final schema is shown in Table 9.1.

The official UK election campaign generally takes place within a four-week window, but in order to minimise the risk of collecting data

*Table 9.1* Content analysis schema for measuring interactivity in local campaign web presences

| **Behaviour** | **Conventional website** | **Facebook** | **Twitter** |
|---|---|---|---|
| Public dialogue | Forum or comment section in which the campaign was actively replying to comments | Replies on a Facebook wall | @replies in timeline |
| Potential dialogue | Email address<br>Contact form | Able to send a Facebook message | Able to send a direct message |
| Site-based interactivity | Download a poster<br>Download a leaflet<br>Complete a poll<br>Sign a petition<br>Make a specific online organisational request<br>Donate money<br>Sign up to email list<br>Join the party | Download a poster on Facebook<br>Download a leaflet on Facebook<br>Complete a poll on Facebook<br>Sign a petition on Facebook<br>Make a specific online organisational request on Facebook<br>Donate money on Facebook<br>'Friend'<br>Link to join the party | Download a poster on Twitter<br>Download a leaflet on Twitter<br>Complete a poll on Twitter<br>Sign a petition on Twitter<br>Make a specific online organisational request on Twitter<br>Donate money on Twitter<br>'Follow'<br>Link to join the party |

from campaigns in differing timeframes and therefore possibly reacting to different events, campaigns were analysed as close together as was possible. Where timelines were present, for instance in a Twitter stream, campaign posts over the previous seven days were included in the analysis. To further manage the workload, only campaigns in the North West of England were considered, and only those from one of the three largest parties: Labour, Conservatives and Liberal-Democrat. Despite these steps, 225 campaigns were identified to analyse using the schema before the end of the election. Campaigns were identified using the information provided by UK polling report,[1] a blog dedicated to electoral politics that contained an up to date database of candidates. Web 1.0 sites were then found using a Google search of the candidate's name and the area. For Web 2.0 sites this was more complex as they both had their own internal search functions. The website Tweetminster[2] acted as a clearing house for candidates' Twitter accounts during the election, but unfortunately there was no such service on Facebook and so Facebook search was seen as the only viable option. With the exception of Tweetminster, the lack of comprehensive databases of campaign sites was one of the greatest challenges of this study. In the focus on developing schemas, more mundane problems such as the identification of cases are easy to overlook. Further complicating the issue, in sub-national campaigns there were often competing Web presences from local, regional and national parties as well as third party actors such as interested citizens and local media. Choosing a single campaign presence from the plethora on offer often relied the judgement of the researcher. As a working rule, sites were chosen on the grounds of what an interested citizen was likely to take as the 'main' site. After they were identified, sites were coded on a spreadsheet using 1 and 0 as indicators of the presence or absence of a particular function.

## Capturing campaigns

As a measure of the effectiveness of this approach for identifying campaigns the outcomes of the content analysis and of a self-reported source of data, the 2010 Electoral Agent Survey (EAS), were compared. There were just over 100 campaigns included on both the EAS and the content analysis, although the precise number varies depending on responses to individual questions on the EAS. The level of agreement between the two data sets is shown in Table 9.2. The results show that for both Web 1.0 sites and Twitter, the content analysis identified more Web presences

*Table 9.2* Comparison of Web use between Content Analysis (CA) and Electoral Agent Survey (EAS) data

| Platform | N | EAS and CA in agreement | Recorded in CA but not EAS | Recorded in EAS but not CA |
|---|---|---|---|---|
| Website | 106 | 84 | 16 | 6 |
| Facebook | 108 | 71 | 16 | 21 |
| Twitter | 107 | 80 | 15 | 12 |

*Source*: Content analysis data and the 2010 Electoral Agent Survey.

than reported by the EAS but not captured by the content analysis. For Facebook, this balance was reversed.

Why do the two methods identify differing numbers of websites? In the first instance, the EAS is addressed to electoral agents[3] specifically (but it is not exclusively completed by them) which begs the question how much can agents be expected to know about what is happening on the Web in their campaigns? It might easily be the case that there are elements of the Web campaign taking place without the knowledge of the agent or even the candidate, with dedicated team members or activists taking matters into their own hands. Equally, it is plausible to see electoral agents bringing their own biases to play in answering the EAS questionnaire, downplaying or over claiming the use of the Web to fit in with their own narratives e.g. the hardened campaigner adamant that shoe leather wins campaigns and the young up and comer attempting to shore up their digital and, therefore, modern credentials.

Putting aside the self-reported data for a moment, the findings of content analysis data are also open to question. The process of identifying Web campaign presences on platforms was fraught with difficulties especially in terms of search tools. Web presences were identified with conventional search tools using the test 'what would an interested citizen be able to find', on social networks the same logic was used but the in-built search tools were used. Identifying Web presences like this always risks missing key sites that agents might assume are easy for the public to find. This is a particular problem where candidates share names with celebrities or sportspeople, who then drown out candidates in search results. There is also a risk that this approach will over-identify websites, taking local party sites or other, non-campaign controlled sites, as being an official campaign Web presence. Central party directory sites were frequently returned in search results raising the question at what point does a directory page on a central party website become a personal campaign site for a candidate? Facebook search was an especially acute problem as it was seemingly less developed than other tools, presumably because the Facebook ecosystem relies on users having previously established social connections. For researchers coming to constituencies 'cold', Facebook search was a frustrating tool. This more than anything explains the high number of Facebook profiles reported on the EAS but missed in the content analysis.

As the research continued, it became increasingly apparent that adopting an approach that relied on focussing on single 'official' presences on platforms missed much of the detail. For example, whereas this approach identified a single official Twitter account presumably managed by the candidate, for every campaign there were likely a good number of unofficial accounts linked to campaign managers, activists, councillors and those politically active. All of them could be thought of as part of the campaign but not official. For Facebook, these accounts might occasionally post on group walls or respond to posts on official profiles, but there is no mechanism for including them. So whereas previous general elections have been relatively centralised online, with campaigns centred on single websites, Web 2.0 has shattered this uniformity. Attached to these centralised accounts are various sub-networks made up of interested citizens, campaigners and opponents, but they remain largely inaccessible to a researcher attempting to content analyse a large number of Web campaigns. In effect, analysis of online campaigns has moved, from the study of single Websites to the study of entire Web presences.

Overall, it seems that the content analysis did a reasonable job in matching the self-reported data but there remains cause for concern. Whilst the self-reported data is unlikely to be completely accurate, content analysis data suffers from problems with site identification, possibly over or under identifying sites. Nevertheless, given the requirements of the main research question, and the specificity of the data required to measure interactivity, the content analysis data remains a good basis for research. There were no other datasets that provided a better representation of interactivity at the constituency level.

## Interactive features in campaigns

Aside from identifying how well content analysis reflects the reality of the Web campaign, a further objective of the study was to uncover the level of interactive features present in Web campaigns in 2010.

Table 9.3 shows the results of applying the schema developed to measure interactivity in campaigns to the North West of England. It groups features into dialogue and site based behaviours and further distinguishes between public and potential dialogue features. The percentages are derived from all campaigns affiliated to the three main parties in United Kingdom that are also online.

Beginning with the public dialogue features, only a small minority of campaigns were engaging in public dialogue features. Websites were the least common platform for public dialogue features, followed by Facebook and with Twitter the most common platform with around 12 per cent of all online campaigns in the North West exhibiting @replies in their Twitter streams. Of the campaigns that used Twitter, 40 per cent of them engaged in dialogue publically. The focus on Twitter is interesting, perhaps symptomatic of campaigns dipping a toe into interactive waters but limiting themselves to just 140 characters to do so. Twitter is public facing but comments and challenges are less intrusive than on media such as Facebook. @replies directed to campaigns will only show up on their notifications and will not be visible to other users unless they search for them, in some ways this is the least public of the public dialogue features.

Potential dialogue features are those that represent a possible point of contact between users and the campaign, but one that takes place in private and is, therefore, hidden from the researcher. Overwhelmingly, this feature was dominated by the provision of an email address though a Web 1.0 site, followed by more restrictive feedback forms that emailed a person's details to a campaign but without giving them an email address. Email is followed by Facebook's messaging system and Twitter's direct messages, both of which are in-built into the platforms (with some restrictions having to do with social connections) and so only reflect the extent to which campaigns are using these platforms more widely. The design of some Web 2.0 services effectively means that, in order to use these services, campaigns *have* to at least provide the opportunity to engage in public dialogue. Email, however, was the standout potential dialogue feature, the provision of an email address over a conventional Web 1.0 site was the most common form of potential dialogue engaged by campaigns. The opaqueness of this communication remains frustrating for researchers in this area who are unable to negotiate special access and the associated ethical concerns required to get more detail.

Site-based interactivity features were the least interactive features considered in this analysis. They represent some kind of limited interactivity but only with the site itself, often taking the form of polls and

*Table 9.3* Interactive features in the NW during 2010 general election campaign (N = 204)

| | | | N | % |
|---|---|---|---|---|
| Dialogue | Public | Interaction on website | 3 | 1.47 |
| | | Interaction on Facebook | 7 | 3.43 |
| | | Interaction on Twitter | 25 | 12.25 |
| | Potential | Email link | 155 | 75.98 |
| | | Feedback form | 67 | 32.84 |
| | | Facebook message | 72 | 35.29 |
| | | Twitter DM | 61 | 29.9 |
| Site based | | Poster from website | 14 | 6.86 |
| | | Leaflet from website | 7 | 3.43 |
| | | Poll on website | 24 | 11.76 |
| | | Petition on website | 13 | 6.37 |
| | | Organisation request on website | 4 | 1.96 |
| | | Friendship mechanism on website | 76 | 37.25 |
| | | Donate money from website | 72 | 35.29 |
| | | Join the party from website | 87 | 42.65 |
| | | Poster from Facebook | 0 | 0 |
| | | Leaflet from Facebook | 0 | 0 |
| | | Poll from Facebook | 0 | 0 |
| | | Petition from Facebook | 0 | 0 |
| | | Organisation request on Facebook | 1 | 0.49 |
| | | Friendship mechanism on Facebook | 72 | 35.29 |
| | | Donate money from Facebook | 1 | 0.49 |
| | | Join the party from Facebook | 0 | 0 |
| | | Poster from Twitter | 0 | 0 |
| | | Leaflet from Twitter | 0 | 0 |
| | | Poll on Twitter | 0 | 0 |
| | | Petition on Twitter | 1 | 0.49 |
| | | Organisation request on Twitter | 1 | 0.49 |
| | | Friendship mechanism on Twitter | 61 | 29.9 |
| | | Donate money from Twitter | 0 | 0 |
| | | Join the party from Twitter | 0 | 0 |

*Source*: Content analysis data.

invitations to join emailing lists. As well as a form of limited interaction for users, site-based interactivity also allows campaigns to collect information about their users, at the very least a highly prized contact email address for future campaign communications, but in some cases extending to credit card information though party joining mechanisms. Site-based features suffer a similar problem to potential dialogue in terms of friendship mechanisms; having a profile on a Web 2.0 site means enabling these kinds of site-based interactivity features by default. Aside from in-built activities, however, Web 2.0 was not used for any kind of site-based interactivity with the bulk of features instead hosted on Web 1.0 sites. The three activities that dominated were formal party joining mechanisms, email mailing lists and opportunities to donate to the party.

Interactive features in 2010 were, therefore, somewhat distant from the interactivity that might have been expected at the first Web 2.0 enabled UK general election. The kind of public dialogue envisaged as becoming the norm has not materialised within political Web presences with only a minority of campaign engaging in public dialogue, primarily using the Web 2.0 social network Twitter. Despite this, less interactive features have flourished, with the majority of campaigns engaging in both potential dialogue behaviours and site-based interactivity. Beyond those features that campaigns are forced to accept in using social networks such as friendship mechanisms and messaging systems, there was very little innovation evident on social networks, campaigns have overwhelming chosen to use Web 1.0 sites, in many cases using centrally provided templates to incorporate relatively sophisticated mechanisms into their sites. It is not possible to conclude from this data that Web 2.0 is driving a more open and interactive form of campaigning. Stromer-Galley's (2000) argument still holds, even when presented with a free and easy method of building up a public dialogue the majority of campaigns eschewed engaging voters in a genuine dialogue. The more limited forms of interactivity going on seemed overwhelmingly designed to gather information on potential voters for future email messages rather than giving users a sense of ownership of the campaign.

These findings must be heavily caveated, however, and this is in large part due to the difficulties of applying content analysis to websites in the Web 2.0 era. First, schema design is complicated by the transition from campaigns focussed around a single website to those based across multiple platforms. This necessitates some careful thought in order to derive meaningful and useful outcomes from the schema and is further complicated by the range of features built into Web 2.0 sites. Whereas every element of a Web 1.0 campaign site represents a decision, either by the campaign or by the designers on their behalf, the same cannot be said of tools such as Facebook. These are effectively delivered to campaigns as a package in the same way they are delivered to other users; the inclusion of a messaging system or a friendship mechanism is far less meaningful here. Researchers must also accept that a lot of what goes on online goes on in private rather than public, necessitating researchers to record the potential effects of features as well as those that are on public display. Providing an email address has the potential to lead to dialogue, but whether it does or not is an unknown as long as researchers are on the outside looking in.

Second, as well as designing the schema, identifying relevant Web presences has also become infinitely more complex. Search related problems are part and parcel of Web content analysis, but they become more confounding when researchers are forced to search ecosystems that do not necessarily want to be searched, for example, Facebook. Without the kind of prior social connections the designers of Facebook rely on, identifying specific campaigns can be difficult. Underlying official presences there is also very often an unofficial layer made up of managers, workers, supporters and interested third parties that is impossible to access without the level of situational awareness normally expected of ethnographers. For wide-scale systematic analysis this level of endeavour is almost impossible. This problem becomes less acute however when content analysis methods are paired with other approaches to the same research questions, for example through the quantitative analysis of secondary data or through following up with quantitative analysis. Given the often-complex networks being analysed, the limited search functions available to content analysis researchers cannot be thought of as being comprehensive.

As a method for analysing future election campaigns content analysis seems sets to grow more difficult to implement. First, the growth in the number of social networking platforms with enough purchase in the mainstream population to be a viable campaign medium looks set to expand the number of platforms content analysis would need to consider. In the short term, new networks such as Google+ or Diaspora may well be able to capture enough market share to become too big for campaigns to ignore. Longer term, technology is notoriously unpredictable and fast moving, the next innovation in social media may well be something that no one sees coming. Of all the issues associated with social media, the preservation of privacy has by far been the most prominent, and in response social networks are constantly redeveloping privacy controls for their networks, which affects the ability of researchers to glean information from them. Although campaigns rely to some extent on being as visible as possible online, any moves to alter privacy settings may reduce the visibility of users' comments or a campaign's responses. In the longer term, this issue is likely to persist or grow worse as privacy concerns make their way further up the agenda of the users of social networks. Online privacy is increasingly becoming one of the greatest challenges faced by those doing research on social media. Finally, and perhaps the greatest threat to content analysis in party political settings, is a complete co-option of constituency campaign Web spaces by the central party either in the form of forcing party templates onto candidates, or through the continued expansion of party networks such as LibDemAct, MyConservatives and MembersNet.[4] It is easy to envisage a 2015 campaign where all Web campaigning takes place through these party networks, satisfying a party's need to control online spaces but leaving little variation between candidate campaigns for researchers to analyse.

## Conclusions and the future

In terms of the substantive research question, the data has shown that whilst any campaigns have been quick to adopt Web 2.0 tools, this has not translated to using interactive features. In public at least, campaigns have been limited to engaging over Twitter. While opportunities for site-based and potential dialogue abounded, on Web 2.0 sites these were restricted mainly to those features designed into sites. Campaigns own efforts at including the voters in polls or getting them to join the party remained Web 1.0 centred. Despite the interactive credentials Web 2.0 was seemingly more a tool for information sharing than for interactivity at the election.

As a method, content analysis of websites is facing a challenging set of circumstances, both for the study of election campaigns, and for the study of online organisations more generally, be they political parties, other institutions or more diverse social movements. Whereas earlier studies needed to capture data from only a single site, or a group of interlinked sites, the Web 2.0 environment presents a different situation. Researchers, perhaps used to thinking about online as a single element are instead going to have to expand their thinking to include a range of platforms; not just websites, but social media profiles, private networking tools (such as MyBO) and third party sites. Daunting as the transition from sites to wider presences may be for those trying to capture and interpret them, there are options.

This study attempted to circumvent the problem of multiple platforms by using a schema based on features rather than Web presences. Although this has met with some success, in particular as a companion piece to a wider study based on both quantitative and qualitative data, this has not been without challenges (Lee 2012). In theory, many of these problems can be conquered with the application of broader and more in-depth schemas, for example expanding search terms or spending longer developing situational awareness in subject constituencies. However, these can only be achieved at a cost in time and resources. Elections, in particular, are relatively sudden events, giving researchers only a narrow window to capture data, the more complex the schema and associated procedure, the more tasks need to be carried out in a short amount of time. Any research attempting to use content analysis to capture specific events is likely to face similar issues. Even where there is a greater focus on institutions themselves and timing is less critical. Researchers need to remember that the malleability of the online word means that their objects of study are always likely to change in response to events.

Another solution might well come from further development of the technology available to researchers, including techniques for the archiving of websites for later analysis, hyperlink network analysis and content analysis of social media posts of the kind made possible by programs such as DiscoverText.[5] Although to some extent exploiting these methods relies on social scientists developing programming and advanced computer skills. A further point to consider is that going down the automated root may lead to research focusing to a greater extent on specific platforms rather than on Web presences as a whole. Whilst researchers are able to gather large amounts of structured data from platforms such as Twitter using specialist tools, the analysis of conventional websites is still very much reliant on researchers to use their own judgement to bring analytical order to what may be inconsistent and difficult to compare material. At the current juncture, researchers looking to develop an in depth understanding of Web presences must keep in mind the limitations of content analysis methods to deal with the Web 2.0 environment. Whereas previous studies may have only had to consider a single website, the advent of Web 2.0 and the growth of the Web more generally has created a far more nebulous environment, with organisations likely to maintain both official and unofficial presences across a range of platforms.

## Notes

1. http://ukpollingreport.co.uk/
2. http://tweetminster.co.uk/
3. In the United Kingdom, election agents are formally responsible for the running of election campaigns and in particular they are responsible for ensuring that campaigns comply with campaign spending limits. Candidates may also act as their own agents.
4. Collectively these tools can be thought of as UK analogues of Barack Obama's MyBO. Each of these platforms presented spaces for supporters of the associated party to organise and develop their campaigns. Although they have not been included as part of this study due to being closed platforms limited only to party members, they remain a potentially interesting basis for future research. In particular the use of these platforms showed a rejection of far more widespread and open commercial social networks, which could be interpreted as candidates from mainstream parties demonstrating their reluctance to engage in un-controlled interactivity with electors in spaces that they cannot fully control.
5. See http://discovertext.com/ for more information.

## References

Anderson, P. (2007) *What Is Web 2.0? Ideas, Technologies and Implications for Education*, available at: www.jisc.ac.uk/media/documents/techwatch/tsw0701b.pdf, date accessed 22 December 2011.

Bartle, J. (2005) 'The Press Television and the Internet', *Parliamentary Affairs*, 58 (4), 699–711.

Berners-Lee, T. (1989) *Information Management: A Proposal*, Online, available at: http://www.w3.org/History/1989/proposal.html, date accessed 11 October 2012.

Chadwick, A. (2009) 'Web 2.0: New Challenges for the Study of E-democracy in an Era of Informational Exuberance', *I/S: A Journal of Law and Policy for the Information Society*, 5 (1), 9–41.

Coleman, S. (2001) 'Online Campaigning', *Parliamentary Affairs*, 54 (4), 679–688.

Crabtree, J. (2010) *David Cameron's Battle to Connect*, available at: http://www.wired.co.uk/magazine/archive/2010/04/features/david-camerons-battle-to-connect, date accessed 10 June 2010.

Foot, K. and Schneider, S. (2006) *Web Campaigning* (London: MIT Press).

Gibson, R., Lusoli, W. and Ward, S. (2008) 'Nationalizing and Normalizing the Local? A Comparative Analysis of Online Campaigning in Australia and Britain', *Information Technology & Politics*, 4 (4), 15–31.

Gibson, R., Ward, S. and Lusoli, W. (2003) 'The Internet and Political Campaigning: The New Medium Comes of Age?', *Representation*, 39 (3), 166–180.

Green, D. and Smith, J. (2003) 'The Professionalization of Campaigns and the Secret History of the Collective Action Problem', *Journal of Theoretical Politics*, 15 (3), 321–339.

Hindman, M. (2009) *The Myth of Digital Democracy* (Princeton: Princeton University Press).

Jackson, N. and Lilleker, D. (2009) 'Building an Architecture of Participation: Political Parties and Web 2.0 in Britain', *Journal of Information Technology and Politics*, 6 (3), 232–250.

Lee, B. (2012) *Are Digital Technologies Supporting Traditional Styles of Electioneering? Measuring and Explaining the use of Interactive Campaigning by Candidates in the 2010 UK General Election*, Ph.D. thesis The University of Manchester.

Lilleker, D. and Jackson, N. (2010) 'Towards a More Participatory Style of Election Campaigning: The Impact of Web 2.0 on the UK 2010 Election', *Policy & Internet*, 2 (3), 69–98.

Margolis, M. and Resnick, D. (2000) *Politics as Usual – The Cyberspace 'Revolution'* (London: Sage).

Margolis, M., Resnick, D. and Tu, C. (1997) 'Campaigning on the Internet: Parties and Candidates on the World Wide Web in the 1996 Primary Season', *Harvard International Journal of Press/Politics*, 2 (1), 59–78.

Negroponte, N. (1996) *Being Digital* (Reading: Hodder & Stoughton).

Norris, P. (2003) 'Preaching to the converted? Pluralism Participation and Party Websites', *Party Politics*, 9 (1), 21–45.

O'Reilly, T. (2005) *What Is Web 2.0? Design Patterns and Business Models for the Next Generation of Software*, available at: http://oreilly.com/web2/archive/what-is-web-20.html, date accessed 22 December 2011.

Rheingold, H. (1993) *The Virtual Community: Homesteading on the Electronic Frontier* (London: MIT Press).

Römmele, A. (2003) 'Political Parties, Party Communication and New Information Communication Technologies', *Party Politics*, 9 (7), 7–20.

Stromer-Galley, J. (2000) 'Online Interaction and Why Candidates Avoid it', *Journal of Communication*, 50 (4), 111–132.

Ward, S. and Gibson, R. (2003) 'Online and On Message? Candidate Websites in the 2001 General Election', *British Journal of Politics and International Relations*, 5 (2), 188–205.

# 10

# New Directions in Web Analysis: Can Semantic Polling Dissolve the Myth of Two Traditions of Public Opinion Research?

*Nick Anstead and Ben O'Loughlin*

An alternative and possibly more apt title for this chapter might well be '1936 and all that', a veiled reference to Sellars and Yeatman's humorous history of England which contained a list more fanciful and cliche-bending answers that students had given in examinations. For our purposes, perhaps the most instructive example to be found in that volume relates not to the eponymous date, but the Battle of Bosworth Field in 1492:

> Noticing suddenly that the Middle Ages were coming to an end, the Barons now made a stupendous effort to revive the old Feudal amenities of Sackage, Carnage, and Wreckage and so stave off the Tudors for a time. They achieved this by a very clever plan, known as the Wars of the Roses.
>
> (Sellars and Yeatman 1930)

The satire relies on a recurring structure in the narrative of Whiggish versions of English history, found especially in school text books and university syllabuses, wherein Bosworth Field represents the hard dividing line between the barbarous late Middle Ages and the flourishing early modern period. Of course, history does not function like this at all, and more recent historiography has been at pains to point out the continuities between the two periods rather than the differences (Watts 2012).

In the history of public opinion research, the date of 1936 could be argued to fulfil a similar symbolic function. The story is well known. The *Literary Digest* magazine polled more than two million of its readers ahead of that year's US presidential election, and predicted that the Republican Alf Landon would comfortably depose the sitting Democratic President Franklin Roosevelt. In contrast, pollster George Gallup surveyed far fewer people and predicted a victory for the incumbent. Instead of being an open poll, his sample was designed to be a microcosm of the US electorate. Not only did Gallup's result prove to be right, but – to confirm the superiority of his method – he was able to 'scoop' the *Literary Digest* by using his data to predict their result before they could publish it (Crossley 1937; Robinson 1999, 39–40). Thus 1936 becomes a dividing date in the history of public opinion research. In this version of history, the age of the representative opinion poll had arrived. Straw polls were taken to be ineffective and inaccurate, and representative samples to be modern and scientific.

This version of events oversimplifies matters greatly. Despite the undoubted methodological weaknesses of their approach, the *Literary Digest* actually had an historically good record of predicting electoral outcomes since their first poll in 1916. Furthermore, straw polls had a far longer history, going back at least as far as 1824 (Smith 1990). It seems likely that the failure of 1936 was caused by the changing nature of the electorate in depression-era America, which was becoming increasingly polarised along class lines. Since the magazine's mailing list was largely constructed from lists of car and phone owners, the sample was disproportionately made up of the increasingly Republican middle classes. It was this development that fatally undermined their poll (Squire 1988).

There is actually very little serious history written about public opinion research (Robinson 1999, 5) and much that does exist is written by the victors. Gallup evangelically wrote and lectured about opinion polling generally and the 1936 election in particular. His argument was always the same, focusing on the scientific nature of opinion polling and – crucially – its role in constructing the good democratic society (see Gallup 1965; and most famously Gallup and Rae 1940). As such, the 1936 election become the foundation stone of a particular mythology of public opinion, combining both a method and a set of political values.

This mythology is significant today. It continues to inform the way we think about public opinion, to the point where it is common to talk in terms of public opinion and opinion polling being synonymous with each other. In both the popular and journalistic imagination, public opinion tends to be thought of as 'what polls try to measure' (Price 1992, 35). However, the *1936 and all that* approach to understanding the history of public opinion research is overly simplistic and has the potential to be damaging, especially at a moment in time when new techniques for understanding public opinion are developing. Certainly, as we shall see, matters were more complicated at the time, with many of Gallup's contemporaries contesting his interpretation of events.

This historically revisionist approach to understanding public opinion research and its role in political life can continue to serve a useful function as we start to consider the emergence and growing use of semantic research techniques, especially what we have termed semantic polling. Broadly, we define semantic research as the mining and analysis of large amounts of social media data through techniques such as natural language processing. Semantic polling is a specialised form of this technique, where the data is harvested in order to make statements about public opinion, especially on political matters (Anstead and O'Loughlin 2011; Anstead and O'Loughlin 2012).

There are four reasons why it is worth looking backwards to older debates about public opinion. First, the very existence of such debates illustrates how both elite and popular discourses can adapt to the emergence of new research methods. Like the survey techniques of the 1930s, it will take some time to understand the new and powerful semantic tools of today, the development of which will be interpreted in multiple and competing manners. Second, that such debates took place indicates that there is in fact neither a monolithic definition of public opinion, nor a single approach to its measurement. As such, this chapter acts as a warning against measuring the success of new techniques against the standards laid out by the old. Third, and as an extension of the previous point, the substance of these earlier debates around opinion polls provide a useful analytical framework as we seek to better understand the meaning and usefulness of semantic research techniques today. Fourth, and of special significance to this chapter, is the particular framing of the discussion around opinion polling. While survey techniques developed in the corporate sector as far back as the late nineteenth century (Converse 2009), it was their entry into political life that demanded a much clearer articulation of a set of values about the research method. Similarly, semantic research methods sit on the cusp of entering into public discourse (Anstead and O'Loughlin 2011), which will raise similar questions.

This chapter therefore identifies some of the most important debates about public opinion research that emerged in the twentieth century, reflecting on them in the context of the emergence of online semantic research techniques. Without denigrating the significance of opinion polls, we will attempt to challenge the reductionist conceptions of public opinion offered by some adherents to this method since the 1930s and, in so doing, start the work of building a broader conception of public opinion, one that is more useful for thinking about semantic research.

The argument will be grouped around five binary relationships that have framed the development of our understanding of public opinion research:

- the parallel development of quantitative and qualitative research techniques;
- the epistemology and ontology of social research;
- individual and collective definitions of public opinion;
- the clash of public and private interests in public opinion research;
- and optimism and pessimism about the democratic process.

While the trajectory of public opinion research for the past 80 years might have made these issues seem like resolved questions, the emergence of new semantic research techniques now demands that these matters are revisited.

## Quantitative and qualitative research techniques

In her history of opinion polling, Herbst argues that '[t]oday the most authoritative tools are quantitative ones' (Herbst 1993, 153). Certainly, numeric data carries great weight in public discourse. Herbst's central thesis is that due to processes of modernisation, numeric data carries a scientific symbolism and thus greater authority. As such, the development of public opinion polls is part of a broader process of quantification across many spheres of society (Robinson 1999, 12–15). The development of public opinion polling was facilitated by new research ideas and techniques in the 1930s that have become synonymous with quantitative research: the ability to measure opinion based on psychological techniques, and the application of scientific sampling theory.

However, it should be noted that recent years have been marked by a growing interest in qualitative public opinion research techniques. Notable among these is the focus group. This has become a particularly common technique, first in advertising and then in politics (Gould 2011). However it is interesting to observe that it has made only limited direct impact on the public sphere. Focus group data is largely gathered for private customers, such as political parties and corporations, and not for publication by media organisations. Researchers have argued that there are good reasons for this, noting that when focus groups are discussed in the media, journalists frequently fail to adequately explain the nature of the data, instead seeking to make it numerical for an audience that is accustomed to opinion poll data (Wilkinson and Kitzinger 2000).

Social media analytics challenges the distinction between quantitative and qualitative research techniques, for a number of reasons. First, the sheer size of the datasets, so-called 'big data', is far more akin to the quantity of information that quantitative social scientists deal with. In contrast, the data fails many of the fundamental tests laid down by survey researchers and pollsters – notably that it is non-representative of the population as whole. Furthermore, given the continuing inequalities of online activity, constructing a genuinely representative online sample using techniques like scaling still seems fanciful.

It would be easy then to characterise social media analysis as the Twenty-First Century version of the *Literary Digest* poll – heavily lopsided in favour of particular social groups and flawed for that reason. But it might be better to characterise the data being gathered as qualitative in nature. Certainly, the datasets look a lot more robust if we start to think of them as providing the types of data that are produced by focus groups, rather than surveys. As such, there has to be a reconceptualisation of research on public opinion away from individual preferences about specific issues and instead asking why people hold those views, or observing the interactions between citizens when they are discussing particular topics.

Indeed, the potential qualitative richness of the data that might be extracted from social media brings to mind another research technique of the 1930s and 1940s, the *mass observation* (Harrison 1986). In this method, citizens were asked to write long diary entries, detailing their daily lives and thoughts, and then post them back to researchers for analysis. There are clear problems with this method – certain groups would be over-represented in the sample and there is no way of checking whether people were telling the truth. However, there is also value. Researchers examining specific things, such as political values, for example, could get a broader understanding of how they fitted into other aspects of people's lives, rather than analysing them in isolation. Social media, because of its nature, offers some of the same opportunities. Semantic polling enables real-time, unobtrusive mass observation.

This raises an interesting question. There is a general reluctance of opinion pollsters (with some exceptions) to countenance the presentation of qualitative research in the public sphere. However, semantic polling can combine big, quantitative datasets with qualitative richness. So, is there a useful role for such analysis in news media? Certainly the polling paradigm is so ubiquitous that journalists have great difficulty explaining the value and significance of qualitative data to the public. The same problems are likely to emerge with social media data. Can journalists and citizens become literate and comfortable examining the new combinations of quantitative and qualitative research that generate semantic polling?

Semantic research methods make citizens' political opinions knowable at an unprecedented level of detail and scope. It offers a far more contextualised opinion of citizens' perspectives than traditional polling methods, not least because people's social media data can be integrated with other data about them. Their shopping and consumption data, reading habits, travel records and other digital traces offer the opportunity for those who own or can buy this data to build rich explanations of a person's political attitudes and behaviours, and the drivers of these. Indeed, the integration of multiple datasets can generate the 'thick descriptions' only traditionally available through labour-intensive qualitative research. While opinion polling has been critiqued for generating false political opinions among people who largely do not think about politics, semantic analysis offers a far greater possibility of developing a richer overview of where politics sits within people's broader identities.

## Epistemology and ontology

George Gallup was very fond of describing what he did as 'fact-finding' (Robinson 1999, 46). This idea was based on two distinct claims. First, it depends on the ontological claim that it is correct to think about the existence of public opinion in society, as a phenomenon existing independently of the researcher. Second, Gallup's 'fact-finding' depends on the epistemological claim that, given the correct methods, public opinion can be discovered and measured. There are, however, three important critiques of both claims suggesting that what we term 'public opinion' is in fact an artefact of different processes.

The first problem is to be found in definition. While Gallup and subsequent generations of survey researchers offered a very specific definition of what public opinion was, built around their methodology, historically, many definitions of public opinion have been offered (Childs 1965). As such, this raises the questions of whether public opinion should be thought of as an innate 'fact' or instead as a historically contingent understanding.

Second, it has been argued that, because the average citizen does not consider political issues very much at all, they have a tendency to spontaneously generate opinions when pressed by a pollster. Perhaps the most famous example of this is to be found in the Public Affairs Act of 1975, on which – although wholly fictitious – the vast majority of those interviewed had an opinion (Bishop et al. 1980). In other words, there is no independently existing phenomenon called public opinion that can be found by researchers; rather, 'public opinion' and individual preferences are created through research methods. Furthermore, because researchers may have the ability to create public opinion through their interventions, it can be thought of as a manifestation of political power. This argument is most forcefully made by Pierre Bourdieu in his essay *Public Opinion Does Not Exist* (1979). The most obvious example of this is to be found in the topics that opinion polls consider and the nature of the political problematic that they assume. These cannot be said reflect the concerns of the public, but rather of the political classes.

Third, in the decade preceding Gallup's new approach to measuring public opinion, John Dewey and Walter Lippmann were making the forceful ontological point that publics only exist to the extent that technology allows them to come together. In the United States of the early twentieth century, citizens could not possess equal, sufficient information about distant, national issues in order to make informed contributions to a national democratic politics, as the circulation of ideas and information depend on technology, transport, and the political and economic forces that shaped them. There is no innate 'democratic spirit'; people living in small independent communities in the nineteenth century may have been able to act as jacks-of-all-trades, akin to 'omnicompetent citizens', but that did not imbue them with knowledge of the wider world (Lippmann 1922, §17.4). The formation of a unitary 'public opinion' would require massive organisation, for 'The truth about distant or complex matters is not self-evident, and the machinery for assembling information is technical and expensive' (Lippmann 1922, §21.1). Information about political problems and leaders' proposals had to reach publics, and publics had to be representable back to political leaders for their will to be brought to bear upon problems. Once complex issues or 'entanglements' drew disparate citizens into politics and the collective task of finding solutions (Dewey 1927), democracy required technology for the representation of them. If democracy proceeds through circuits of accountability (Warner 2002), a looping rhythm wherein citizens' views cohere into 'public opinion' which mandates representatives to perform tasks and then holds representatives to account, then public opinion must be mediated, and how this is done depends on the technologies of the day.

This means there is no *a priori* ontology to publics – their character depends on techniques and methods of mediation and representation. While political theorists such as Habermas or Arendt might suggest politics and publics exist in a distinct sphere or domain of life, one constituted by the claims and counterclaims of political subjects, Lippmann and Dewey directed attention to the mix of human and non-human subjects and objects through which 'the public' comes into being. More recently, their approach has been taken up enthusiastically by scholars following Latour and the application of Actor Network Theory to political practices (Latour 2005; Marres 2005; Callon et al. 2009; Marres and Lezaun 2011).

Even if we did assume public opinion exists as a social phenomenon independently of researchers or techniques of representation, discovering 'it' through a survey methodology raises a number of problems. The history of research into opinion polling is replete with examples that have questioned the effectiveness of opinion poll methodology at generating unbiased datasets. Indeed, as early as the 1940s, researchers were discovering that the answers people gave were heavily conditioned by who interviewed them. Daniel Katz (1942) noted that white collar interviewers tended to illicit more conservative answers, while blue collar interviewers generated a more left-wing response. Certainly, it is clear that the design and order of questions can have a great impact on the ultimate findings of the survey (Schuman and Presser 1996). Semantic research analysis faces some of the same questions about ontology and epistemology. At the very least, however, it offers an opportunity to rethink what public opinion is and might look like, developing the narrow definitions offered by opinion pollsters and, in turn, challenging those who rely on those definitions to mount their critique of the idea of public opinion generally.

It is also worth noting one possible major advantage that the technique has over more traditional survey methodologies. Unlike surveys or even focus groups, semantic polling is research in the 'natural' environment. It gathers data people produce in everyday situations as they debate the day's events or whatever is on TV. In other words, it does not use artificial stimuli, such as survey questions or a moderator to generate responses, but instead relies on harvesting data that people are producing as they go about their daily lives, independent of public opinion researchers. As such, it has the potential to overcome the epistemological problem of researchers 'contaminating' their data in an effort to gather it. However, as semantic polling analyses become more regularly published in mainstream media, so citizens may become more reflexive about how their routine social media activities are being harnessed to produce 'public opinion'. Semantic polling avoids delimiting a 'sphere' of politics and political debate – political talk can happen in any social media interaction. But does this simply entail a new form of invasiveness? If this question becomes a matter of public debate, the independence of public opinion as social reality from its representation will begin to collapse again.

Finally, our understanding of the ontology of publics must be open to the technical, as Lippmann and Dewey argued. Technology developers and electoral regulators as well as political scientists and methodologists need to pay attention to how settings, devices and emergent behaviours around new social media help shape how political discussion happens. Semantic polling might not immediately contaminate naturally occurring conversations, but those conversations depend on hashtags, devices to share content, and norms of searching, linking, and sharing. Digital environments and infrastructures enable and constrain political action and communication in ways citizens, pollsters and regulators might take for granted. Perhaps Marres and Lezaun exaggerate when they write:

> [T]echnology *silently* replaces the legal coercions that bind politics subjects; artefacts, settings and socio-material architectures exert a semi- or juridical form of constraint on action [. . . they] have become a sort of 'second nature' for political subjects.
>
> (2011, 494–495)

However, the broader ontological point remains: Dewey and Lippmann in the 1920s and Latour and Marres today are correct to argue that the ontology of 'public opinion' must account for both its human subjects and its material, technological structures. Indeed, by refusing to begin with a fixed ontology of public opinion but instead an interest in the different ways public opinion is formed and performed, researchers may also realise there is no need for a fixed, positivist epistemology and be reflexive about how their methods for knowing public opinion may affect it too.

## Individual and collective definitions of public opinion

The victory of methodological individualism in public opinion research is one of the most significant legacies of the 1930s. This is perhaps not surprising, as the relationship between understandings of whether public opinion is an individual or collective phenomenon is highly historically contingent, reflecting the social and political environment that fostered them. The pollster's methodological individualism represented a rejection of two pre-existing and previously dominant understandings of 'the public'. First, there was the long-standing idea of the deliberating public. This is the public as imagined in Habermas's eighteenth-century coffee shops and salons, made up of rational, deliberating actors (Habermas 1991). As such, the very act of arriving at an opinion was a collective endeavour, which could not be carried out in isolation. Second, in the decades prior to the development of public opinion surveys, public opinion had been conceived in a very different way, built around the work of crowd theorists, such as Le Bon (1897/1972, see also Canetti 1992). These were focused on the behaviour of the public as a collective, unified entity.

The emergence of survey research techniques led to a disciplinary reorientation of public opinion studies, however. Pollsters' skills were based on the science of psychology, rather than the Enlightenment's philosophy or the crowd theorist's sociology. Thus the focus of attention shifted from the interactions within a group to the individual, and the public came to be understood as nothing more than the accumulation of individual preferences. This commitment was perhaps most clearly stated in Floyd Henry Allport's article in the first issue of *Public Opinion Quarterly*, the house journal of American Association for Public Opinion Research. In it, Allport argued:

> The term public is given its meaning with reference to a multi-individual situation in which individuals are expressing themselves, or can be called upon to express themselves, as favouring or supporting (or else disfavouring or opposing) some definite condition, person or proposal of widespread importance, in such a proportion of number, intensity, and constancy, as to give rise to the probability of affecting action, directly or indirectly, toward the object concerned.
>
> (1937, 23)

This commitment to methodological individualism was as deep-rooted as it was unsurprising. While only a few decades before the implications of mass-suffrage democracy and participation had seemed horrifying to Le Bon, pollsters (and especially American pollsters) were committed to the one-man-one-vote principle. These values were further enshrined by the rise of mass consumerism and the accompanying industry of market research from which polling emerged (Price 1992; Curtis 2002).

However, it would be wrong to assume that debate about the merits of individual and collective definitions of public opinion were at an end. The leading voice opposing a methodological individualist consensus was Herbert Blumer (1946, 1948). Drawing on the sociological tradition, he argued that pollsters made 'no effort, seemingly, to try to identify public opinion as an object' and went on to claim that 'Public opinion must obviously be recognised as having its setting in a society and being a function of that society' (Blumer 1948, 542–543).

In contrast to Allport, Blumer's definition of the public was constructed within a broader framework, based on the types of interactions that were occurring between people. He drew a tripartite distinction between the crowd, the public, and the mass. The crowd was defined as an emotionally bound group of a single opinion, while the public was a group that would contain disagreements over any given issue, but existed within a network which facilitated debate. In this sense, Blumer's definition is more akin to Habermas's idea of the public (Habermas 1991). Finally, the mass – constituting the vast bulk of the citizenry – was made of people who, while they might be aware of important issues of the day, existed in isolation, so could not engage with their peers, as citizens did (Blumer 1946).

Blumer's argument is interesting because he also disagreed with older sociological theorists, such as Le Bon, for whom modern societies faced a danger from the crowd. Blumer was more concerned by the disengagement of the mass. However, Blumer's definition of the mass is actually very close to Allport's definition of the public, especially since both treat individuals in isolation, as opposed to being part of broader social environments. In other words, the growing role of opinion polling in the body politic was the very process that Blumer was most concerned about.

While some survey researchers have long since been happy to declare the battle over and settled in their favour (Converse 1987), Blumer's conception of public opinion and critique of the narrow methodological individualism of the opinion pollsters seems pertinent today. The social media space challenges simple and inherently contradictory definitions of the individual and collective. Instead, people online are more akin to what Wellman et al. 2003 have referred to as 'networked individuals' (2003), producing what Castells calls 'mass self-communication' (Castells 2007).

Certainly, the online space is replete with Blumer's three kinds of collective action. Crowds, defined through their unified purpose, have appeared. While some scholars have questioned the quality of debate online (Hindman 2008), a debating public is also observable through environments such as blogs and social networks. And perhaps the closest thing to Blumer's definition of the mass is to be found in so-called 'clicktivism' and low-threshold actions (Gladwell 2010).

Nor is the online space an environment of equals. Blumer argued this was the case in the offline world nearly 70 years ago, when he claimed:

> we know essentially nothing of the individual in the sample . . . We do not know whether the individual has the position of an archbishop or an itinerant Laborer; whether he belongs to a powerful group taking a vigorous stand on the issue or whether he is an attached recluse with no membership in a functional group.
>
> (Blumer 1948, 546)

While survey researchers would have claimed such considerations are not important provided a representative sample was gathered, Blumer's concern is somewhat different. While polling data allows the measurement of opinion, it does not measure the potential impact that particular person holding a particular opinion might have. In contrast, the online space has the potential to measure both opinion and, to some degree at least, the impact of that opinion on other citizens. Indeed, many of the techniques used in semantic analysis are particularly focused on identifying 'influencers' – namely individual that wield greater power within the network (Anstead and O'Loughlin 2012).

The most hopeful reading would suggest it is possible that semantic research has the potential to transcend the individual and collective definitions of public opinion. Many online spaces are inherently discursive environments, and so may have the potential to offer more than snapshots of individuals' thoughts, but instead a more subtle and evolving measure of opinion and how it is influenced by interactions with others. As such, semantic analysis may hold open the potential of a hybrid model of public opinion measurement, which, while relying on data generated by individual citizens is not inherently methodologically individualist; and which, while able to generate claims about the opinion held by specific collectivities, is not methodologically holist (Sawyer 2005; Al-Lami et al. 2012).

## The clash of public and private interest

One of the central claims made by early opinion pollsters was that they acted in the public interest, providing a counterbalance to more powerful vested interests within a society. This assertion was always dubious. The development of opinion polling was closely intertwined with particular vested interests. Two standout as being particularly significant: big business and mainstream media institutions.

In contrast to the rhetoric of populism and devolving power to citizens, early pollsters were embedded in corporate America. This is hardly surprising; the origin of opinion polling was closely related to business interests. The science of opinion polling grew out of the market research techniques that had developed in the earlier part of the century, in order to fuel the more advanced capitalism that was emerging (Converse 2009). This had two important ramifications.

First, pollsters had no real interest in constructing a sample that was representative of the population, but instead sought to construct a sample that reflected the voting population of a country. Thus their definition of citizen was closer to the marketeer's idea of a consumer. Consequently, their datasets reflected (and continue to reflect), the structural inequalities that exist in contemporary society. So, for example, Gallup's sample under-represented women and African-Americans relative to their numbers in the US population. The former group was less likely to vote and the latter were barred from voting in the South. While such a weighting made sense if the aim of the poll was to predict election results, it undermined the claims that survey methods enhanced democracy and gave voice to the powerless. Polling research techniques were developed to meet the needs to corporate clients, not of civic life.

A second issue relates to the expense of opinion polls. It should be remembered that polling was carried out by corporate actors existing in a market economy. It was in the interest of these firms to satisfy their clients. While George Gallup never admitted his own political preferences, details of his firm's findings in the years after its creation are instructive. Few questions were ever asked about corporate America, while labour union power was a regular preoccupation (Robinson 1999).

An extension of this tension is to be found in opinion polling's interaction with a particular type of corporation found in the media sphere. While 1936 can be interpreted as the triumph of scientific methodology, the showmanship displayed by Gallup in challenging the *Literary Digest* prior to the election clearly demonstrates how the measurement of public opinion was always a highly mediated activity. This has continued to be the case. However, the dual role of the polls as both rigorous research and media artefacts creates many tensions. Mainstream media are, understandably, interested in the newsworthy elements of polling findings. As such, there is a tendency to play up the sensational.

What makes this argument even more pertinent is that pollsters derive a tiny portion of their revenue from political work. Most of their income is generated by contracts with private sector clients. Their relationship with news media is therefore driven by the objective of raising their profile. Pollsters have an interest in appearing to be accurate, rather than necessarily unearthing more complex information about public preferences.

These elements of the history of opinion polling bear a close relationship to contemporary social media analysis. They also offer warnings about how the techniques might develop. Like their opinion polling forebears, many of the firms currently conducting such work have their origins not in civic activity, but instead in market research. Political work is only a small proportion of their business, largely undertaken to raise their profile and recruit more corporate clients.

The nature of the research techniques employed by these firms also raises issues about their relationship with news media. Techniques such as data mining and natural language processing are complex. Few members of the public, or indeed journalists, will understand them in great depth. In turn, this means that findings might be badly reported without the necessary caveats and explanations as to their meaning.

Indeed, in some ways, the reporting of semantic polling raises greater concerns than the early days of opinion polling, simply because of the dominance that the traditional notion of opinion polling has achieved in political discussion. In other words, the way in which journalists, politicians and the public understand data is framed by the dominant opinion polling paradigm of public opinion. This paradigm is wholly inappropriate for understanding semantic polling. The data might be measured against the norms of opinion polling and, therefore, found wanting and dismissed as, for example, being unrepresentative.

## Democratic optimism and pessimism

Throughout the history of public opinion research, arguments have been made to link the data gathered to democratic processes. Participants in these discussions have historically taken either an optimistic view, seeing certain types of data about public preferences as a democratic good, or a pessimistic view, critiquing the methods used to gather this data or the way it is employed as damaging to democratic life.

The pollsters of the 1930s were not neutrals in their political ideology. They were committed to a form of democratic populism, derived from their own claims to having a scientific methodology. At the heart of this was the idea that all citizens were equals and should have an equal say in political decisions. Prior to the advent of the representative opinion poll, they argued that there was no mechanism for the discovery of public opinion, so the concept was nothing more than a rhetorical device that could be adopted by political elites with access to the metaphorical megaphones required to broadcast it (Gallup and Rae 1940). As such, the ideology of opinion polling is a logical development of the progressive politics of the early part of the twentieth century in the United States – distrustful of elites and keen to decentralise power. One of the most significant consequences of the events surrounding the 1936 presidential election was that it gave pollsters the new role of acting as the sages who would 'decipher their [citizens'] future votes and opinions' and 'suggested a confluence of forces promoting popular democracy' (Robinson 1999, 40).

Gallup and his supporters believed that the people were wise and their judgement sound, arguing that

> [i]f government with the consent of the governed is to be preserved and strengthened, then the common man, the farmer, the industrial worker, the stenographer, the clerk, the factory hand, must become as politically articulate as the professional, the businessman, and the banker.
>
> (Gallup and Rae 1940)

As such, their views were part of a far broader political debate, which encompassed the likes of Walter Lippmann's argument that the public lacked the knowledge, awareness or time to cope with complex political questions (Lippmann 1927), and John Dewey's belief that the public had as yet untapped civic capabilities (Dewey 1927). The pollsters of the 1930s believed that they had discovered the mechanism to tap this resource.

This view was to be long-lasting. Indeed, this optimistic reading of the power of public opinion polling is still embedded in the rhetoric deployed by modern pollsters. Writing after the 2010 UK general election, for example, a number of pollsters commented on the value of polls released immediately after each of the three televised leaders debates, arguing that they undermined attempts by political elites to 'spin' the result of the debate and claim victory for their own side (Kellner et al. 2011; Lawes and Hawkins 2011).

The democratic value, as opposed to the harm done, by opinion polls has remained hotly contested for decades. Modern scholars, for example, frequently accuse polls of undermining discussion about policy during election campaigns (Broh 1980), while the most obvious policy manifestation of this are countries that attempt to ban polls in the run-up to elections (Bale 2002).

It should be noted though that these debates emerged very rapidly with developments in survey technique. Even before the election in 1936, Congressman Walter Pierce was seeking to pass legislation banning polls. In 1936, an article in the *Atlantic* was referring to polls as 'instruments of power' (Childs, cited in Robinson, 1999, 59). Many of these discussions were motivated by partisanship, since opinion polling had a tendency – somewhat ironically, given the events of 1936 – to underestimate the Democratic Party vote share, and there was a concern this could have a direct effect on political outcomes. A second critique of opinion polling as a democratic instrument relates to the way in which the data came to be used by the professional political class, especially those managing communications. Gallup's idealised use of opinion polling suggested that public opinion would be given a voice that would influence the course of political debate. However, the reality was that polling became a tool that was used not to inform decision-making, but instead to discover the best ways of communicating decisions that had already been taken, what has been referred to as 'crafted talk' (Jacobs and Shapiro 2002).

The emergence of semantic research techniques echoes this earlier debate. There have been those who have seen social media data as a powerful democratic good. Indeed, the Web's ability that allows citizens to produce and publish their own content has led to similarly strong populist rhetoric as was evident in the 1930s (Armstrong and Moulitsas 2006; Trippi 2008). Gallup's belief that the collective citizenry are wiser than political elites has a modern echo in the idea of *the wisdom of crowds* (Surowiecki 2004).

Critiques today also echo the earlier debate. Just as Lippmann argued that publics were too ill-informed to partake in complex policy decisions some have bemoaned the move away from expertise that the Internet has facilitated (Keen 2007). Similarly, it is likely that the future will see increased concern about the use to which semantic data will be put to once harvested, and whether it will feed into the policy-making process in a positive manner or just be used as another tool to find new ways of packaging pre-existing policies.

## Conclusion

How we remember and order history is frequently different to the course of events themselves. The history of public opinion research is a good example of this. Each of our five binaries is indicative of contested understandings about what the development and rise to prominence of opinion poll techniques meant. Furthermore, tensions evident at the birth of modern public opinion research in the 1930s help us understand some of the dilemmas emerging around semantic polling today. In short:

- Semantic polling blurs the distinction between quantitative and qualitative research techniques. Instead, it points towards the possibility of quantitative levels of data providing qualitative richness.
- Both ontological and epistemological claims were embedded in early opinion polling ideas. Public opinion was thought to exist independently of the researcher. It could be discovered through opinion polling. The conflation of public opinion with opinion polling has never gone uncontested, but remains dominant. Semantic polling not only points toward the possibility of new conceptions of public opinion and new ways of measuring it, but also challenges these narrower understandings.
- Survey methods were built on the assumption of methodological individualism. Public opinion was also defined through this understanding, being seen as nothing more than the sum total of individual preferences. Semantic polling techniques challenge this because they capture the social: relationships, communities and networks and patterns of influence, opinion and even emotion. This challenges us to think about our definition of public opinion.
- The role of vested interests in semantic research techniques and the possible tensions this creates has strong echoes in the history of opinion polling. The majority of pollsters' revenue comes from private clients, not public opinion research. Media clients have a particular set of objectives, focused on the news value of findings. Since semantic polling is emerging from market research, the same tensions are likely to abound.
- Public opinion research has always been inseparable from questions of democracy. Early pollsters made strong claims as to the populist

power of their tools. However, these claims were not uncontroversial. Similarly, semantic analysis firms entering the democratic sphere have to engage with broader democratic questions.

Beyond these specifics, the broader point of this chapter is to note that methods for understanding public opinion cannot be separated from their social context (Law et al. 2011), as they are never value-neutral, and are subject to power and interests. Despite his protestations of striving for democratic equality, Gallup's polling method actually lent greater weight to male, white, middle-class voices. Embedded in opinion polling is a particular representation of 'the public', so it seems likely that semantic polling will create the representation or image of a different kind of public or publics. This recognition will be both a strength and a weakness – it will discourage critiques of social media research based wholly on the norms of survey research techniques, yet it will also challenge any claims made by social media researchers to have a unique ability to tap the public mind.

One further point needs to be made. Much of the mythology of 1936 is based on the predictive value of the poll. It seems inevitable that public opinion research during election periods is always going to be used to address the question 'who is going to win?' Yet semantic polling techniques open new horizons for how we understand public opinion. These techniques generate data upon which we can develop theories of how individual and collective opinions form and change, as well as of the role of communities, networks and individuals with varying levels of credibility, authority and information to affect the views of others.

## References

Al-Lami, M., Hoskins, A. and O'Loughlin, B. (2012) 'Mobilisation and Violence in the New Media Ecology: The Dua Khalil Aswad and Camilia Shehata Cases', *Critical Studies on Terrorism*, 5 (2), 237–256.

Allport, F. (1937) 'Towards a Science of Public Opinion', *Public Opinion Quarterly*, 1 (1), 7–23.

Anstead, N. and O'Loughlin, B. (2011) 'Semantic Polling and the 2010 UK General Election', *ECPR General Conference*. Reykjavik.

Anstead, N. and O'Loughlin, B. (2012) *Semantic Polling: The Ethics of Online Public Opinion*, Media Policy Brief, 5 (The London School of Economics and Political Science, London).

Armstrong, J. and Moulitsas, M. (2006) *Crashing the Gate* (White River Junction, VT: Chelsea Green).

Bale, T. (2002) 'Restricting the Broadcast and Publication of Pre-election and Exit Polls: Some Selected Examples', *Representation*, 39 (1), 15–22.

Bishop, G.F., Oldendick, R.W., Tuchfarber, A.J. and Bennett, S.E. (1980) 'Pseudo-Opinions on Public Affairs', *Public Opinion Quarterly*, 44 (2), 198.

Blumer, H. (1946) 'Elementary Collective Behavior', in A.M. Lee (ed.), *New Outline of the Principles of Sociology* (New York: Barnes Noble), 166–222.

Blumer, H. (1948) 'Public Opinion and Public Opinion Polling', *American Sociological Review*, 13 (5), 542–549.

Bourdieu, P. (1979) 'Public Opinion Does Not Exist', in A. Mattelart and S. Siegelaub (eds.), *Communication and Class Struggle* (New York: International General), pp. 124–130.

Broh, C.A. (1980) 'Horse-Race Journalism: Reporting the Polls in the 1976 Presidential Election', *Public Opinion Quarterly*, 44 (4), 514.

Callon, M., Millo, Y. and Barthe, Y. (2009) *Acting in an Uncertain World: An Essay on Technical Democracy* (Cambridge, MA: MIT Press).

Canetti, E. (1992) *Crowds and Power* (Harmondsworth: Penguin).

Castells, M. (2007) 'Communication, Power and Counter-power in the Network Society', *International Journal of Communication*, 1, 238–266.

Childs, H.L. (1965) *Public Opinion: Nature, Formation and Role* (Princeton, NJ: D. van Nostrand).

Converse, J. (2009) *Survey Research in the United States: Roots and Emergence 1890–1960* (Piscataway, NJ: Transactions Publishers).

Converse, P. (1987) 'Changing Conceptions of Public Opinion in the Political Process', *Public Opinion Quarterly*, 51 (2), S12–S24.

Crossley, A.M. (1937) 'Straw Polls in 1936', *Public Opinion Quarterly*, 1 (1), 24.

Curtis, A. (2002) *The Century of the Self* (London: BBC Television).

Dewey, J. (1927) *The Public and its Problems* (Athens, OH: Ohio University Press).

Gallup, G. (1965) 'Poll and the Political Process-Past, Present and Future', *Public Opinion Quarterly*, 29 (4), 544–549.

Gallup, G. and Rae, S. (1940) *The Pulse of Democracy: The Public Opinion Poll and How It Works* (New York: Greenwood Press).

Gladwell, M. (2010) 'Small Change: Why the Revolution Will Not Be Tweeted', *The New Yorker*, 4 October, 44–49.

Gould, P. (2011) *The Unfinished Revolution: How New Labour Changed British Politics Forever* (London: Abacus).

Habermas, J. (1991) *The Structural Transformation of the Public Sphere: An Inquiry into a Category of Bourgeois Society* (Cambridge MA: MIT Press).

Harrison, T. (1986) *Britain by Mass Observation* (London: Cressnet).

Herbst, S. (1993) *Numbered Voices: How Opinion Polling has Shaped American Politics* (Chicago: University of Chicago Press).

Hindman, M. (2008) *The Myth of Digital Democracy* (Princeton, NJ: Princeton University Press).

Jacobs, L.R. and Shapiro, R.Y. (2002) 'Politics and Policymaking in the Real World: Crafted Talk and the Loss of Democratic Responsiveness', in J. Manza, F. Lomax Cook and B.I. Page (eds.), *Navigating Public Opinion: Polls, Policy, and the Future* (Oxford: OUP), pp. 184–200.

Katz, D. (1942) 'Do Interviewers Bias Poll Results?', *Public Opinion Quarterly*, 6 (2), 248.

Keen, A. (2007) *The Cult of the Amateur* (New York: Currency).

Kellner, P., Twyman, J. and Well, A. (2011) 'Polling Voting Intentions', in D. Wring, R. Mortimore, and S. Atkinson (eds.), *Political Communication in*

*Britain: The Leader Debates, the Campaign and the Media in the 2010 General Election* (Basingstoke: Palgrave MacMillan), pp. 94–110.

Latour, B. (2005) 'From Realpolitik to Dingpolitik or How to Make Things Public', in B. Latour and P. Weibel (eds.), *Making Things Public: Atmospheres of Democracy* (Cambridge, MA: MIT Press), pp. 14–41.

Law, J., Ruppert, E. and Savage, M. (2011) *The Double Social Life of Methods* (Manchester/Milton Keynes: Centre for Research on Socio-Cultural Change).

Lawes, C. and Hawkins, A. (2011) 'The Polls, the Media and the Voters: The Leaders Debate', in D. Wring, R. Mortimore and S. Atkinson (eds.), *Political Communication in Britain: The Leader Debates, the Campaign and the Media in the 2010 General Election* (Basingstoke: Palgrave MacMillan), pp. 56–76.

Le Bon, G. (1897/1972) *The Crowd: A Study of the Popular Mind* (New York: Viking).

Lippmann, W. (1922) *Public Opinion* (London: Allen & Unwin).

Lippmann, W. (1927) *The Phantom Public* (New Brunswick and London: Transaction Publishers).

Marres, N. (2005) 'Issues Spark a Public into Being', in B. Latour and P. Weibel (eds.), *Making Things Public: Atmospheres of Democracy* (Cambridge, MA: MIT Press), pp. 208–217.

Marres, N. and Lezaun, J. (2011) 'Materials and Devices of the Public: An Introduction', *Economy and Society*, 40 (4), 489–509.

Price, V. (1992) *Public Opinion* (Thousand Oaks, CA: Sage).

Robinson, D.J. (1999) *The Measure of Democracy: Polling, Market Research, and Public Life 1930–1945* (Toronto: University of Toronto Press).

Sawyer, R. (2005) *Social Emergence* (Cambridge: Cambridge University Press).

Schuman, H. and Presser, S. (1996) *Questions and Answers in Attitude Surveys: Experiments on Question Form, Wording, and Context* (Thousand Oaks, CA: Sage).

Sellars, W.C. and Yeatman, R.J. (1930) *1066 and All That: A Memorable History of England, Comprising all the Parts you can Remember, Including 103 Good Things, 5 Bad Kings and 2 Genuine Dates* (London: Methuen and Co).

Smith, T.W. (1990) 'The First Straw? A Study of the Origins of Election Polls', *Public Opinion Quarterly*, 54 (1), 21.

Squire, P. (1988) 'Why the 1936 Literary Digest Poll Failed', *Public Opinion Quarterly*, 52 (1), 125.

Surowiecki, J. (2004) *The Wisdom of Crowds* (New York: Doublesday).

Trippi, J. (2008) *The Revolution Will Not Be Televised* (New York: William Morrow).

Warner, M. (2002) 'Publics and Counterpublics', *Public Culture*, 14 (1), 49–90.

Watts, J. (2012) 'One Cygnet to Many: Review of Winter King: The Dawn of Tudor England by Thomas Penn', *London Review of Books*, 34 (8), 25–26.

Wellman, B., Quan-Hasse, A., Boase, J., Chen, W., Hampton, K. and de Diaz, I. (2003) 'The Social Affordances of the Internet for Networked Individualism', *Journal of Computer-Mediated Communication*, 8 (3), available at: http://onlinelibrary.wiley.com/enhanced/doi/10.1111/j.1083-6101.2003.tb00216.x/

Wilkinson, S. and Kitzinger, C. (2000) 'Clinton Faces Nation: A Case Study in the Construction of Focus Group Data as Public Opinion', *The Sociological Review*, 48 (3), 408–424.

# Index

Note: Locators with letter 'n' refer to notes.

Printed and bound by CPI Group (UK) Ltd, Croydon, CR0 4YY